MW01120520

# Preventing Ideological Violence

International Law, Crime and Politics

*Preventing Ideological Violence: Communities, Police and Case Studies of "Success"*
Edited By P. Daniel Silk, Basia Spalek, and Mary O'Rawe

# Preventing Ideological Violence

## Communities, Police and Case Studies of "Success"

Edited by

*P. Daniel Silk, Basia Spalek, and Mary O'Rawe*



palgrave
macmillan

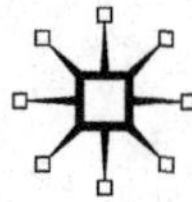



First published in 2013 by
PALGRAVE MACMILLAN®
in the United States—a division of St. Martin's Press LLC,
175 Fifth Avenue, New York, NY 10010.

Where this book is distributed in the UK, Europe and the rest of the world, this is by Palgrave Macmillan, a division of Macmillan Publishers Limited, registered in England, company number 785998, of Houndmills, Basingstoke, Hampshire RG21 6XS.

Palgrave Macmillan is the global academic imprint of the above companies and has companies and representatives throughout the world.

Palgrave® and Macmillan® are registered trademarks in the United States, the United Kingdom, Europe and other countries.

ISBN: 978–1–137–29037–3

Library of Congress Cataloging-in-Publication Data is available from the Library of Congress.

A catalogue record of the book is available from the British Library.

Design by Newgen Imaging Systems (P) Ltd., Chennai, India.

First edition: April 2013

10 9 8 7 6 5 4 3 2 1

Transferred to Digital Printing in 2013

# Contents

*Series Introduction* vii

Introduction 1
*Mary O'Rawe, P. Daniel Silk, and Basia Spalek*

**Part I**

1 The Role of Communities and Police in Preventing Ideological Violence: Considering the Literature, Policies, and Potential 15
*Mary O'Rawe, P. Daniel Silk, and Basia Spalek*

2 The Sociopolitical Contexts Affecting Police-Community Engagement in Northern Ireland, Britain, and the United States 33
*Tara Lai Quinlan, Basia Spalek, and Mary O'Rawe*

**Part II**

3 Police, Community, Conflict, and Context: Some Thoughts on British Muslim and Irish Comparisons 55
*Mark McGovern*

4 The Muslim Safety Forum: Senior Police and Muslim Community Engagement during the War on Terror 67
*Robert Lambert*

**Part III**

5 Communities and Policing in Transition: The Northern Ireland Experience 91
*Noel Rooney and Liam Maskey*

6 Making Sense of Models of Community-Police Engagements in North Belfast 105
*John Loughran*

7 Lessons Learned from Loyalist-Police Engagement in Northern Ireland: The Connect Program 127
*Winston Irvine*

8 Prevent and Police-Community Partnerships in Birmingham 137
*Zubeda Limbada*

9 Community Partnerships Thwart Terrorism 151
*Deborah Ramirez, Tara Lai Quinlan, Sean P. Malloy, and Taylor Shutt*

10 Pioneers Always Take the Arrows: LAPD Outreach to Muslim Communities in Los Angeles 171
*Mark G. Stainbrook*

11 Hearing Community Voices to Identify Best Practices: Building Antiterrorism Partnerships with American Muslims 191
*Alejandro J. Beutel*

12 Building Bridges: The Experience of Leaders in Detroit, Michigan 209
*Ihsan Alkhatib*

13 Lessons Learned and Best Practices: The Outreach Efforts of the Los Angeles County Sheriff's Department Community Policing Method with Emphasis on the Muslim Community 227
*Mike Abdeen*

Conclusion 239
*P. Daniel Silk, Mary O'Rawe, and Basia Spalek*

*Notes on Contributors* 265

# Series Introduction

It is almost certainly a cliché by now that the September 11, 2001, terrorists attacks on the United States changed the world. These events did so in many ways, including the launching of a multinational war in Afghanistan against al-Qaeda. But perhaps the most significant change was in the eroding of the traditional boundaries between domestic policing and criminal justice and international security concerns. In countries such as the United States, Great Britain, and Spain, three countries that experienced terrorist attacks, political and legal pressures were placed on the government to protect the borders, maintain law and order, and also respect domestic and international human rights and law.

But well before the events of 9/11 and the appearance of al-Qaeda on the international scene, other countries faced what they considered to be domestic terrorist or other threats that challenged the capacity of law enforcement agencies to respond. This included Great Britain and its effort to address violence and unrest in Northern Ireland inspired by Republican or Loyalist forces in Belfast. How the American and British authorities and the police responded to their threats is the subject of *Preventing Ideological Violence: Communities, Police and Case Studies of "Success,"*, edited by P. Daniel Silk, Basia Spalek, and Mary O'Rawe.

Silk, Spalek, and O'Rawe have produced an edited volume of academics and practitioners who collectively examine counterterrorism techniques in three contexts—Britain, Northern Ireland, and the United States of America. But they do so from the perspective of community policing. Community policing as a law enforcement strategy came to fore in the 1980s in response to arguments that there needed to be closer collaboration between the police and the community. Instead of police simply responding to crime, a more effective technique to maintaining order would be fostering closer collaboration between the people and the authorities. Encouraging police to get to know their community and the public to trust them would result in a more effective model of preventing not only traditional forms of crime but also perhaps domestic terrorism.

Community policing effected a law enforcement revolution across the world as many jurisdictions adopted it. Some heralded it as responsible for declining crime rates, yet questions persisted to why. *Preventing Ideological Violence* provides an excellent examination of how community policing really works. It offers contrasting perspectives of the theories behind community policing as well as specific case studies from those in charge of actually implementing them and putting them into practice. The book yields important lessons, both practical and academic, regarding why community policing works and perhaps how to improve its techniques.

*Preventing Ideological Violence* is a compelling book inaugurating the new Palgrave book series "International Law, Crime, and Politics." The editorial series publishes single-author and edited monographs for scholarly or classroom use that explore the interrelationships between international politics, and criminal justice issues. It widely examines the boundaries and intersections between international law, domestic crime, and global political issues. Topics in the series will include but not be limited to exploring human rights, international law, terrorism, globalism and globalization, international political economy, NGOs, crime and international affairs, and international politics and international institutions such as the World Court, International Criminal Court, European Court of Justice, and the European Court of Human Rights.

The editorial goal of this book series is to publish the most relevant and important scholarly works that examine these topics. It will provide readers the intellectually best research that investigates a new world of scholarship that reflects a world that has blurred old boundaries and has created a new global order.

DAVID SCHULTZ,
Professor and Series Editor
Hamline University,
St. Paul, Minnesota USA
dschultz@hamline.edu

# Introduction

*Mary O'Rawe, P. Daniel Silk, and Basia Spalek*

## Introduction

Given recent efforts by governments in the United Kingdom and the United States to develop counterterrorism policies that contain distinct, locally emphasized police engagement practices (see, e.g., Lowe and Innes 2008; Spalek, El Awa, and McDonald 2008; HM Government 2011; The White House 2011; Spalek 2012), this book is designed to explore the application of "community policing" activities as a means to address the causes of ideologically inspired violence. The book seeks to encourage deeper exploration and debate around the roles that communities and the police (and the "state" more broadly) should, and should not, have in the "pre-crime" arena. This is especially important in circumstances where ideological influences are increasingly becoming the concern of government, and certain sections of communities garner more law-enforcement attention, pertaining to the prevention of extremist violence.

Like many other academic books, this one assesses the effects of particular laws, policies, and practices against the backdrop of relevant literature. More than this, it also includes first-hand input and experiences from practitioners "on the ground" in three jurisdictions—Britain, Northern Ireland, and the United States of America. To assist in the development of a unique and contextualized picture, the book, therefore, not only employs academic commentary, but additionally provides an opportunity for practitioners (both police and civilian) to speak for themselves, as among those whose voices are often missing from broader discussions of where we are going and why. In this book, *Preventing Ideological Violence: Communities, Police and Case Studies of "Success,"* we hope that the inclusion of the views of practitioners in this arena will both enhance dialogue, and, at the same time, contribute to a more holistic understanding and analysis of government security efforts as filtered through the lens of police-community partnerships at the local level.

## Overview

Part I of *Preventing Ideological Violence* sets the scene for this discussion from a largely academic perspective, and attempts to place some of the case study realities that follow within a broader, theoretical context. Chapter One surveys the relevant academic literature for significant themes and challenges, while Chapter Two addresses those meanings and definitions that have come to be accepted and embedded in the promotion of police-community engagement to tackle violent extremism. These initial chapters highlight the unique and communal challenges of the case study jurisdictions, and identify some of the themes, questions, and paradoxes that require further analysis in terms of arriving at any understanding of "success." Among these are issues around defining and framing appropriate parameters for intervention, including questions around participants, stakeholders, and the particular task at hand. These considerations are fundamental to our understanding and acceptance of how police organizations perform their work, how and which roles are facilitated, and what police responsibilities actually are, or should be. How are priorities for engagement chosen? By whom? To serve what purposes? What makes for "equal" partnership? How are "resilient" citizens created? Why are some forms of violence deemed more important for attention (from communities and/or police) than others? Is it right to single out specific communities for special attention in the context of counterterrorism efforts in the post-9/11 era? What are the ethical considerations that are attached to such targeted policing efforts? The questions are myriad, but significant, and often bypassed. They deserve more attention.

Chapter Two also considers the importance of context. It is in the interests of both state and nonstate policing actors to situate themselves so as to be seen, by those deemed to matter, to be on the "right" side of conflict, and to be doing the "right" thing. But "success" in a given context will ultimately be defined by whose version of "right" holds sway. Many of the police personnel and community members who speak in this book would be quick to concede that their ambitious projects challenge conventional thinking, and that they might also occasionally be seen—perhaps proudly—as departing from the law and order status quo. Are they, therefore, somehow, not "right"? This issue of what is "right" may be straightforward when communities and police are in general agreement regarding the need to address violent crime. But what happens when society seeks to focus on factors that are considered potential predicates to violence, such as political ideologies and faith? The lines become very murky when defining right and wrong, cross into areas of thought and belief not traditionally held to be within the purview of police attention, and are largely outside the accepted role of government concern.

In Chapter Three of Part II, Mark McGovern draws some interesting conclusions in this respect, identifying parallels between assumptions made about Muslims in Britain and the experience of the Irish in Britain during the "Troubles" in Northern Ireland. McGovern suggests lessons to be learned from the Irish experience, which, deliberately or otherwise, do not appear to have not been fully considered in the UK government's current counterterrorism agenda (see also O'Connor and Ruhmann 2005). This discussion is important, and might just as easily be drawn from the experience of other "suspect" communities (see, e.g., Hakim 1995; Irons 1993; Weglyn 1996; Spalek and McDonald 2009) who can, too easily, be made scapegoats in times of crisis.

In Chapter Four, Lambert continues the theme of questioning how national agendas can overshadow local attempts to reach accommodation, understanding, and shared practices that can be harnessed to build safer communities. Using the example of the Muslim Safety Forum (MSF) in London, Lambert—himself both a PhD academic and also a retired, long-time counterterrorism officer in London—simultaneously looks at the MSF experiment as a practitioner *and* as a researcher, and he points out that for all the successes over the years of work building this initiative

> [T]he efforts of police and Muslim community representatives to succeed were hampered by government policy in regard to the war on terror. That impediment is the thread that runs through this account of MSF dialogue and which helps explain the most crucial failure: a failure to build adequate trust which in turn helps explain the forum's eventual demise.

While Lambert looks specifically at the London experience, like McGovern in Chapter Three, he provides a backdrop, which illustrates broader concerns that deserve attention in other jurisdictions as well. Though both authors would be quick to concede their views may not represent the mainstream, they are indeed reflective of a critical strand of counterterrorism thought that is deserving of more attention—perhaps particularly by policy makers and legislators.

In Part III of this book, community activists and policing personnel put forward concrete examples of initiatives they have been involved in or have thorough knowledge of, and reflect on the learning coming from these processes. They do this in the voice they each select as most comfortable. Therefore, some chapters are more conversational, first-person accounts (such as Limbada in Chapter Eight), while others seek to bring in multiple voices to provide a helpful review in a slightly more "academic" framework (see Alkhatib in Chapter Twelve). The tone of each chapter should not be confused as a reflection of its value, content, or even intent. In these case study chapters, the goal is merely to let the contributors speak for themselves, highlighting the experiences of a number of people in different jurisdictions and in different roles currently engaged in this type of work. In providing a space for the voices of those striving to make a difference in Northern Ireland, Britain, and the United States, the book attempts to hold a magnifying glass up to the work happening in jurisdictions which are both actively involved in counterterrorism, and to a greater or lesser extent, perhaps also seeking to rebuild societies after terrorist atrocity.

We do not claim this book to be a comprehensive analysis of all initiatives in the case study jurisdictions. Nor do we necessarily endorse all of the views or models for engagement featured in the various chapters. Given that the definition of success can be so contested, it may be that the reader will wonder why certain chapters have even been included as examples of good practice. The ultimate consensus among us has been that "success" means different things to different people, and it is part of the function of the book to point out what passes for success in this arena as well as what might, with deeper research and understanding, be more universally accepted as such. What we do agree upon is that these and similar initiatives merit more consideration and reflection.

In this regard, the Žižak (2008) thesis on violence may be instructive. He suggests that rather than, unthinkingly, responding to violence or to the threat of subjective violence by immediate action, often in an ad hoc manner (e.g., in the face of the seemingly urgent demands of the "war on terror"), actors should instead resist the pressure to always be "doing something." His work suggests that the constant "busy-ness" and push for action distracts us from having the space to begin to understand what causes violence, and consider what kind of violence actually causes the most harm. We wonder how many of the contributors in Part III have themselves felt pushed to immediately "act" when they would have preferred time to "think," and what effect this has had on their professional practices. We hope this book offers both the contributors *and* the readers an opportunity to take the time to reflect on engagement and counterterrorism, the role of police and communities, and the results of these and similar initiatives.

## THEMES AND CHALLENGES

The "success" theme is taken up, explicitly and implicitly, in the case study chapters themselves. In large measure, success is relative and linked inextricably with context. Indeed, the importance of context in each contribution is key to realizing the potential value of this book.

Part of this context is represented by police and community activists who seek to work in areas in which some person (or group) has been subjected to becoming "the other" in the response to a violent conflict—whether that is within a sectarian Catholic/Protestant context in Northern Ireland, or the more recent marginalization of Muslim communities in Britain and the United States. This "othering" represents a sad reality, and underlines one facet of the human side of the policing equation, and therefore also, the value of selecting the right people to work in this arena. In this spirit, Stainbrook, speaking from a US law enforcement perspective in Chapter Ten makes a key point: "Personnel are the key to a successful outreach unit. They will make or break the unit... finding the right people can be difficult, but recruiting outstanding officers is imperative"; many other contributors to this book would agree. One of the important strands seen throughout this work is how forward-leaning members of communities, police forces, universities, and other organizations are challenging the dichotomizing trend of framing government and community responses to violence as issues of "us versus them." This point is important.

In this context, the multiagency approach to partnering on societal problems is showing positive results in Northern Ireland, and there is evidence that police and community partners in the United States and Britain are seeking to harness similarly broad initiatives (see HM Government, 2011; The White House, 2011). As well as rounding out a problem and its possible solutions, engaging police powers and services as one strand in a much more layered approach also appears to take the "sting" out of alienated and distrustful communities engaging with the police, who are not universally viewed as "the good guys." Moving the debate out of a two-dimensional criminal justice forum can, as suggested by certain case studies here, facilitate a paradigm shift beyond the unhelpful yet ubiquitous "us and them"/"for us or against us" rhetoric that so polarizes viewpoints and heightens, rather than addresses, conflict in any meaningful way. This can allow space for knowledge of "the other side(s)" to grow, prejudices to be broken down, and strong relationships to begin to be formed.

In Chapter Six, John Loughran focuses on his experiences with the cross-community organization, Intercomm, in Belfast, Northern Ireland, and gives us an early glimpse into how this type of work might be approached. Intercomm works with a range of constituencies who historically would have been deeply suspicious of each other and had their own highly conflicted and dysfunctional relationships with policing and the state (see also McGovern in Chapter Three). The idea of these groupings coming together voluntarily to forge and pursue a common agenda would, a number of years ago, have been unthinkable in Northern Ireland. Adding police into the equation as an important and willing partner has had enormous risks attached for all involved—but it has also brought important gains, as Loughran shows, developing community safety in the highly segregated, conflicted, and economically deprived interface areas in North Belfast.

In Chapter Five, Rooney and Maskey showcase another particular initiative, working with police, community activists, and other representatives of statutory agencies north and south of the Irish border. The Communities and Policing in Transition (CAPT) project drew much of its strength and ability to take risks from being funded independently of national government. The project, externally evaluated as having met its own indicators for success, has, importantly, identified the need for tailored training, awareness raising, and networking opportunities to be provided specifically to young people in order to impact deeply ingrained beliefs and attitudes, and lead to concrete action and partnering at a local level.

The disaffection and sense of alienation felt by many in the Loyalist community in Northern Ireland, in terms of the new policing arrangements, is a feature of Winston Irvine's contribution in Chapter Seven. The potential of a "new dispensation" to devalue the experience and relative loyalty of the Unionist community to the erstwhile Royal Ulster Constabulary (RUC), is keenly felt and well-articulated in Winston Irvine's analysis. Here, again, a community at the hard edges of the conflict has, working with local police, taken innovative and thoughtful steps toward recasting the die. In the process, the potential for diminishing alienation and adding value to a more inclusive vision of policing has been highlighted, where people can be brought to carve space and build capacity to understand each other's realities.

In Chapter Eight, Limbada offers a unique perspective as a Muslim female employed by the local authority in Birmingham, England. Her view is insightful and nuanced as she spent time "seconded" to a police counterterrorism squad, all the while well aware of the potential effects of counterterrorism efforts on Muslim communities. She questions simplistic, one-dimensional models of community safety and counterterrorism, and highlights that partnerships are complex affairs, in which all involved have a great deal to learn.

Ramirez, Quinlan, Shutt, and Malloy offer an overview of examples of "successful" community-police partnerships for counterterrorism in the United States in Chapter Nine, while drawing some comparisons to efforts in the United Kingdom. Their contribution is important in its own right, but it is also worth noting their affiliation with Northeastern University's "Partnering for Prevention and Community Safety Initiative" (PfP), which has been involved in related programs and research for several years—indeed, even before the "Prevent" initiative became institutionalized in the UK. Unabashed advocates for a community policing response to terrorism, they also display their own skepticism regarding the correct mechanisms through which such initiatives can be utilized.

In Chapter Ten, Stainbrook—a retired Los Angeles Police Department lieutenant and experienced practitioner of community engagement within a large police force—relates a frank assessment of the challenges often experienced when innovative projects for this purpose try to get off the ground. It is clearly an environment in which "failures" offer opportunities for learning and later success. Indeed, in Stainbrook's chapter, it seems reflection is part and parcel of defining "success," as is questioning the public safety *status quo*. In the words of Los Angeles Police Department deputy chief, Michael Downing, quoted by Stainbrook:

> In the past we have relied on interventions based on "experts," logic or previous programs that are either generic or insensitive to the constellation of issues. This has consistently produced unremarkable results. Public safety pays a high cost for this business practice.

Police and communities alike clearly continue to have much to learn, especially as they seek to collaborate on programs to prevent ideological violence. But the potential results are, in Stainbrook's estimation, worth the effort nonetheless.

In Chapter Eleven, Beutel follows Stainbrook's candid recognition that there are deep challenges to trust building between law enforcement agencies and Muslim communities in the United States. His viewpoint is especially instructive as a former staff member of an influential and politically active Islamic affairs organization in the United States. Through his "overview of the complex factors that inhibit the development of trust between law enforcement and American Muslim communities," followed by a selection of interviews with Muslim leaders from across the United States, Beutel is able to offer a snapshot of the key facets of trust building between Muslims and law enforcement in the United States, from the viewpoint of Muslim community leaders themselves.

Alkhatib, like Beutel, relies on interviews as well as his own experience as a practitioner (and attorney) in community engagement in Chapter Thirteen. Alkhatib specifically relies on the example of the Detroit-area BRIDGES (Building Respect In Diverse Groups to Enhance Sensitivity) program as a foundation for his contribution—a program that started soon after 9/11 between law enforcement and Arab Americans in Detroit, and served as an early example of the type of programs that have developed in other areas of the United States since. Regarding Islamophobia in the post-9/11 world, Alkhatib quotes a community member in Detroit, Michigan, who views the success of outreach primarily associated with

> [B]ring[ing] about a better and a more accurate understanding of the culture, religion, norms, traditions and the way of thinking of people from the Middle East region [and]...creat[ing] awareness that being different should not be viewed as being non-patriotic, inferior, or hostile.

This theme, utilizing police-community outreach as a vehicle for learning about one another is powerful and also pervasive among our contributors here, and is therefore addressed again in the conclusion to this book.

Where the investment in police-community partnerships is in building relationships, clearly the need to choose the right partners is of prime importance. In Chapter Thirteen, Abdeen, a Los Angeles Sheriff's department sergeant and Arab American, demonstrates the difficulties with assuming that members of a certain community or organization necessarily can be viewed as representative of grassroots opinion, or sufficiently influential to do what needs to be done. Like other contributors, he concedes the real-world influence of disparate interests, recognizing that first attempts at outreach are often imperfect. He also points out that police-community relations cannot be built exclusively on narrowly defined issues. Abdeen offers an example of how innovative thinking can be seen to pay dividends, especially in the realm of building trust between potentially alienated communities and local law enforcement.

In their totality, the case studies identify how initiatives can be politically charged and inspired, and may be more or less successful as a function of the personalities involved (see also Lambert in Chapter Four on this point). Claiming any kind of durable success in such contexts can be deeply problematic, as influence shifts and agendas wane. Initiatives that contain the seeds of something very valuable can disappear overnight depending on which way the wind is blowing, politically and/or organizationally. At the same time the existence of a number of initiatives can appear to evidence a fuller consensus on one country's counterterrorism agenda than actually exists. Costly initiatives can be undertaken and either reproduced or replaced, based on flawed or skewed analysis, without lessons being sufficiently learned from past experience.

On the other hand, joint community–police projects can also pay unexpected dividends, surprising even the most hardened of critics. Success may "fly under the radar" as a program with little fanfare or attention, might provide opportunities for developing deep trust and truly affecting the roots of violent crime. In reality, there is no way of knowing with any certainty before an initiative starts whether it will bear fruit, and all involved are assuming some level of risk. While success is hard to quantify, there is little doubt that it requires open-minded thinking and innovation.

In Chapter Ten, Stainbrook speaks of a range of different units within a given police organization needing to send out the same signals in order not to marginalize or undermine the work being done by a particular community-focused police unit. He also refers to the Los Angeles Police Department moving deliberately to a policy of engagement with all communities impacted by terrorism, not just those who happen to be Muslim. This dynamic can also work both ways, with communities moving, on occasion, from making assumptions that police are the correct (or indeed the only possible) partners, to thinking about how a non-law enforcement approach with multiple other statutory partners might be more appropriate in terms of preventing violence and addressing quality-of-life issues in a more holistic way (see Loughran in Chapter Six). There is some evidence, especially from Northern Ireland, of success related to the philosophical call in the UK Prevent agenda (HM Government 2011) and White House "Empowering Local Communities to Prevent Violent Extremism" (The White House 2011) strategy to harness strength from organizations outside of law enforcement to support the broad public safety mandate. This is valuable, but politically fraught and, in the end, success will be a measure of the extent to which forward-thinking people, "on the ground," are properly empowered and resourced to develop and sustain sensitive, inclusive, and multilayered interventions, across a range of sectors.

As Stainbook acknowledges, there is a danger in rushing headlong into outreach initiatives in an attempt simply to engage with Muslims (or any community, for that matter). Building partnerships are challenging, and the work is complex. He asks the question: "How do you attempt to have positive interactions with Muslims in Los Angeles when you don't know who they are, where they are, or even what is important to them?" More than this—why are Muslims in the post-9/11 era the focus of such initiatives in the first place, when firstly they are not a monolith and, generally speaking, as Abdeen points out in Chapter Thirteen, far from being a "problem community" in terms of law enforcement anyway? Seeking opportunities to learn about one another can signal an acceptance of the need to value different experiences of being human. Equally, information gathering can have more sinister or problematic connotations that need to be explored and upfronted in the dialogue.

A variety of contributors suggests the importance of realizing that the best-intentioned outreach and community partnering initiatives often start off "on the back foot" from the point of view of needing to both justify their existence and restore trust. This, itself, speaks to failures, based in utilizing extremely ineffective law enforcement approaches, which Beutel (Chapter Eleven) refers to as: "[a] combination of broad-brushed surveillance, poor training, negative police experiences, internal disagreements over the utility of engagement, and anti-Muslim politics at the national level." Abdeen highlights the importance of using the right terminology so as not to create fear and suspicion in communities that they are being *targeted* rather than *partnered*. These suggestions are insightful. However, the issue goes beyond one of using the right language (Spalek 2012).

In Chapter Ten, Stainbrook uses the example of the problematic dynamics emanating from how communities tend to be depicted in the case study jurisdictions and the dangers of, even well-meaning law-enforcement initiatives, buying into and perpetuating these unhelpful myths and stereotypes:

> Vulnerability of a community to the effects of terrorism, does not imply they are more likely to become terrorists; it means that they are

> more likely to be impacted socially, economically, mentally, and yes, possibly to the point wherein some individuals believe that violence is an acceptable alternative. *However, statistically very few actually resort to physical violence.* One source of frustration for us was, and still is, the perpetuation of the myth that Muslim communities are somehow more susceptible to becoming violent in support of Islam. This has never been academically proven, but is continually perpetuated by far-right extremists on the Internet and via pseudo-intellectual books.

Stainbrook, like other contributors, offers a concern that is worth noting. The grafting of a counterterrorism agenda onto community policing efforts might seem to make complete sense on one level or to one group of people, but it might equally present unique challenges. Overlaying this agenda onto something which started off as a means of building bridges, getting officers to respond more sensitively to different religious practices and cultural realities, and introducing communities to a more positive view of local law enforcement, can contain its own problematic dynamics. Similarly, allowing law enforcement to be pigeonholed into narrowly framed national security concerns, such as terrorism, runs the risk of minimizing its potential contributions to the broader public safety mission. It is worth stating repeatedly throughout this book: the context matters, as does formulating a more holistic understanding of violence and its triggers (see e.g., Gilligan 2000). In the Conclusion, we return to these issues, and emphasize several recurring themes and points that deserve more attention.

## REFERENCES

Gilligan, James. 2000. *Violence: Reflections on Our Deadliest Epidemic.* London: Jessica Kingsley Publishers.

Hakim, Joy. 1995. *A History of Us: War Peace and All That Jazz.* Oxford, UK: Oxford University Press.

HM Government. 2011. *Prevent Strategy.* Norwich: TSO.

Irons, Peter. 1993. *Justice at War: The Story of the Japanese American Internment Cases.* Berkeley: University of California Press.

Lowe, Trudy, and Martin Innes. 2008. "Countering Terror: Violent Radicalisation and Situational Intelligence." *Prison Service Journal 179*: 3–10.

O'Connor, Michael, and Celia Ruhmann. 2005. "Into the Fire: How to Avoid Getting Burned by the Same Mistakes Made Fighting Terrorism in Northern Ireland." *Cardozo Law Review 24*: 1657–1751.

Spalek, Basia (Ed). 2012. *Counter-Terrorism: Community-Based Approaches to Terror Crime.* Hampshire, UK: Palgrave Macmillan.

Spalek, Basia, Salwa El Awa, and Laura Zahra McDonald. 2008. *Police Muslim Engagement and Partnerships for the Purposes of Counter-Terrorism: An Examination*. Birmingham, UK: University of Birmingham.

Spalek, Basia, and Laura Zahra McDonald. 2009. "Terror Crime Prevention: Constructing Muslim Practices and Beliefs as 'Anti-Social' and 'Extreme' through CONTEST 2." *Social Policy and Society* 9(1): 123–132.

Weglyn, Michi. 1996. *Years of Infamy: The Untold Story of America's Concentration Camps*. Seattle:University of Washington Press.

The White House 2011. *Empowering Local Partners to Prevent Violent Extremism in the United States*. Washington, DC: The White House. http://www.whitehouse.gov/sites/default/files/empowering_local_partners.pdf.

Žižak, Slavoj. 2008. *Violence*. London: Profile Books.

# Part I

# 1

# The Role of Communities and Police in Preventing Ideological Violence: Considering the Literature, Policies, and Potential

*Mary O'Rawe, P. Daniel Silk, and Basia Spalek*

## Exploring the Parameters

Engagement and partnership are complex concepts. When applied to preventing concerns such as "terrorism" or "ideologically driven violence," especially in the context of community policing strategies, they become even more so. This book, through including the voices of both academics and practitioners, seeks to simultaneously address current practices in this field and explore the effect of straightforward conceptualizations of some of the terms related to and underpinning such practices. This is not done to add obfuscation to an area that is already sufficiently challenging. Instead, it is designed to highlight the fact that there are foundational questions that require philosophical consideration before we can launch into examples of "success." Policing, community policing, terrorism, and counterterrorism are all ideas largely accepted as "understood" in their common usage in modern society, yet they can also be dangerously imprecise in both application and discussion. The ambiguities, nuances, and, on occasion, diametrically opposed positions that may be adopted in relation to these terms deserve further consideration; this chapter begins that analysis.

## Terrorism, Counterterrorism, and the Power of Terminology

"Terrorism" itself has been notoriously difficult to define in universally accepted terms (e.g., LaFree and Ackerman 2009; Schmid and Jongman 1988; 2005). Indeed, within the United States alone, the Central Intelligence Agency, the Department of Justice, and the Department of Defense all have their own distinct definitions (United States General Accounting Office 2003), and Perry (2003) has enumerated 22 separate definitions or descriptions of terrorism at the federal level. Definitions have also shifted in legislation over time, with all manner of previously legitimate activity coming increasingly within a proscriptive statutory purview (e.g., the UK "Terrorism Act 2000"; "United and Strengthening America" or "USAPATRIOT Act of 2001"). In this complex and contested arena, all involved—practitioners and commentators alike—use vocabulary to describe terrorism and counterterrorism efforts as if they were clear-cut, rather than moving, shifting, evolving, and, above all, context dependent.

Disagreements and polarized positions regarding the rights and wrongs of ideologically motivated violence, not to mention what terrorism *is* (and therefore, who the terrorists are), are not confined to the legal, policy, or academic domains. It is trite logic to suggest that "one person's terrorist is another person's freedom fighter," but even this slogan reflects a real-world complexity that has direct application in joint police-community endeavors to prevent ideological violence. Who is right and who is wrong is not always simple, and should not be assumed to be so. Even in terms of trying to document consistency of viewpoints over time, yesterday's pariah, against whom counterterrorism methods were adopted and applauded, can become tomorrow's dignitary or statesman (see examples in Northern Ireland, Afghanistan, and Iraq)—and this phenomenon can also work in reverse.

Given the extent and depth of differing opinions and positions, mainstream terrorism studies tend to consider terrorism fairly myopically, as something perpetrated almost exclusively by nonstate actors. As Spalek et al. (2008, 15) point out:

> [W]ithin counter-terrorism arenas, research has often been dominated by state-centric perspectives founded on secondary sources and lacking the input of primary data collection and analysis. For this reason, traditional terrorism studies has been criticised for being analytically and methodologically weak, relying too heavily on secondary information and failing to understand terrorism and counter-terrorism not

> only through the perspectives and experiences of practitioners, but also through those experiencing state repression. (Breen-Smyth 2007; Jackson 2007)

However attractive, one-dimensional views of terrorism and counter-terrorism that fail to consider the complexity of multiple experiences and conflicted realities serve a minimized purpose. For our purposes here, the related phenomenon of the "securitization" of particular issues at certain points in history, leading to the creation of "suspect communities" (e.g., Hillyard 1993), is also important, well documented, and of concern. However, insufficient attention is still paid to understanding the causes of violence and what lies behind support for (or rejection of) certain types of violence over others (Žižak 2008; Gilligan 2000; Boyle 2012).

It is clear, both in the jurisdictions under study in this book and elsewhere that societies, groups, and individuals can harbor inconsistent and even hypocritical views as to which types of violence and related views are acceptable. Dominant power groups in society will continue to determine which views of violence and violent crime "matter" the most, and which should be prioritized for action. Police personnel face this type of quandary when political influence is exerted on them to address one criminal issue over another, as do communities who witness state efforts to address one type of crime, while another appears to receive scant attention. These examples, however, only hint at the philosophical complexity that is attached to this issue. Gilligan (2000) argues that the key difference between criminal violence as opposed to other, sometimes state-sanctioned, violent behavior is only differentiated by what governments declare illegal—while motives and means may be the same in both instances. However difficult it may be to consider, there may be something to be learned from Gilligan's point, even if only to underline that dominant theories of crime, violence, and fault are far from universal, and may, on further exploration, prove at many levels to be counterproductive in terms of any overarching aim to diminish violence in our societies.

Within this framework, the kinds of violence projected as most problematic by governments, media, and other commentators tend to be subjective rather than objective, structural, or systemic (Žižak 2008). Fear is manipulated at many levels (Hamber 2006), to ensure focus remains on state-defined wrongdoers, while less attention is paid to concerns identified by communities. This is another phenomenon that can work in reverse to posit a given state or group of states as the fount of all evil. While it may be true that democratically elected leaders in some way dictate the security priorities of the constituencies they represent—therefore representing "the people"—at the same time, communities, or sections of communities, in those same areas may actively question what receives political and police attention and why. This can apply equally, and sometimes more so, when the crime at hand is terrorism or, to use today's terminology, violent extremism. Whether it ever helps to label someone a terrorist (and/or a "violent criminal"), and the extent to which traditional counterterrorism approaches are productive of enhanced security, rather than insecurity, are important, but generally moot points (O'Connor and Ruhmann 2005). In the end, terms such as "terrorism" and "extremism" have a hegemonic hold, and are part and parcel of the current vocabulary in the jurisdictions under study. Simply put, these are the terms that rightly or wrongly, are used at a societal level to label and categorize. So while we may appear to have little choice in whether or not we use the term "terrorist" or "fundamentalist," we are at least obligated to question whose definitions are used and how descriptive they truly are—particularly before seeking to apply and utilize these meanings in terms of practical endeavors aimed at eradicating ideological extremist violence.

If defining terrorism is difficult, putting a precise framework around counterterrorism, much less *effective* counterterrorism, clearly cannot be viewed as straightforward either. This is all the more so as counterterrorism efforts have traditionally been carried out in the shadows, operating covertly, often on a strictly "need to know" basis. This can be important in terms of protecting systems, procedures, and sources, but secrecy and the dictates of clandestine practice make full spectrum understanding, accountability, and evaluation nearly impossible. Kevin McNamara, a UK member of Parliament has pinpointed some of the problems associated with a lack of transparency in the area of counterterrorism policing when it comes to trying to independently evaluate the effectiveness of intelligence collection efforts:

> The upside of...secrecy is that terrorists might be led to believe that the intelligence agencies are all-seeing and all powerful. They do not know where the subterfuge begins and ends, how deeply agent penetration goes or what are the agencies' objectives at any time. The downside of the policy is that we do not know either. We do not know to what extent, if at all, the agencies are overrunning ethical boundaries. There is a plethora of agencies in the field, each running agents,

> collecting information and conducting operations. The terrorist might be confused over who is who, but so are we, especially when something goes wrong and we want to find out who is responsible. (2002, 5)

While this concern is valid, we must also consider that an overreliance on the covert and secret runs the risk of distortion, devaluation, and diminishing proactiveness and overt engagement with the community so as to undermine the co-creation of more imaginative and effective forms of community safety.

## Considering the Shape of Community Policing

As challenging as it may be to agree on what constitutes terrorism and effective counterterrorism, we must similarly concede that no consensus exists in the literature, either, as to what community policing is, or what is required for such policing to be effectual (e.g., MacKenzie and Henry 2009; García Chávez 2012). The US National Research Council is of the view that community policing is too nebulous a term to be evaluated empirically (National Research Council Committee to Review Research on Police Policy and Practices 2004).Besides this, there are disparate understandings of even the base concepts of "community" and "policing" viewed as entities in their own right. When a counterterrorism agenda is grafted onto an already fluid concept, the potential for definitional mistakes or misunderstandings multiply exponentially. This consideration is vital as the reader continues into the case studies that follow, as each of the practitioners who have contributed to this collection are, themselves, working in a gray area, where their innovation may march ahead of clearly defined government policies or academic concepts.

For some, community policing is a philosophy (Friedmann 1992), orienting police organizations toward a more outward-looking and community-responsive means of doing business (Alderson 1979; Myhill 2006; García Chávez 2012). It arguably includes any initiative or process geared to facilitate a better understanding of, and responsiveness to, community needs and/or encourage civilians to trust and cooperate with police in a joint societal policing endeavor—though on this point see MacKenzie and Henry (2009) on the importance of distinguishing between, for example, community policing, community policing "lookalikes," and problem-oriented policing (as in Goldstein 1990).

Broadly, community policing has been framed in a variety of ways, but in general it tends to be seen as

> [A] partnership between the police and the people they serve. This partnership is designed to improve the quality of life in the community through the introduction of strategies designed to enhance neighborhood solidarity and safety. It is expected that the police and citizens of the community will work together to address issues of crime and social disorganization. (Vito, Walsh, and Kunselman 2004, 2)

Put like this, what's not to like? Community policing was, indeed, widely vaunted as the dominant policing philosophy, at least in the United States in the years leading up to 9/11, with some commentators suggesting: "Community policing could arguably be called the new orthodoxy of law enforcement in the United States" (Sadd and Grinc 1996, 1). However, more critical voices signal unresolved and often unarticulated tensions in the philosophy of community policing. To what extent might community policing be a distraction from the "real" business of policing—if that work in some way is at odds with a community-centric strategy? How much is it about recruiting a volunteer labor pool to be the eyes and ears of an overwhelmed police force, who may candidly concede they need the help? Where are the boundaries between awareness raising within a community and intelligence gathering about that same community? To what extent are such initiatives owned and subject to direction by police or government as opposed to the community? What does any of this say about whose agenda is being served and how success can be defined? How can co-option by national security programs be avoided, or encouraged, depending on the perspective of which is more desirable?

There is a sense that police rendering themselves more approachable or accessible, attending community events, and building trust with a number of community representatives will result in a payback of further trust of their organization and more information coming from a heretofore unavailable, insufficiently exploited, or reluctant source. This, in turn, is intended to make police more effective in terms of identifying, detecting, and increasingly, preventing crime (Innes 2006). However, at the same time Myhill suggests that one of the issues that must be considered when police hope to effectively take part in community engagement is "sharing power with communities," which suggests that "engagement is not something to be done 'to' communities; they [the community] must participate in planning and choosing approaches and feel equal ownership of the process" (2006, vi). If police and communities are to work collaboratively on counterterrorism efforts, citizens are (or should be) equal stakeholders in the planning and process of a truly community-centered program.

What becomes clear, both from the broader literature and from the empirical research carried out for this book, is that similar kinds of methodologies are being utilized by police in this arena toward removing mystique on "both sides," improving channels of communication with select individuals perceived as important links into broader community experience and knowledge, and ingratiating police more fully into a given community's everyday experience. To be sure, there are many potential positive outcomes from this approach. Trust and human empathy are clearly important (see, e.g., Spalek, El Awa, and McDonald, 2008; Silk, 2010), but how these are best garnered and sustained, and for what purpose, is not easily reduced to a simple formula. It is very difficult to pinpoint when these strategies and tactics can, or should, be applied under the guise of community policing to support counterterrorism efforts, and many important questions have to be considered here.

One of the important questions requiring clarity here is this: Who are the subjects of such an outreach, and why do the underlying reasons behind the choice vary over time and place? For example, community engagement projects can serve to identify certain sectors and groupings viewed by police as having particular legitimate expectations of law enforcement, which are currently not being met. Those approached by police to remedy this state of affairs are deemed able to both articulate the problems and be part of the solution in terms of assisting police to understand the difficulties and find appropriate means to address them. Such persons may well have further value to contribute to the overall policing of their local community. However, their engagement often does not go beyond participation of this nature (DuBois and Hartnett 2002). Increasingly, there has been an innovative, but needed, move toward engaging those more distrustful of policing, and/or those whom police distrust, with the most recent manifestation of this phenomenon more explicitly geared toward police working with individuals and communities deemed, by the new discourse on "terror," as "at risk" of committing acts of violence (Spalek 2012). If such approaches are not thoughtfully applied, these individuals and groups may continue to be viewed more as part of the problem than the portion of the solution they actually may represent (see, e.g., Lambert 2008a; 2008b). Given the difficulty with shaking off entrenched stereotypes, there is still a tendency to balk at the active recruitment of individuals and groups deemed too "extreme" or too "radical." These groups tend to be "othered," kept at arm's length, and further alienated from engagement processes.

Their potential contributions, as members of communities with shared concerns about safety and security like other members of their neighborhoods, are not given due consideration.

Clearly, different understandings and methodologies in utilizing community outreach for preventing ideological violence are required, depending on the objectives and constituencies involved. However, the possibility exists, in reality, of overly generic community policing efforts being applied where they are far from appropriate and might actually cement mistrust. A level of further ambiguity, and concern, enters the process when, in the context of counterterrorism, national or local law-enforcement leaders decide that police organizations need to know more about Muslims living in their area of jurisdiction (see the recent NYPD example in Powell 2012). Is increased contact with Muslims about recognizing the need to be more inclusive? Is it fueled by an understanding that policing or broader government agendas have failed or are failing Muslims in particular? Is it about improving efforts to combat Islamophobia? The questions do not stop there. Are Muslim communities good potential partners because they can assist police to respond more effectively and sensitively to policing issues, in general, or in respect to policing "the Muslim community" in particular? Are they a good potential source of previously unexploited intelligence? Maybe the answer is all of the above—but herein inherent tensions and competing agendas lie.

On the community side, engagement with the police can equally be motivated by a range of factors: altruistic, selfish, personal, organizationally driven, or otherwise. Some of these may be in tension with one another other or differ from a law-enforcement agenda. Some may want a seat at the table simply to receive or impart information and advice. Others may be motivated by a wish to impact more directly on policy and practice and/or render police more sensitive to or appreciative of a community's culture, needs, or experience.

The potential for overlap, misunderstanding, and mutually exclusive motivations, in the above respects alone, make it all the more necessary to question whether, and in what circumstances, real engagement and partnership are fundamentally necessary, desirable, and successful or, at the other end of the spectrum, even possible. The inherent danger here is that well-intentioned initiatives, or even those with ulterior motives, are equally susceptible to being mediocre, counterproductive, or affirming of stereotypes and assumptions, themselves requiring to be more fully tested.

Clearly all is not doom and gloom. Positive results can be generated by police and community partners coming together. Lives can be changed, or even saved, and real differences can be made in communities and in police ways of thinking. The "humanizing" and educational effect of such encounters can often result in a sufficient degree of mutual satisfaction for those involved to stay involved (see, for example, Irvine in Chapter Seven). Often this is as far as the analysis goes. However, the affective domain is a significant factor for further study in terms of measuring the success and potential for success of such engagements.

In this context, bringing academia into more direct conversation with those practicing engagement and partnership in a counterterrorism context, whether or not specifically framed as such, can provide a useful avenue for learning at multiple levels. Whether policies and initiatives more cognizant and mindful of, or open to situating themselves within a more theorized framework, stand a better chance of "success" depends on myriad factors, some of which will be explored in the course of this book, and drawn more fully together in its conclusion.

## Community Policing: Themes and Challenges

Community engagement in policing is often characterized by a fundamental absence of agreement on what such initiatives are required to effect, or what precisely these labels actually mean in content or intent (e.g., Trojanowicz and Bucqueroux 1990, 2–3; Eck and Rosenbaum 1994, 5; Myhill 2006). Myhill (2006, 9) boils this paucity of consensus down to both the definition of community being contested, and also the multiplicity of levels and methods of engagement adopted (Home Office 2008; Northern Ireland Policing Board 2008).

The literature does seem to suggest that partnership and engagement strategies can be effective (Myhill 2006), and are at the high end of effective police-community approaches. Spalek et al. (2008, 12–13), on the basis of their empirical work in the United Kingdom, point out the following as key to sustainable and effective community engagement and partnership:

- The centrality of dialogue and trust building between partners.
- The need to acknowledge grievances on both sides, for example, the frustration with foreign policy for some community members, and the perception by some police officers that community members may apportion too much responsibility regarding political matters to police rather than politicians.

- Understanding and making space for emotions: counterterrorism and related issues are emotive subjects and areas of work. Recognizing emotions on the part of police and community members allows participants to address negative sentiments, and use the energy and commitment underpinning positive emotion to drive partnership work.
- Developing individual and community empowerment: supporting independent community interests, especially within the highly politicized environment of counterterrorism, may be particularly problematic for police officers.
- Identifying those members of communities who can partner with police: in-depth knowledge of the complexities of communities allows for strategic partnering between police and communities, and the development of relations with those best placed to counterterrorism, including, in some cases, Muslim groups normatively deemed "radical."
- Building on the mutual goal of the prevention of violent actions and drawing upon and utilizing community experiences, ideas, and knowledge.
- The importance of a multiagency approach, whereby the police, communities, statutory, and other agencies work in partnership to address violent extremism.

In the current collection, the Northern Ireland case studies, in particular, point to the benefits to be gained by a multiagency approach that frames problems other than in a specifically criminal justice or antiterrorist context.

## What Is Community?

The policing literature tends to focus little attention on defining the term "community" or, with notable exceptions (e.g., Adelman et al. 2003), using its vagaries to interrogate the standing of partners within a given context with any specificity. The literature also tends not to consider the police as (a separate) community, with their own codes for belonging and being. Failures in this regard, however, permit a view of communities (both police and nonpolice) as homogenous and monolithic, with community policing initiatives presupposing that there is a community view of what is wanted and expected of policing and a matching corollary of what police do and should expect of the community in terms of quid pro quo. If this leads, for example, to assuming that a well-settled, law-respecting, relatively affluent Muslim community will know anything more than anyone else about terrorist activity, it would appear counterintuitive on many levels. It further begs the question of why engagement with such individuals is often deemed preferable to attempting to engage with Salafis and those deemed more "radical" or alienated from policing structures.

Often, labels and signifiers envisioned and operationalized for policing purposes operate in very black and white terms, clearly separating out "criminals," "terrorists," and all who are conceived of as bad or evil from law-abiding citizens in fairly binary terms—even if police personnel themselves recognize that their world is not so easily divided. In the counterterrorism sphere, enemies are not just individuals who commit atrocities but may be conceived of as groups—concretized, or more nebulous in form. Without sufficient insight, oversight and care, group characteristics such as race, religion, ethnicity, or other forms of difference can be used in a discriminatory or arbitrary manner in profiling (Open Society 2005; Powell 2012), thereby stereotyping and often ultimately demonizing communities deemed suspect by the powers that be (Hillyard 1993).

In practice, false assumptions and a lack of awareness can lead to many community-focused police initiatives employing quite crude understandings about what defines a person as representative of or even as belonging to a certain community. Any sense of essentialism, whether of police or community, needs to be deeply questioned. Otherwise, the tendency in practice can be, for instance, to see Muslims as a monolithic entity, with little thought about how engaging with a small number of Muslim men can provide insight into the views of Muslim women, young Muslim boys or girls, the poor, members of a different branch of Islam, or indeed the Muslim man living next door. Spalek et al. (2008) criticize engagement strategies influenced by "new terror" discourses that make normative assumptions about what kinds of Muslim identities should be engaged, and which help sustain a binary between "Muslimness" and "Britishness" or "Americanness." Adelman et al. (2003) make the point that those favored by police, or those who are self-selected as community partners, may not actually be reflective of a full range of different views of those whom they are deemed to represent. They argue that engagement on such terms can cement stereotypes and the more dysfunctional aspects of relationships between men and women, or with regard to dissident and dissonant members of a given community, under the guise of cultural sensitivity. Spalek et al. (2008) highlight the value of policies that strive to build connections with true grassroots individuals rather than appointed community representatives.

A different view is that community is a "warm and fuzzy" place, and that being seen to police in line with community demands can only be a good thing—part of the "community policing as cherry pie" thesis (Brodgen 1999). However, Bruce and Neild (2005) point out that often the most vocal members of a community, or those feeling particularly besieged, can call for a tough, quite authoritarian approach to policing when this might be neither appropriate nor representative of the views of many others living within or coming from that community. Nor would an adoption of populist sentiment necessarily be in keeping with human rights imperatives more generally. Indeed, police personnel may be the ones to first recognize that community demands are patently unconstitutional. Other commentators equally point out that there is a real risk that community policing can become problematic "if it moves away from a genuine problem-solving ethos towards pseudo-problem-solving through simply appeasing public appetites for enforcement that may function as unduly exclusionary" (MacKenzie and Henry 2009, 1).

O'Rawe and Moore (1997) make the point that, often, "community" can be a very dangerous place to be, particularly for those marginalized or otherwise alienated from mainstream experience. Community, therefore, can neither be viewed as benign and value free, nor monolithic. Selecting which parts to engage with therefore involves, of necessity, a range of value judgments and sites of exclusion, which themselves may be contested. This is not to suggest that police, as a manifestation of state, are the only factor at work in the societal construction of folk heroes and devils (Cohen 2002). However, just as police rely on societal representations and understandings of good and evil to position themselves, so also they may contribute to those understandings and articulations of who is the enemy and who can be permitted to be friend.

We must carefully consider the extent to which community members are treated as agents in their own right, or only valued inasmuch as they can be prevailed upon to provide a volunteer labor force for the police. Baden argues convincingly:

> Good governance is founded on citizens' ability to claim entitlements in three broad areas: the right to participate in public decision-making; the inclusion of people's needs and interests in policy; and the allocation of resources. (Baden 2000, 37)

But community-police initiatives may operate at such a localized or junior-rank level that they do not succeed in meeting, in a meaningful way, even the first two of these indicators. Power over resource allocation is rarely on the agenda, except to the extent that it ticks police boxes. The Communities and Policing in Transition (CAPT) project, outlined in Chapter Five, indicates that very different dynamics and possibilities can hold sway where communities have access to a funding stream independent of the police. The Independent Commission on Policing in Northern Ireland (1999) had set out an important and internationally resonant blueprint in this respect, in terms of conceptualizing *policing* more broadly than "the police," and providing conditions for a broad-based policing budget to be raised, administered, and deployed beyond the normal criminal justice dictates. This vision is still a long way from coming to fruition (Ellison and O'Rawe 2010), but it surely contains the seeds of something very significant if it were ever to be rolled out.

Whether, or to what extent, community policing actually works is difficult to say, partly due to the ongoing confusion, both in the literature and in reality, as to what community policing or engaging the community actually means in application. The lack of clarity of the concept means that a range of initiatives can take place under the broad umbrella of community policing, while serving a variety of competing agendas. Where valuable initiatives do take hold and bed down, they tend not to be mainstreamed within policing systems as a whole. Indeed, police personnel in each of the areas described here have themselves likely felt marginalized if their dedication to community policing seemed to put them too firmly at odds with more traditional policing strategies. Things often seem to work best where they are localized and personality driven. This can prove difficult where community officers are transferred in and out of areas at will, with insufficient consideration for the value of continuity or the damage high staff turnover might do to relationships painstakingly built up. A focus on pockets of local "successes" might equally be evidence, at some level, of police leaders and managers balking at the extent of the paradigm shift that would actually be necessary, internally, to a police organization, and otherwise, to truly embed human rights compliant, community-oriented practice in a more systemic and holistic way (e.g., Green and Mystrofski (eds) (1988); Myhill 2006: vi; O'Rawe 2007).

## Violence—The Need for a Public Health Approach

The confusions and conundrums pouring through the literature suggest a need to go back to first principles, and ascertain what we actually do know about violence and how to counter it. Gilligan (2000) argues that our responses to terrorism and extremist violence are ill-conceived, as they are not based to any real extent on a theorized understanding of what violence is or how best it can be tackled. Žižak (2008) posits three forms of violence: subjective, objective (systemic), and symbolic. While we may be very prone to focus on subjective violence by an identifiable agent (e.g., crime and acts of terror), instead, Žižak argues:

> [W]e should learn to step back, to disentangle ourselves from the fascinating lure of this directly visible "subjective" violence, violence performed by a clearly identifiable agent. We need to perceive the contours of the background which generates such outbursts. A step back enables us to identify a violence that sustains our very efforts to fight violence and promote tolerance. (2008, 1)

This willingness and ability to "step back" and look more holistically at the roots and sources of violence may be one of the less-examined keys to making community policing initiatives work to address ideological violence.

Gilligan (1996, 2000) also has much to share in striving to reorient our responses to violence and how it is conceptualized. Perhaps we need to view violence, not in terms of a criminal justice issue, but, instead, as a public health epidemic, requiring the same kind of understandings and responses. Nobody expects doctors to develop a scathing rhetoric about how bad and evil cancer is, as this is going to do nothing to help them cure it. Similarly with violence, heaping opprobrium on certain classes and groups of people as undesirable or evil is not going to bring them to see the wisdom of any more fundamental message or need. Gilligan points out that shame is the central motive for collective as well as individual violence, and that this can be documented throughout history. Nor is it only terrorist violence that is subject to the same motivations. Greg Boyle (2010), a Jesuit priest with a history of success in rehabilitation work with gang members in Los Angeles, also describes the same issues at work with recognizing where the violence of gang culture comes from and what is needed to eradicate it. He also situates gangs very squarely, not as a crime issue, but as a community health issue. He considers the shame that leads people to seek belonging and pride in gang activity, and the need for unconditional love to take the place of punishment and further humiliation and contempt.

We are perhaps not going to develop policing and community engagements on the foundation of unconditional love—but the point is instructive in arguing the need to question the premise behind such engagement, to factor in the complexity in the humanity of all involved in (or excluded from) such initiatives and, perhaps, to challenge ourselves and our governments in terms of the extent to which we might need to seek more inclusive and holistic solutions to the problem of radical violence.

## References


Adelman, Madelaine, Edna Erez, and Nadera Shalhoub-Kevorkian. 2003. "Policing Violence against Minority Women in Multicultural Societies: 'Community' and the Politics of Exclusion." In *Police and Society 7*: 105–133.

Alderson, John. 1979. *Policing Freedom*. Plymouth: Macdonald and Evans.

Baden, Sally. 2000. "Gender, Governance and the Feminization of Poverty." In *Women and Political Participation: 21st Century Challenges*. New York: UNDP. http://www.undp.org/governance/docs/Gender-Pub-21stcentury.pdf.

Boyle, Gregory. 2010. *Tattoos on the Heart: The Power of Boundless Compassion*. New York: Free Press.

Breen-Smyth, Marie. 2007. "A Critical Research Agenda for the Study of Political Terror." *European Political Science 6*: 260–267.

Brogden, M. 1999. "Community Policing as Cherry Pie." In *Policing across the World: Issues for the 21st Century*. Edited by R. I. Mawby. 167–186. London: Routledge.

Brown, Ben. 2007. "Community Policing in Post September 11 America: A Comment on the Concept of Community Oriented Terrorism." *Police Practice and Research 8*(3): 239–251.

Cohen, Stanley. 2002. *Folk Devils and Moral Panics*. London: Routledge.

Bruce, David, and Neild, Rachel. 2005. *The Police That We Want: A Handbook for Oversight of Police in South Africa*. Johannesburg, South Africa: Centre for the Study of Violence and Reconciliation. http://www.ssrnetwork.net/document_library/detail/2520/the-police-that-we-want-a-handbook-for-oversight-of-the-police-in-south-africa.

DuBois, Jill, and Susan M. Hartnett. 2002. "Making the Community Side of Community Policing Work: What Needs to Be Done." In *Policing and Community Partnerships*. Edited by Dennis J. Stevens. 1–16. New York: Prentice Hall.

Eck, John E., and Dennis Rosenbaum. 1994. "The New Police Order: Effectiveness, Equity and Efficiency in Community Policing." In *Community Policing: Testing the Promises*. Edited by Dennis P. Rosenbaum. 3–23. Thousand Oaks, CA: Sage.

Ellison, Graham, and Mary O'Rawe. 2010. "Security Governance in Transition: The Compartmentalizing, Crowding Out and Corralling of Policing and Security in Northern Ireland." *Theoretical Criminology 14*(1): 31–57.

Friedmann, Robert, R. 1992. *Community Policing: Comparative Perspectives and Prospects*. New York: Harvester Wheatsheaf.

García Chávez, Tania Guadalupe. 2012. *Perspectives on Community Policing: A Social Constructivist and Comparative Analysis*. Unpublished PhD dissertation. University of Birmingham.

Gilligan, James. 2000. *Violence: Reflections on Our Deadliest Epidemic*. London: Jessica Kingsley Publishers.

Goldstein, Herman. 1990. *Problem Oriented Policing*. New York: McGraw Hill Publishing.

Greene, Jack R., and Stephen D. Mastrofski (Eds). 1988. *Community Policing: Rhetoric or Reality?* New York: Praeger.

Hamber, Brandon. 2006. "Flying Flags of Fear: The Role of Fear in the Process of Political Transition." *Journal of Human Rights* 5(1): 127–142.

Hillyard, Paddy. 1993. Suspect Community: People's Experience of the Prevention of Terrorism Acts in Britain. London: Pluto Press in Association with Liberty.

Home Office. 2008. *Community Engagement in Policing*. www.community engagement.police.uk.

———. 2010. "Channel: Supporting Individuals Vulnerable to Recruitment by Violent Extremists. A Guide for Local Partnerships." Norwich, UK: The Stationery Office, in partnership with Association of Chief Police Officers.

Independent Commission on Policing (Patten Commission). 1999. *A New Beginning for Policing in Northern Ireland*. Norwich, UK: The Stationery Office.

Innes, Martin. 2006. "Policing Uncertainty: Countering Terror through Community Intelligence and Democratic Policing." *The ANNALS of the American Academy of Political and Social Science 605*(1): 222–241.

Jackson, Richard. 2007. "The Core Commitments of Critical Terrorism Studies." *European Political Science 6*: 244–251.

LaFree, Gary, and Gary Ackerman. 2009. "The Empirical Study of Terrorism: Social and Legal Research." *Annual Review of Law in the Social Sciences 5*: 347–374.

Lambert, Robert. 2008a. "Empowering Salafis and Islamists against al-Qaeda: A London Counterterrorism Case Study." *PS: Political Science & Politics 41*(1): 31–35.

———. 2008b. "Salafi and Islamist Londoners: Stigmatised Minority Faith Communities Countering al-Qaida." *Crime, Law and Social Change 50*(1–2): 73–89.

MacKenzie, Simon, and Alistair Henry. 2009. Community Policing: A Review of the Literature (Web only publication). Edinburgh, Scotland: Scottish Government Social Research. http://www.scotland.gov.uk/Publications/2009/11/19091609/0.

Manning, Peter. 1977. Police Work: The Social Organisation of Policing. Cambridge, MA: MIT.

McNamara, Kevin. 2002. House of Commons Hansard Debates for 11 July, 2002. http://www.publications.parliament.uk/pa/cm200102/cmhansrd/vo020711/debtext/20711-28.htm.

Myhill, Andy. 2006. *Community Engagement in Policing: Lessons from the Literature.* London: Home Office. http://police.homeoffice.gov.uk/news-and-publications/publication/community-policing/Community_engagement_lit_rev.pdf?view=Binary.

National Research Council Committee to Review Research on Police Policy and Practices 2004. *Fairness and Effectiveness in Policing: the Evidence.* Washington, DC: National Academic Press.

Northern Ireland Policing Board. 2008. *Best Value Review of Community Engagement.* http://www.nipolicingboard.org.uk/final_nipb_best_value_community_engagement_function_bvr.pdf-2.pdf.

O'Connor, Michael, and Celia Ruhmann, 2005. "Into the Fire: How to Avoid Getting Burned by the Same Mistakes Made Fighting Terrorism in Northern Ireland." *Cardozo Law Review 24*: 1657–1751.

Open Society Justice Initiative. 2005. *Ethnic Profiling by Police in Europe.*

O'Rawe, M, and L. Moore. 1997. *Human Rights on Duty.* Belfast, Northern Ireland: Committee on the Administration of Justice.

O'Rawe, Mary. 2007. "Human Rights, Transitional Societies and Police Training: Legitimating Strategies and Delegitimating Legacies." *St John's Journal of Legal Commentary 22*(1): 199–259.

Perry, Nicholas. 2003. "The Numerous Federal Legal Definitions of Terrorism: The Problem of Too Many Grails." *Journal of Legislation 30*: 249.

Powell, Michael. 2012. "Police Monitoring and a Climate of Fear." *The New York Times*, February 27. http://www.nytimes.com/2012/02/28/nyregion/nypd-muslim-monitoring-and-a-climate-of-fear.html?_r=0.

Sadd, S., and R. M. Gricc. 1996. *Implementation Challenges in Community Policing: Innovative Neighborhood-Oriented Policing in Eight Cities.* Washington, DC: US Dept of Justice, National Institute of Justice. http://www.ncjrs.gov/pdffiles/implcp.pdf.

Schmid, Alex P. and Albert J. Jongman. 1988. *Political Terrorism: A New Guide to Actors, Authors, Concepts, Data Bases, Theories and Literature.* Amsterdam: North Holland Publishers Company.

———. 2005. *Political Terrorism: A New Guide to Actors, Authors, Concepts, Data Bases, Theories and Literature.* Piscataway, NJ: Transaction Publishers.

Silk, Phillip, D. 2010. Planning Outreach between Muslim Communities and Police in the USA and the UK. Unpublished PhD Dissertation. University of Georgia.

Spalek, Basia (Ed). 2012. *Counter-Terrorism: Community-Based Approaches to Terror Crime.* Hampshire: Palgrave Macmillan.

Spalek, Basia, Salwa El Awa, and Laura Zahra McDonald. 2008. *Police Muslim Engagement and Partnerships for the Purposes of Counter-Terrorism: An Examination.* Birmingham: University of Birmingham.

"Terrorism Act 2000." 2000. http://www.legislation.gov.uk/ukpga/2000/11/contents.

Trojanowicz, Robert C., and Bonnie Bucqueroux. 1990. *Community Policing: A Contemporary Perspective.* Cincinnati, OH: Anderson.

United and Strengthening America by Providing Appropriate Tools Required to Intercept and Obstruct Terrorism (USA PATRIOT ACT) Act of 2001. 2001. http://www.gpo.gov/fdsys/pkg/PLAW-107publ56/pdf/PLAW-107publ56.pdf.

United States General Accounting Office. 2003. *Combating Terrorism: Interagency Framework and Agency Programs to Address the Overseas Threat.* Washington, DC: United States General Accounting Office. http://www.gao.gov/new.items/d03165.pdf.

Vito, Gennaro. F., William F. Walsh, and Julie Kunselman. 2004. "Community Policing: The Middle Manager Perspective. *Police Quarterly* 6(X): 1–22. https://louisville.edu/advising/justiceadministration/faculty-staff/vita/g.vito/COP %20Middle%20Manager.pdf.

Žižak, Slavoj. 2008. *Violence.* London: Profile Books.

2

# The Sociopolitical Contexts Affecting Police-Community Engagement in Northern Ireland, Britain, and the United States

*Tara Lai Quinlan, Basia Spalek, and Mary O'Rawe*

Counterterrorism is a challenging arena characterized by deep disagreements regarding "truth," tactics, and the appropriate roles of governments and communities. Despite this, as a state-led national and international approach to conflict, counterterrorism tends, in fairly black-and-white terms, to situate terrorism as the "problem" and "terrorists" as the enemy. The politically charged calls to defeat terrorism are replete with diametric language, such as former president Bush's argument that the world is cleanly divided in matters of terrorism: you are either for us or against us. This simplistic characterization, however attractive it may be to some, overshadows the complexities that confront governments, police, nongovernmental organizations, and communities in their efforts to work collaboratively to reduce violence.

After the September 11, 2001 attacks in the United States, a "war on terror" was unleashed in response to what was seen to be a global terrorist attack. Over the last 11 years, the pursuit of this war has involved wide-ranging counterterrorism measures across North America, Europe, Asia, the Far East, and Australia. However, beneath the rhetoric and political posturing, deep contestations regarding "truth" have continued, with the wide interest in conspiracy theories representing just one facet of the opposing views regarding the source and nature of the terrorist threat. Concurrent with the post-9/11 counterterrorism efforts, Northern Ireland has been involved in the arduous task of trying to construct a viable and peaceful society following over 30 years of violent political conflict stemming from the "Troubles." Policing has been high on the agenda in terms of reforms initiated, with the International Commission on Policing positing 175 recommendations on how to establish acceptable and effective policing arrangements on the twin pillars of respect for human rights and policing with the community (Independent Commission on Policing 1999). Perhaps the most difficult and long-standing task for any peace process, and certainly for that in Northern Ireland, continues to be that of establishing "truth" in the postconflict environment. Where truth begins and ends, and whose truth should be privileged, is deeply challenging in all these contexts, for there are always multiple truths in relation to the causes and casualties of conflict. Among the truths that tend to be most unpalatable for governments the world over, is any suggestion that what is done by the state under the guise of "counterterrorism" is potentially not above the conflict, but instead part and parcel of its continuance and, at times, even its exacerbation.

Indeed, there is no one "truth" for policy makers, practitioners, and communities to agree upon regarding "right," "wrong," causes, and blame. In part, this is due to the problems associated with defining what terrorism is. Many researchers argue that terrorism should be approached as a concept or idea rather than a label (Wilkinson 2006). Viewing terrorism as a concept involves an understanding that there are many state and nonstate actors and agencies (e.g., policing bodies, government institutions, international bodies, researchers, community members, and so on) who define terrorism and counterterrorism differently, although there may be points of convergence as well as divergence. Definitions of terrorism can include violence that is committed by nonstate and state actors, a form of threat and violence-based communication used to create terror (Schmid and Jongman 2005). However, there is still a tendency for established scholars, governments, and others to view terrorism as predominantly the actions of nonstate actors rather than as acts committed by states themselves (Breen-Smyth 2007; Jackson 2008).

## Definitions and Positions

This discussion is important in understanding the challenges for police and community engagement in relation to counterterrorism in the jurisdictions under study. Due, in part to the definitional and conceptual challenges of "terrorism" itself (Chomsky 1991; Friedrichs 2006; Kellner 2004, 42; Mills and Miller 2009, 417), counterterrorism is a necessarily contested field, with wide chasms often separating police and other practitioners, community members, and policy makers regarding what is effective, appropriate, or even ethical in prosecuting a counterterrorism agenda. These differences can lead to differing perspectives upon the kinds of initiatives that should be implemented to reduce terrorism-related violence. For example, after 9/11 there have been significant differences of opinion over the causes of violent radicalization, among Muslim youth in particular. While some policy makers, community members, and practitioners have viewed Salafism and Islamism as key risk factors in the violent radicalization of young people—and therefore as the object of counterterrorism and counterinsurgency measures—others have viewed some forms of Salafism and Islamism as being the solutions to the potential of violent radicalization as opposed to the cause (Lambert 2008, 2011; Baker 2011). These positions sharply diverge over the extent to which certain sections of the Muslim population can or should be viewed as either the "problem" or as the "solution." This foundational disagreement is just one example of how fundamentally different viewpoints can be expressed in the counterterrorism arena, and it also offers a small glimpse into the complexities involved.

## The Role of the State in Counterterrorism

It is perhaps unsurprising, therefore, that there are disagreements in the United Kingdom and the United States over the extent to which the state should even be involved in community engagement for counterterrorism purposes. For example, it may be that communities are best placed to deal with the sensitive issues affecting them, among themselves, and therefore, state, and more particularly police, involvement may be perceived as state intrusion. In Britain, for example, there has been some concern that while some mosques have been dealing with extremism, they have been doing so largely on their own, without involving the police. Moreover, in these cases, often the police are not made aware of community interventions through the community contacts that they have (Innes et al. 2011). In other instances, it may be the case that state involvement in community security is indeed important, for security is something that may need to be coproduced by state and nonstate actors to ensure due process and regard for the rights of all involved. Such efforts may be usefully furthered by engagement and partnerships between police officers and community members. This raises an important question: If it is important for community members to act credibly with their key audiences and groups, then might it be the case that it is be essential for them to act independently—perhaps meaning the freedom to act independently from the police to address community concerns (Spalek 2013)?

## Coproduction of Security

This, of course, is a controversial point, and it raises the issue of what is meant by the coproduction of security. Coproduction may, in certain circumstances, indeed, require community members acting independently of the police. It might also mean that in some cases community members deliver those projects that police would like to see delivered, but without too much police involvement, so as to maintain the credibility of those community members concerned (Spalek 2013). Credibility is clearly a key concept to consider when discussing police counterterrorism efforts. Credibility helps determine the extent to which a person's message, viewpoint, or initiative really can influence behavior, particularly among those deemed at risk of vulnerability to violent radicalization. Credibility can play an important transformative role within conflict precisely because this is about state and nonstate actors maintaining integrity and trust, despite considerable pressures to conform to dominant norms that may include repression, human rights abuses, violence, or its promotion. The engagement of former paramilitary prisoners in Northern Ireland, in various strands of the peace process is a case in point, and may be instructive on many levels. Credibility can be an important resource through which to build and maintain important connections with wide-ranging actors for the purposes of conflict transformation and of offering peaceful responses to social norms and practices that are unjust and even violent. However, all this happens in a context where state responses to terrorism can, at times, negatively impact the credibility that state and nonstate actors have worked hard to build (Spalek 2013).

In these and similar discussions, it is useful to make a distinction between *community-focused* and *community-targeted* approaches to counterterrorism. A *community-targeted* approach might be characterized as one that ignores the issue of gaining the consent of those communities that are being targeted, with the well-being of targeted communities often being compromised through striving to achieve the broader goal of maintaining nation-state security (e.g., Hillyard

1993, on the experience of the Irish in Britain under the Prevention of Terrorism legislation). At the same time, a community-targeted approach is characterized by distrust between communities and security officials and practitioners. *Community-focused* approaches, on the other hand, can be characterized by partnership between communities and state officials, harnessing community consent and participation in the actual governance of the various strategies and approaches that are applied, by building and sustaining trust between state officials and security practitioners and community members. A community-focused approach therefore embraces communities for their complexities in relation to ethnicity, religion, politics, emotions, grievances, locales, histories, and so forth. This approach seeks to work with, rather than manipulate, communities (Spalek, El-Awa, and McDonald 2009; Spalek 2012; but see Adelman, Erez, and Shalboud-Kevorkian 2003, where initiatives in a range of countries worked only with mainstream Muslim men under the guise of cultural sensitivity). It may be that state involvement in outreach as a counter-terrorism tactic is valid as long as there are enough safeguards in place to ensure a community-focused rather than a community-targeted approach. The question that remains is this: What constitutes sufficient safeguards, and to what extent do they enhance or suppress the thoughtful risk-taking that is sometimes required of all involved?

## The Role of "Active" Citizens and Resilience

Another issue within the sociopolitical contexts shaping police and community engagement in the United States and the United Kingdom is that of the increasing focus upon "active" citizenship in relation to counterterrorism policies and practices. Within the national counterterrorism strategies of Britain and the United States in particular, individuals as citizens are expected to act responsibly in the face of threats from terrorism, spotting signs of vulnerability within their family, work, and other cohorts, and working with appropriate authorities (HM Government 2011; The White House 2011b). As argued by Briggs, Fieschi, and Lownsbrough in 2006, the notion that "communities can defeat terrorism" has become a popular counterterrorism maxim. Similar to other areas of social policy—crime, health, and welfare, for example—individuals are being viewed as an important resource for preventing terrorism, as part of their responsibilities as active citizens and as concerned members of wider communities.

Within the US and British counterterrorism strategies, there is also a focus on resilience. In the US counterterrorism strategy, building a culture of resilience is a core guiding principle: "The United States and its partners are engaged in the full range of cooperative CT activities—from intelligence sharing to joint training and operations and from countering radicalization to pursuing community resilience programs" (The White House 2011a, 6). Furthermore, the *National Strategy for Counterterrorism* contends, "We will continue to assist, engage, and connect communities to increase their collective resilience abroad and at home" (The White House 2011a, 10). In the review of Prevent, a core strand of the British counterterrorism strategy, the following phrases can be found: "vulnerability to violent extremism includes a lack of resilience in some places and communities" (Home Office 2011, 18); "resilience in the context of this document means the capability of people, groups and communities to rebut and reject proponents of terrorism and the ideology they promote"(Home Office 2011, 108); "a stronger sense of 'belonging' and citizenship makes communities more resilient to terrorist ideology and propagandists. We believe that Prevent depends on integration, democratic participation and a strong interfaith dialogue" (Home Office 2011, 27).

The focus on resilience, and in particular community resilience, illustrates the importance placed upon individuals from within communities to be responsible and active citizens, to be moral agents, and to help prevent terrorism. This focus heralds a radical shift from traditional counterterrorism policies and practices, which have pursued "hard-ended" policies and practices involving surveillance and the use of informants among other tactics (Hewitt 2010).

While the overall effectiveness has yet to be seen, there is little doubt that the post-9/11 era has seen a policy shift to incorporate "soft" counterterrorism strategies to supplement "hard" approaches (see Spalek and Imtoual 2007). The question is, to what extent have hard approaches been supplanted by a realization that softer approaches work better, and to what extent are soft approaches simply broadening the field for additional covert activity, coopted at a range of levels to the services of a broader more furtive national security agenda?

## Singling out Communities?

Within this shift, in the United States and in Britain, counterterrorism policies and practices have focused predominantly over the past decade upon Muslim communities, thereby singling them out as being especially responsible for preventing terrorism (Pantazis and Pemberton 2009; Harris 2010; Tyler, Schulhofer, and Huq 2010, 365–66; Choudhury and Fenwick 2011, 9). The language of community resilience and citizenship presumes that all individuals have equal choice in deciding whether to help counterterrorism or not. However, it might be argued that in a post-9/11 world, Muslim minorities living within Western democratic states have much less freedom and choice in relation to counterterrorism initiatives, because many of these focus explicitly on Muslim communities. These Muslim communities may retain some choice to participate or not in counterterrorism initiatives, but they certainly were not consulted in government strategies, which, for example, state that the "paramount terrorist threat we have faced" (The White House 2011a, 1) is the questionably Islamic(ist) group al-Qaeda. This is despite the fact that terrorism is a threat that emanates not just from al-Qaeda-linked violence, but also from threats posed by separatist, left wing, and anarchic groups, and indeed, individuals who have never come within the police radar prior to committing mass murder, such as happened in Norway in the summer of 2011. Is the mere fact of violence seeming to be employed for explicitly political ends (and even more exclusively emanating from those possibly linked to al-Qaeda) somehow more of a threat or social harm than violence perpetrated every day and night on our streets and in our homes? Gender-based violence is a global problem, killing more women and children year on year than terrorism—yet the drive for and level of police community engagement to deal with the issue of patriarchy, whether in the form of domestic violence, honor killings, or sexual abuse is nowhere of the same magnitude. Is it more important to focus attention on "terrorist violence" than on other forms, which in terms of actual harm perpetrated impact on the daily lives of so many more citizens (and noncitizens)? Would a more holistic approach to the epidemic that is violence in our communities and in our world be more effective in allowing connections to be made between terror-based violence and its other manifestations (Gilligan 2000; 2001)?

Despite all of this, a number of research studies highlight that Muslim communities have experienced differentiated citizenship post-9/11 as a result of the "securitization" of their communities. Securitization involves the implementation of emergency politics whereby a particular social issue that becomes securitized is responded to above and beyond established rules and frameworks that exist within what might be called "normal politics" (Jutila 2006). It is the Muslim communities, following on in the United Kingdom from the Irish in Britain and Nationalists in Northern Ireland, who have predominantly experienced "hard-edged" counterterrorism policies and practices (Pantazis and Pemberton 2009; Spalek, El-Awa and McDonald 2009; Kundnani 2009; McGovern and Tobin 2010; Choudhury and Fenwick 2011; Hickman, et al. 2011). This discussion raises some further important questions. Can members of Muslim communities take a proactive civil stance toward national counterterrorism strategies and work toward preventing terrorism? Or, should citizens—Muslim and non-Muslim alike—critique state-driven counterterrorism policies and practices? Although government messages may suggest that communities are needed to help prevent terrorism, the reality on the ground is that communities continue to experience state-led "hard-ended" approaches that include surveillance, the use of informants, the use of stop and search, and other intrusive measures. If citizens do critique and challenge state-led approaches do they run the risk of potentially being viewed as "subversives" by the state?

Irish communities have had to face these problems and similar questions and issues, over a much longer period of time. As a report by McGovern and Tobin (2010) highlights, the depth of wide-ranging laws and state powers in relation to the perceived threat from "Irish" terrorism has criminalized vast sections of Irish communities. Therefore, it is important to understand that seeking for citizens to engage in counterterrorism is not necessarily a straightforward demand. This quest for participation can be particularly tough where their own relationship with state and/or state practice is conflicted or contested; the very proposition might be something that is just too controversial and too challenging for many. There may need to be significant social, political, policing, and other reforms before many individuals as citizens can or would wish to engage with counterterrorism. The phenomenon of political vetting in Northern Ireland (e.g., the Glor na nGael case) that came to public attention in the 1980s, the number of Irish arrested each year under antiterrorism legislation before being released without charge (see O'Connor and Ruhmann 2003), or the number of those imprisoned through miscarriage of justice (e.g., the cases of the Birmingham 6, Guilford 4, Maguire 7, and Judith Ward) provide examples of the very real economic and other consequences that can attend being deemed subversive ). These are issues that members of Muslim communities, in particular, have increasingly had to face over the last 12 years or so (see Morris 2010), and these circumstances are key to consider when one seeks to better understand the complexities involved in expecting community participation in countering terrorism.

It is, therefore, not so straightforward to insist that "if you're not for us you're against us." The vexed issue of Catholic unwillingness to neither join nor cooperate with the Royal Ulster Constabulary during the years of the conflict in Northern Ireland is further instructive in this regard. The police force in Northern Ireland was 92 percent Protestant when the Independent Commission on Policing reported in 1999 (ICP 1999). This was clearly not because Catholics as a group instead supported or belonged to the IRA and other paramilitary groupings, but was instead symptomatic of something else. To what extent was Catholic disengagement and alienation a function of terrorist threat and intimidation with the ever-present reality that they could not so engage and continue to live in their own communities, under the highly segregated living conditions of Northern Ireland? To what extent was the clear British and Protestant ethos of the Royal Ulster Constabulary as an organization a barrier in itself to someone who considered themselves Irish rather than British? How much was it about the counterinsurgency, paramilitary style of policing that characterized the RUC, particularly, though not exclusively, in Catholic areas throughout the decades of the Troubles? Similar questions pertain and require to be more fully explored in the post-9/11 era.

## The Role of Locally Driven Initiatives

Interestingly, there are examples of citizens implementing local initiatives that might challenge dominant nation-state policies (McDonald 2012; Spalek 2013), thereby perhaps offering a solution while at the same time bypassing the reluctance of some to partner with the police. In the case of Northern Ireland, community restorative justice schemes, which arose both in the context of wide-ranging policing and criminal justice reforms, and also as a necessary antidote to reforms being perceived by certain sections of the community as not going far enough, are also noteworthy (Mika 2006; McEvoy and Shirlow 2009). Given the sensitive and politicized context of counterterrorism, trust-building and relationship-building activities between state and nonstate actors appear to be of vital importance where they can be made to work (Silk 2010; Spalek 2010). However, there needs to be recognition that at certain points in time, state-driven solutions will be neither possible nor desirable, and other ways of doing business must be found.

Another issue in relation to police-community engagement in the counterterrorism context that has manifested in the United States and the United Kingdom is to do with how police identify community partners for engagement approaches, and on what bases. Community partners can be a source of valuable community intelligence, serve as law enforcement's eyes and ears in the community, speak representatively on the community's behalf, and tap into community networks that otherwise would not be available to law enforcement (Meares 2002, 1612; OSCE 2008, 23; Ramirez et al. 2012).

Voluntary and transparent police-community engagement efforts are distinct from covert approaches like surveillance or use of confidential informants because they require police and local authorities to actively and openly select community partners. But how do police select partners, and based on what criteria? While government first and foremost seeks credible community partners that it can trust (Brodeur and Dupont 2006, 17; HM Government 2011), what determines a community partner's credibility and trustworthiness? Governments seem to select community partners for a variety of reasons that do not necessarily ensure the most effective police-community partnerships. Effective police-community engagement requires engaging a sufficiently broad network of community partners to adequately address the communities' problems (Lasker and Weiss 2003, 18), which may or may not be primarily linked to terrorism prevention and antiradicalization. When the scope of community partners is too limited, it becomes much more difficult for partnerships to be effective in addressing the problem, particularly the underlying roots of the problem (Lasker and Weiss 2003, 18). In the case of terrorism prevention, police-community engagement necessitates that a broad array of individuals and community organizations be engaged, but this often proves challenging for several reasons.

First, politics plays a role in which organizations police engage with. Too often, police and local government opt to engage with the most politically active or prominent community organizations, to the detriment of less vocal, less politically active, or minority community voices (Lasker and Weiss 2003, 20). Some critics have argued that law enforcement partnership programs in the counterterrorism context have focused on "acceptable" and "favorable" viewpoints rather than engaging a broader range of views and philosophies within Muslim communities (Kundnani 2009). Critics argue that the government has alienated some viewpoints within the Muslim community deemed too unpopular or too far outside the mainstream (Choudhury and Fenwick 2011, 49; Lambert 2012). This not only has the effect of marginalizing minority voices with Muslim communities, but also generates or reinforces long-term radicalization issues related to the most marginalized community voices (Spalek, McDonald, and El Awa 2011, 24). For example, some have criticized the United Kingdom's terrorism prevention community engagement efforts for their selective engagement of certain Muslim organizations while excluding other representative Muslim organizations from partnering efforts (Lambert 2012). In the counterterrorism context, for police-community engagement to be effective in local Muslim communities, police must engage with groups with varying viewpoints, intentionally seeking to include nonmainstream and minority views (Thiel 2009, 41; Spalek, McDonald, and El Awa 2011, 24). But police have been criticized for engaging with so-called radical or extremist organizations or individuals, attacks that cannot necessarily be substantiated (Bright 2007). Moreover, such general criticism of partnerships with Muslim communities misses the very point of community engagement. In the counterterrorism context, it is precisely when police engage with the broadest variety of groups with the broadest range of viewpoints that police-community partnerships engage a much broader range of community members, and are more likely to succeed (Thiel 2009, 40; Lambert 2012).

Second, police-community engagement programs too often rely exclusively on community experts or gatekeepers, as opposed to soliciting the involvement and participation of regular community members (Lasker and Weiss 2003: 21). In the counterterrorism context, community partnering programs have been criticized for relying exclusively on community gatekeepers for access to Muslim communities (Innes 2006, 234; Kundnani 2009). In limiting community engagement to community leaders, community engagement efforts relegate regular community members to mere recipients and consumers of government services, not partners (Lasker and Weiss 2003, 20). Too frequently, regular community members are simply treated by government as if they "have little or nothing to do or say concerning setting policy or making decisions, these approaches devalue and discredit their contributions and breed feelings of helplessness and dependency" (Lasker and Weiss 2003, 20). In police counterterrorism efforts, this means that too few Muslim community members may be engaged in transparent police-community engagement programs and left uninformed and without any input in the process. Effective police-community engagement must therefore endeavor to engage with the broadest feasible range of community groups and viewpoints to not only gain the broadest possible insights from community members, forge a wide range of community ties, and develop significant trust from different actors within Muslim communities, but also to give community engagement efforts in counterterrorism the most credibility.

## ONE SIZE DOES NOT FIT ALL

Even when police seek to genuinely partner with a wide variety of communities, they must still question whether community engagement efforts provide sufficient opportunities for different approaches for different communities with different needs. In the post-9/11 context in particular, police must realize that Muslim communities are not homogenous, but instead comprise many diverse groups potentially hailing from a large number of nations, with different ethnicities and cultural groups, histories, socioeconomic and education levels, and belief systems within Islam (Briggs, Fieschi, and Lownsbrough 2006, 29; Choudhury and Fenwick 2011, 5–7). The notion of one singular Muslim community with a single set of interests, experiences, and views is highly problematic and very much contested (Spalek, McDonald, and El Awa 2011, 11). Police-community engagement efforts in the counterterrorism context cannot, then, apply a one-size-fits-all community engagement model with the expectation that it will be highly effective (Lasker and Weiss 2003, 19).

The nature of any nationally funded counterterrorism program poses a variety of risks, not the least of which is the implementation of a one-size-fits-all police-community engagement program at the local level. Indeed, nationally funded community engagement programs increase the risk of creating a top-down infrastructure driven by the national agenda, not community needs. This is particularly problematic when the national agenda itself is so contested. Police-community engagement is by nature an issue that plays out in local communities, and is most effective when the particular needs of the local communities are addressed (Thacher 2005, 637; Innes 2006). For nationally funded community engagement programs to work, they require local community buy-in and participation. Where the national government uses a top-down approach with little local community input, this frequently results in very limited local community buy-in to the program, and often limited program effectiveness (Lasker and Weiss 2003, 19; Choudhury and Fenwick 2011, 52). Without grassroots-level community input incorporated into nationally funded police-community engagement strategies, such programs have minimal chance of long-term effectiveness in solving the underlying problems (Lasker and Weiss 2003, 19; Spalek, McDonald, and El Awa 2011). Even then, a national strategy is not guaranteed to succeed and avoid the pitfalls of other forms of more locally generated intervention.

In the United Kingdom, for example, some have criticized the Prevent counterterrorism strategy for being driven completely by the national government's agenda, which they argue was set completely independent of input from local Muslim communities (Briggs, Fieschi, and Lownsbrough 2006, 27–28; Kundnani 2009). Such criticisms raise questions about the legitimacy and viability of the program as a long-term counterterrorism strategy. Nonetheless, the Prevent program is an endeavor by the national government to provide the overarching guidelines, infrastructure, and funding, and by local authorities and police departments to work with local community groups and religious institutions to develop approaches tailored to fit a particular community's needs (HM Government 2011). National programs like Prevent require local flexibility to be successful even in their own terms.

In the United States, there is currently no overarching national police-community engagement infrastructure in the counterterrorism context, although the Obama Administration has recently committed to integrating police-community engagement efforts into its national counterterrorism strategy (The White House 2011a; 2011b). The existing US counterterrorism partnership models in cities like Los Angeles, Dearborn, Michigan, Minneapolis, and Northern Virginia have thus been developed locally through grassroots efforts and with community input, which has allowed each local community to adopt a structure and practices best suited to that community's particular needs (Ramirez et al. 2004). While some common "best practices" have emerged from these independent local efforts, for the United States to be successful in implementing a national police-community engagement counterterrorism strategy, it would need to retain the local flexibility of existing police-community engagement programs while providing appropriate funding and guidance to creative and sometimes risky partnership efforts.

## Power

A final issue related to police and community engagement in the counterterrorism context in the case study jurisdictions is the power dynamics between the police and the community in the partnership context. In terrorism prevention there is an inherent tension between the traditional counterterrorism approach that targets particular communities with covert surveillance and infiltration, and the voluntary, transparent police-community engagement approaches discussed in this chapter (Thacher 2005; Spalek, McDonald, and El Awa 2011, 13). In this context, community members repeatedly express concerns that their input is not sought by law enforcement, and that government unilaterally makes decisions behind closed doors without local community input (Kundnani 2009). Unbalanced community partnerships where government makes most of the decisions can significantly harm police-community relations in the long term (Harris 2010). Indeed, if the community does not feel it is having sufficient input into a police-community partnership, it poses the real risk of the community disengaging from the process entirely. The longevity of a project, not necessarily an indicator of its success, as durability might be, attests to a "coziness" in relationships that might flourish by very virtue of the fact that they do not rock the boat too unduly, whether in the maintenance of a comfortable status quo or an uneasy truce. Effectiveness is limited where deeper or politically contentious issues remain "no-go" areas and where contradictory realities on all sides remain unaddressed. As local community partnerships have limited effectiveness if the community does not buy-in and support the effort (Lasker and Weiss, 19), effective community partnerships therefore require community empowerment and capacity building to be an important aspect of the calculus, and to be accounted for (Lasker and Weiss 2003, 21; Briggs, Fieschi, and Lownsbrough 2006; Kundnani 2009; Spalek, El-Awa, and McDonald 2009; Thiel 2009, 40; Choudhury and Fenwick 2011, 16). There must be sufficient checks and accountability mechanisms in regard to partnership efforts to ensure that community participants are facilitated and empowered to ensure that decisions are not made unilaterally by the police.

Moreover, beyond the risk of unilateral police decision making, partnerships also pose the risk of police-community partnership programs being used to gather information and intelligence on members of the targeted communities (Kundnani 2009; Choudhury & Fenwick 2011, 47; Spalek, McDonald, and El Awa 2011, 19). Experts agree that the danger posed by police-community engagement programs in the counterterrorism context is that they become "co-opted into intelligence-led, covert, policing under the auspices of the neighborhood policing model" (Spalek, McDonald, and El Awa 2011, 19). For police-community engagement programs to work, there must be trust between the police and the community, and safeguards to prevent exploitation of the police-community engagement process (Thacher 2005, 644; Innes and Thiel 2011, 566). If the former is difficult, the latter is virtually impossible to ascertain with any degree of certainty. However, without mutual trust and exploitation-prevention mechanisms, police-community partnerships in the counterterrorism context will not be effective, and police will lose legitimacy in communities (Briggs, Fieschi, and Lownsbrough 2006, 15–16; Kundnani 2009; Choudhury and Fenwick 2011, 80; Spalek, McDonald, and El Awa 2011, 19).

If mutual trust can be established and exploitation avoided in police-community engagement, the long-term benefits to terrorism prevention could be significant. Indeed, where police-community engagement is based on real trust, there are the mutual benefits of positive two-way information flow between police and the community (Choudhury and Fenwick 2011, 16; Spalek, McDonald, and El Awa 2011). However, can success be measured by the fact that certain community members are kept apprised of (and asked to comment on) important developments, while helping be the eyes and ears of police in the community, based on their ability to gain information and observe occurrences that the police are likely not privy to (Meares 2002, 1612; OSCE 2008, 23; Ramirez et al. 2012)? Community members may or may not have unique knowledge, information, and access within a community that law enforcement does not. This can be extremely helpful to law enforcement if a two-way trust relationship is established (Brodeur and Dupont 2006, 17; Spalek, McDonald, and El Awa 2011; Ramirez et al. 2012), but equally can be problematic if overjudicious information sharing results in wrong conclusions being drawn as to who is dangerous and who is not.

## CONCLUSION

In the post-9/11 world, success in preventing ideologically inspired violent extremism depends on the success of the coproduction of security, particularly with affected communities (Mueller 2006; Harris 2010, 127), as well as minimal recourse to covert policing measures, which must themselves be appropriate, ethical, and subject to sufficient effective scrutiny. Because communities and law enforcement have shared interests in safety from terrorism, radicalization, and other problems like violence, gangs, blight, youth truancy, and a host of other community problems, community partnerships are an important problem-solving mechanism (Meares 2002, 1595; Thiel 2009, 41). However, to be successful, post-9/11, police-community engagement must represent only one strand in a much bigger tapestry of effective government and community programs and interventions. Further, there must be "a deep commitment to the idea that success in public safety efforts of any kind can only occur when strong, positive connections exist between police and those whom they serve—that is, through partnerships based on trust" (Harris 2010, 134).

## References

Adelman, Madelaine, Edna Erez, and Nadera Shalboud-Kevorkian. 2003. "Policing Violence against Minority Women in Multicultural Societies: 'Community' and the Politics of Exclusion." *Police and Society 7*: 105–133.

Baker, Abdul Haqq. 2011. *Extremists in Our Midst: Confronting Terror*. Basingstoke: Palgrave Macmillan.

Breen Smyth, Mary. 2007. "A Critical Research Agenda for the Study of Political Terror." *European Political Science 6*(3): 260–267.

Briggs, Rachel, Catherine Fieschi, and Hannah Lownsbrough. 2006. *Bringing It Home: Community-Based Approaches to Counter-Terrorism*. Demos. London: Demos.

Bright, Martin. 2007. *When Progressives Treat with Reactionaries: The British State's Flirtation with Radical Islam*. London: Policy Exchange.

Brodeur, Jean-Paul, and Benoit Dupont. 2006. "Knowledge Workers or 'Knowledge' Workers?" *Policing and Society 16*(1): 7–26.

Chomsky, Noam. 1991. "International Terrorism: Image and Reality." In *Western State Terrorism*. Edited by Alexander George. 12–38. Oxford: Polity Press.

Choudhury, Tufyal, and Helen Fenwick. 2011. *The Impact of Counter-Terrorism Measures on Muslim Communities*. London: Equality & Human Rights Commission.

Friedrichs, Jorg. 2006. "Defining the International Public Enemy: The Political Struggle behind the Legal Debate on International Terrorism." *Leiden Journal of International Law 19*(1): 69–91.

Gilligan, James. 2000. *Violence: Reflections on Our Deadliest Epidemic*. London: Jessica Kingsley Publishers.

———. 2001. *Preventing Violence: Prospects for Tomorrow*. London: Thames and Hudson

Goldstein, Herman. 1979. "Improving Policing, A Problem-Oriented Approach." *Crime & Delinquency 25*(2): 236–258.

Ellison, Graham, and Mary O'Rawe. 2010. "Security Governance in Transition: The Compartmentalising, Crowding Out and Corralling of Policing and Security in Northern Ireland." *Theoretical Criminology 14*(1): 31–57.

Hamber, Brandon, Paddy Hillyard, Amy Maguire, Monica McWilliams, Gillian Robinson, David Russell, and Margaret Ward. 2006. "Discourses in Transition: Re-Imagining Women's Security." *International Relations 20*(4): 487–502.

Harris, David. 2010. "Law Enforcement and Intelligence Gathering in Muslim and Immigrant Communities After 9/11." *New York University Review of Law & Social Change 34*: 123–190.

Hewitt, S. 2010. *Snitch ! A History of the Modern Intelligence Informer.* London: Continuum.

Hickman, Mary, Lyn Thomas, Sara Silvestri, and Henri Nickels. 2011. *"Suspect Communities"? Counter-Terrorism Policy, the Press, and the Impact on Irish and Muslim Communities in Britain.* London: London Metropolitan University. http://www.londonmet.ac.uk/fms/MRSite/Research/iset/Suspect%20Communities%20Findings%20July2011.pdf.

HM Government. 2011. *CONTEST: The United Kingdom's Strategy for Counterterrorism.* London: The Stationery Office. http://www.homeoffice.gov.uk/publications/counter-terrorism/counter-terrorismstrategy/strategy-contest?view=Binary.

Independent Commission on Policing. 1999. *A New Beginning for Policing: Northern Ireland Report of the Independent Commission on Policing for Northern Ireland.* Belfast: The Stationery Office. http://www.nio.gov.uk/a_new_beginning_in_policing_in_northern_ireland.pdf.

Innes, Martin. 2006. "Policing Uncertainty: Countering Terror through Community Intelligence and Democratic Policing." *The ANNALS of the American Academy of Political and Social Science 605*(1): 222–241.

Innes, Martin, and Darren Thiel. 2011. "Policing Terror." In *Handbook of Policing.* Second Edition. Edited by Tim Newburn. 553–579. Cullompton, UK: Willan Publishing.

Innes, Martin, Colin Roberts, and Helen Innes, with Trudy Lowe and Suraj Lakhani. 2011. *Assessing the Effects of Prevent Policing: A Report to the Association of Chief Police Officers.* London: The Association of Chief Police Officers. http://www.acpo.police.uk/documents/TAM/2011/PREVENT%20Innes%200311%20Final%20send%202.pdf.

Jackson, Richard. 2008. "An Argument for Terrorism." *Perspectives on Terrorism 2*(2): 25–32.

Jutila, Matti. 2006. "Desecuritizing Minority Rights: Against Determinism." *Security Dialogue 37*(2): 167–185.

Kellner, Douglas. 2004. "9/11, Spectacles of Terror, and Media Manipulation." *Critical Discourse Studies 1*(1): 41–64.

Kundnani, Arun. 2009. *Spooked! How Not to Prevent Violent Extremism.* London: Institute of Race Relations.

Lambert, Robert. 2008. "Empowering Salafis and Islamists against Al-Qaida: A London Counter-Terrorism Case Study." *PS: Political Science and Politics 41*(1): 31–35.

———. 2011. *Countering Al-Qaeda in London: Police and Muslims in Partnership.* London: Hurst and Company.

———. 2012. "Time to End Exceptional Security Policies Targeting Muslims: They Don'tWwork,."*Open Democracy*, February 28. http://

www.opendemocracy.net/opensecurity/robert-lambert/time-to-end-exceptional-security-policies-targeting-muslims-they-dont-wo.

Lasker, Roz, and Elisa Weiss. 2003. "Broadening Participation in Community Problem Solving: A Multidisciplinary Model to Support Collaborative Practice and Research." *Journal of Urban Health: Bulletin of the New York Academy of Medicine 80*(1): 14–47.

McDonald, Laura Zahra. 2011. "Listening to the Experts: Muslim Youth Work in the UK and Its Implication for Security." *Religion, State & Society, Special Edition*. Edited by B. Spalek and M. Shterin. 177–190. 2/3 2012.

McEvoy, Kieran, and Peter Shirlow. 2009. "Reimagining DDR: Ex-Combatants, Leadership and Moral Agency in Conflict Transformation." *Theoretical Criminology 13*(1): 31–59.

McGovern, Mark, and Angela Tobin. 2010. *Countering Terror or Counter-Productive: Comparing Irish and British Muslim Experiences of Counter-insurgency Law and Policy*. Report of a Symposium held in Cultúrlann McAdam Ó Fiaich, Falls Road, Belfast, June 23–24, 2009. Edge Hill University, Ormskirk.

Meares, Tracy. 2002. "Praying for Community Policing." *California Law Review 90*: 1593–1634.

Mika, Harry. 2006. *Community Based Restorative Justice in Northern Ireland*. Belfast: Queens University.

Miller, David, and Tom Mills. 2009. "The Terror Experts and the Mainstream Media: The Expert Nexus and Its Dominance in the News Media." *Critical Studies on Terrorism 2*(3): 414–437.

Morris, Nigel. 2010. "Anti-Terrorism Law Arrests Fail to Secure Convictions." *The Independent*, August 13. http://www.independent.co.uk/news/uk/home-news/antiterrorism-law-arrests-fail-to-secure-convictions-2051336.html.

Mueller, Robert S. 2006. "Critical Partnerships, Fighting Crime Together." Speech, Boston, Massachusetts, October 17.

O'Rawe, Mary. 2010. "The Importance of Gender in the Transformation of Policing." In *Policing the Narrow Ground: Lessons from the Transformation of Policing in Northern Ireland*. Edited by John Doyle. 212–241. Dublin: Royal Irish Academy.

Organization for Security and Co-Operation in Europe. 2008. *Good Practices in Building Police-Public Partnerships*. Austria: Organization for Security and Co-Operation in Europe, Office of the Secretary General. http://www.osce.org/spmu/32547.

Pantazis, Christina, and Pemberton, Simon. 2009. "From the 'Old' to the 'New Suspect' Community: Examining the Impacts of Recent UK Counter-Terrorist Legislation." *British Journal of Criminology 49*(5): 646–666.

Ramirez, Deborah, Sasha O'Connell, and Rabia Zafar. 2004. *Developing Partnerships between Law Enforcement and American Muslim, Arab, and Sikh Communities: A Promising Practices Guide Executive Summary*. Boston: Northeastern University.

Ramirez, Deborah, Tara Lai Quinlan, Sean Malloy, and Taylor Shutt. 2012. "Community Partnerships Thwart Terrorism." In *Preventing Ideological Violence*. Edited by P. Daniel Silk. Hampshire: Palgrave Macmillan.

Schmid, Alex, and A. J. Jongman. 1988. *Political Terrorism: A New Guide to Actors, Authors, Concepts, Data Bases, Theories and Literature*. Amsterdam: North Holland Publishers Company.

Silk, Phillip Daniel. 2010. *Planning Outreach between Muslim Communities and Police in the US and the UK*. University of Georgia. https://getd.libs.uga.edu/pdfs/silk_phillip_d_201005_phd/silk_phillip_d_201005_phd.pdf.

Spalek, Basia. 2010. "Community Policing, Trust and Muslim Communities in Relation to 'New Terrorism.'" *Politics & Policy 38*(4): 789–815.

———. 2013. *Governing Terror: Community, Trust and Counter-Terrorism*. London: Bloomsbury Academic.

Spalek, Basia, and Alia Imtoual. 2007. "Muslim Communities and Counter-Terror Responses: 'Hard' Approaches to Community Engagement in the UK and Australia." *Journal of Muslim Minority Affairs 27*(2): 185–202. Doi 10.1080/13602000701536117.

Spalek, Basia, Laura McDonald, and Salwa El Awa. 2011. *Preventing Religio-Political Extremism Amongst Muslim Youth: A Study Exploring Police-Community Partnership*. Birmingham: University of Birmingham.

Spalek, Basia, and Robert Lambert. 2008. "Muslim Communities Under Surveillance." *Criminal Justice Matters 68*(1): 12–13.

Spalek, Basia, Salwa El Awa, and Laura McDonald. 2009. *Engagement and Partnership Work in a Counter-Terrorism Context*. Birmingham: University of Birmingham.

Thacher, David. 2005. "The Local Role in Homeland Security." *Law & Society Review 39*(3): 635–676.

Thiel, Darren. 2009. "Policing Terrorism: A Review of the Evidence." In *The Police Foundation*. London: The Police Foundation.

Thornton, Sara. 2010. *Project Champion Review*. Thames Valley Police. http://www.west-midlands.police.uk/latest-news/docs/Champion_Review_FINAL_30_09_10.pdf.

Tyler, Tom, Stephen Schulhofer, and Aziz Huq. 2010 "Legitimacy and Deterrence Effects in Counterterrorism Policing: A Study of Muslim Americans." *Law & Society Review 44*(2): 365–402.

The White House. 2011a. *National Strategy for CounterTerrorism*. Washington, DC: The White House. http://www.whitehouse.gov/sites/default/files/counterterrorism_strategy.pdf.

———. 2011b. *Empowering Local Partners to Prevent Violent Extremism in the United States*. Washington, DC: The White House. http://www.whitehouse.gov/sites/default/files/empowering_local_partners.pdf.

Wilkinson, Paul. 2006. *Terrorism versus Democracy: The Liberal State Response*. Second Edition. Oxon: Routledge.

# Part II

# 3

# Police, Community, Conflict, and Context: Some Thoughts on British Muslim and Irish Comparisons

*Mark McGovern*

## From Then to Now, and There to Here: Learning from the Past?

In February 2011, British prime minister David Cameron delivered a keynote speech on "terrorism and radicalisation" to an audience, including many of his fellow EU leaders, at a European Security Conference in Munich (Cameron 2011). In it, Cameron trailed the current British government's strategy for "preventing violent extremism," fleshed out with the publication of updated versions of CONTEST[1] and Prevent[2] in July and June 2011 respectively (Home Office 2011b, 2011c). As with the prime minister's Munich speech, the new versions of Prevent and CONTEST make for depressing reading, although not perhaps as was intended. Designed to serve as a stark warning of the existential threat ("not only to lives but to our way of life," [Cameron 2011]) of "Islamist extremism," Cameron's Munich speech and the updated *Prevent* and *Contest* policies were depressingly familiar in how they sought to examine, explain, and legislate for the potential challenge of political violence.

In essence, the argument goes as follows. In a context where "state multiculturalism" has allegedly done little to provide an antidote to a sense of disjuncture, dislocation, and isolation for (particularly young, male) Muslims, radicalizing, extremist activist leaders exploit perceived grievances and, through a series of small group social networks (both in "social reality" and cyberspace), disseminate an

Islamist ideology that leads a small, vulnerable section of the Muslim population down the path of violence. "Preventing violent extremism" therefore, is concerned with preventing the spread of that ideology and intervening where needed with those potentially vulnerable to its dangerous message.

While some of this was new (notably, and worryingly, the focus on "non-violent extremists" as potential "facilitators of terrorism" and the equally worrying allegations of universities and colleges as ripe breeding grounds for radicalization), much of it was not. Seeing the roots of "violent extremism" in the supposed failures of multiculturalism and diversity, and arguing that an "ideology of extremism" should be regarded as the "root cause of the problem," reflected an intensification of a state approach to dealing with "Islamist terrorism" (and other aspects of the lives of British Muslims) that has been prevalent for much of the past decade. Typified by an integrationist argument that lays the blame for British Muslim alienation and grievance at the door of "self-segregation," a lack of "shared values," and an inability to develop a cohesive sense of identity and belonging, such analyses have a lineage dating back at least to the aftermath of the riots at Bradford, Burnley, and elsewhere in the summer of 2011 (Kundnani 2007; Hewitt 2008; McGhee 2008; Fekete 2009). Heightened in the wake of the attacks of 9/11 and 7/7, this integrationist approach to policymaking in relation to the Muslim community today constitutes what Arun Kundnani has called the contemporary "politics of anti-Muslim racism" (Kundnani 2007, 121).

In certain key ways, this focus on supposed "self-segregation;" questions of meaning, identity, and belonging; the overdetermining impact of a malign ideology; and the vulnerability of certain sections of the community (particularly the young) to "radicalisation" mirrors the manner in which the British state understood, represented, and policed the conflict in the North of Ireland through most of the period from 1968 to 1998 (McGovern 2010b). There are echoes here of the dominant, official "explanations" of the conflict in Northern Ireland as a sectarian war, a conflict of "two traditions" driven toward violence by the *politique du pire* logic and quasi-religious martyrdom myths of Irish Republicanism, that left the British State with little choice but to use state force and emergency laws as a nonself interested neutral "pig-in-the-middle." It is an analysis that, it will be argued, is equally as flawed. This is because what is specifically missing in all of this is the cause and impact of grievance and injustice itself. Not least in terms of a sense of injustice generated by government policy and, most relevant, in terms of reactions to the very measures introduced by the state to supposedly "counter terrorism."

What relevance does this have for police-community engagement at a local level? Whatever the undoubted significance that operational decision making, local conditions, and interpersonal interaction and bonds of trust are likely to have upon police-community engagement, the overarching framework of government policy and practice will invariably shape, frame and, in large part, ultimately determine any localized agenda. Institutionally, policy frames define the limits of the permissible and give overall direction and impetus to the practice of state agencies, not least of course, in terms of policing.

Equally, long-term experience of state policy and practice will invariably shape community perceptions of policing. Communities are sites of (often diverse, sometimes conflicting and by no means homogenous) collective knowledge, memory, and experience. As the human rights lawyer Gareth Peirce has argued, whenever we are looking at the experience of the "new suspect community" of British Muslims, comparisons with the Irish (the "old suspect community") should be kept in mind (Peirce 2010; see also Greer 1994; 2010; Hillyard 2005 1993; Hickman et al. 2011). This is, not least, because of the circulation of knowledge that is often obscured (and little enough researched) to those outside:

> Just as Irish men and women, wherever they lived, knew and registered every detail of each injustice as if it had been done to them, long before British men and women were even aware that entire Irish families had been wrongly imprisoned in their country for decades, so Muslim men and women here and across the world are registering the ill-treatment of their community here, and recognising, too, the analogies with the Irish experience. (Peirce 2010, 52–53)

If police and community are both to benefit, this world of community knowledge and experience (and by that I specifically *do not* mean "intelligence") needs to be taken into account when considering how best to even consider the ways in which "partnership" might work. It is something of those experiences that this chapter will reflect upon.

In doing so it is primarily based upon the findings of a symposium held in Belfast exploring comparisons between Irish and Muslim experiences of counterinsurgency law and policy (McGovern 2010a).[3] These discussions (involving representatives of a number of community, human rights, and victims organizations) explored the impact of counterterrorism measures in what were, in many ways, quite distinct circumstances. Nevertheless, it soon became clear that the analogies noted by Gareth Peirce were ones that made a great deal of sense to those who took part. Included in the conversations were some (e.g., Irish Republican political ex-prisoners) who had in the past been in direct confrontation with the state and the police but were now deeply committed to postconflict transformation. This inclusion was deliberate. Not only because of the validity of such voices in and of themselves, but also given that, despite a wealth of insight and experience (not least into why it is that some may resort to political violence), they are all too often excluded from dialogue on such matters. Such exclusion is, indeed, part of the problem.

The sum of the discussions might, from the outset, be considered as a warning against efforts to integrate community-based approaches to policing with counterinsurgency and intelligence-gathering strategies. This is particularly so where the latter are driven both by the supremacy and prioritization of national security interests and a (perhaps willful) misreading of the causes of political violence.

## Emergency Laws, Dual Track Systems, Due Process, and Torture

Community experience of the various laws and practices specifically introduced as "counter-terror" measures will invariably have a significant impact on police-community engagement. Despite claims to the contrary (not least with the new *Prevent* strategy document itself) the nature and application of such powers, and of the practices of counterinsurgency and counterterror, can often have distinctly counterproductive consequences.

Counterterror measures are something of which Northern Ireland has long experience. Even before the partition and the foundation of the state, and ever since, Northern Ireland has always had "emergency powers" that have, as a result, become "normalised" (Hillyard 1993; Walsh 2000; Donohue 2007). In turn, such laws, and particularly those introduced during the 30 years of conflict between 1968 and 1998 (such as the 1973 Emergency Provisions Act and the 1974 Prevention of Terrorism Act), have provided the basis and the "architecture" of current counterterror measures (Hillyard 2006; CAJ 2008). However, one significant change introduced with the 2000 Terrorism Act was that this was a permanent piece of legislation. "Sunset clauses" been part of earlier legislation and required a periodic review and parliamentary renewal for emergency powers. While having little enough effect in determining or deterring the passage of such legislation, the dropping of "sunset clauses" from the more recent swathe of antiterror laws has emphasized the permanence of "emergency powers."

Emergency legislation can be counterproductive for police-community relations by engendering a greater sense of alienation (making antagonism and violence more, not less, likely) and in undermining community confidence in the rule of law (CAJ 2008). Undermining the due process of the criminal justice system and a lack of accountability, transparency, and oversight of state agencies engaged in counterinsurgency and counterterror work were identified as common complaints. At its most extreme, the evidence of widespread collusion between security and intelligence agencies with (particularly Loyalist) paramilitary organizations in Northern Ireland can be seen as indicative of a wider problem emerging where intelligence takes precedence over "ordinary policing."

The development of "dual track" criminal justice systems can similarly lead to community distrust. Extending powers of detention, altering the rules governing interrogations, and changing the makeup and practice of the courts can fundamentally undermine civil liberties. Certainly, the use of internment in Northern Ireland could be seen as a pivotal policy in engendering alienation among the nationalist community in the early 1970s, and the power to detain people without charge for up to seven days, under the original PTA (1974), was a focus for long-standing grievance. While its use may be on a very different scale, the substantial expansion of the period of detention without charge in more recent counterterror legislation (up to 28 days under the 2006 Terrorism Act, since allowed to "lapse" to 14 days in 2011) represents a similar cause for concern today.

A dual-track legal system, particularly in the creation and operation of the Diplock no-jury courts in the North (combined with the creation of interrogation centers), was also seen by critics as doing much to have undermined confidence in the rule of law. Again, while on a very different scale, the adaption and "securitisation" of elements of the immigration system (particularly in the use of Special Immigration Appeals Commission) in the treatment of non-British nationals raises question marks over the operation of due process and the protection of civil liberties (Fekete 2009).

As Gareth Peirce suggests knowledge of, and concerns over, abusive interrogation techniques, the practice of state torture and extraordinary rendition have a deeply alienating impact within "suspect communities." In Northern Ireland, allegations of torture were a feature of human rights concerns from the early 1970s onward.

This was highlighted by the case of the "hooded men," detainees who were subjected to new techniques of physical and psychological brutality (McGuffin 1974; Murray 1974). The failings of successive British public inquiries into these and other allegations of torture again contributed significantly to a widespread distrust of the rule of law within the nationalist community. The increasing reliance of the Diplock courts on uncorroborated confessions to obtain convictions also drew attention to the systematic abuses alleged to have taken place within interrogation centers as part of a coherent and comprehensive subversion of rule of law norms. Such knowledge shaped community attitudes toward, and relations with, the state.

Similarly, a widespread awareness of cases of torture, miscarriages of justice, and the practice of rendition as part of the "War on Terror," needs also to be seen as inevitably shaping Muslim community attitudes toward state agencies. This is also closely connected to the "elephant in the room" framing Muslim community perspectives on state agencies, Western, and specifically British, foreign policy, and actions in and toward Muslim communities (Hewitt 2008). This is particularly the case for Diaspora communities, transnational households, and people in Muslim communities who come from, and maintain ongoing interconnections with, many of those regions of the world in which the impact of foreign policy in the post-9/11 period has been most directly felt.

## Stop and Search Powers, Intelligence, Informers, and Vetting Communities

For most members of a "suspect community," the emergency measures that are most likely to impact directly upon them are "stop and search" powers. The widespread and habitual use made of stop and search powers (under the Emergency Provisions Act) in the North was noted for having contributed significantly to tense and antagonistic relations between the police, the army, and (particularly young) people in nationalist working-class areas. This might be understood as a frontline experience of oppression and harassment. Indeed, as a Human Rights Watch Report noted in 1992, the street harassment of children was "endemic" in parts of the North and one of the most frequent causes of complaint and resentment they received, although "lodging harassment complaints against security forces [was] generally seen as useless" (Human Rights Watch 1992, 18).

The coalition government's recent review of counterterror legislation, published in early 2011, recommended a series of changes to the "stop and search" powers allowed for under Section 7 and Section 44 of the 2000 Terrorism Act (Home Office 2011a). Section 7 provided for the designation of areas in which people could be stopped and search without the requirement of reasonable suspicion. Section 44 allowed officials at ports and airports to detain people for questioning for up to 9 hours without charge. Throughout the last decade, both sections 7 and 44 were routinely employed by police forces (and in terms of Section 44 by other state officials) throughout the country. Wide geographical areas (such as the whole of London) have been designated for the use of Section 7 and the powers then routinely renewed. Their impact has been felt by hundreds of thousands of people, drawn disproportionally from Muslim communities and, here again, often been felt most by young people. Nor have such "stop and search" practices had any evident practical impact on "preventing terrorism," with few if any arrests for terrorism-related offenses being made as a result. The full practical outworking of the recommendations of the Government Review have yet to be seen, but in itself, the level of concern that gave rise to those changes reflected the counter-productive impact the sweeping use of "stop and search" powers has had within communities.

Mirroring the experiences of Muslim communities in Britain, there was a significant increase in the use of stop and search powers in the North in the mid- to late 2000s (PSNI 2012). For example, between 2007–8 and 2010–11, there was an increase of over 250 percent in the total number of people stopped under a range of legislative measures, from 19,012 to 53,855. In the same period, those stopped and searched under Section 44 of the Terrorism Act rose almost tenfold, from 3,358 to 28,770. The decision by the European Court in 2010 that Section 44 was illegal (given the lack of a requirement for even "reasonable suspicion") brought an end to its use. While this did lead to an overall decline in the numbers stopped, in Northern Ireland it also saw a shift to the use of alternative, Northern Ireland–only legislation, in the form of the 2007 Justice and Security Act (JSA) (*Belfast Newsletter* 2010). In 2009–10, 621 people had been stopped under the JSA, in 2010–11 the number rocketed to 11,721. While 2011–12 has seen a decrease in stop and search, the total of 35,268 is still almost twice what it was in 2007–08.

Of great concern to many has been the nature of the questions people have been asked (concerning, for example, political and religious attitudes and affiliations) when stopped at ports and airports, and allegations that these occasions were used to try and recruit people as informers. This reflects a far wider issue. Along with "stop and search" powers themselves, nothing has greater potential for generating distrust and alienation within communities than attempts to integrate the actions and practices of a wide range of state agencies (and most obviously police-community engagement) with intelligence-gathering activities.

In Northern Ireland, the findings of a number of recent inquiries into allegations of collusion have highlighted the deeply corrosive consequences for the rule of law of a culture of policing where a reliance on informers and the prosecution of a counterinsurgency campaign took precedence over virtually everything else. A strategy of intelligence gathering that relied on developing networks of informers had an impact on communities subject to such strategies at an everyday level. This was again most evident among young people. A drive for low-level intelligence has in the past led to the police pressuring young people, who had been involved in antisocial behavior, to act as informers. The prospect of exposing that role to paramilitary organizations subsequently served as an additional threat.

The vulnerability of young Muslims to the abuse of intelligence strategies predicated on the use of informers is also a concern. There have been, for example, allegations of attempts by MI5 to recruit from several sections of the Muslim population, including students, prisoners, and asylum seekers. The vulnerability of young Muslims can also be felt in the context of criminalization of accessing material on the web and the growing focus on universities and colleges as supposed hotbeds of radicalization. Again, there have been allegations that Muslim students are placed in potentially vulnerable situations by attempts to recruit them as intelligence informers. The cumulative effect is the sense that such phenomenon can contribute to a pervasive culture of surveillance and fear that has a wide range of consequences for community life.

It is a cumulative effect of a "culture of fear" that the *Prevent* agenda, certainly for some observers, has brought in its wake. The silencing of debates and creation of "taboo" subjects may also generate a reticence on the part of many to engage openly and honestly in criticism of police-community engagement itself. The danger of funneling funding for community development through counterradicalization programs has similarly been noted as a major area of concern for its wider impact on community life, attitudes, and activities (Kundnani 2010). Northern Ireland has had some experience of these issues in the past too. The "political vetting" of community groups in the North was an issue that first emerged in the mid-1980s and continued to be a problem for many years. A range of cultural groups and organizations was affected, and it was not until an evident lack of transparency over funding decisions, which appeared to be primarily politically motivated but were ultimately the subject of legal challenges, that the policy was changed.

In such a context the fear pervading may be that community development structures themselves become integrated with intelligence gathering. This is particularly so if combined with the securitization of a wide range of government agencies and agendas and pursuing policies that are ultimately based on a deeply flawed grasp of what constitutes, and leads to, "radicalization" and "extremism." Learning from past experience, a path whereby "community engagement" may actually mean becoming part of such a "policing nexus" is one best not taken.

## CONCLUSION: FROM HERE TO THERE AND BACK AGAIN?

One last area of concern must be that, far from policy being informed by the lessons learnt from past mistakes made in Northern Ireland, the current official mood may in fact be for things to be moving in the other direction. While much of both, the recently updated *CONTEST* and *Prevent*, has remained the same, "Northern Ireland–related terrorism" is given a greater prominence than before. The scope of *CONTEST* had been expanded beyond "international terrorism" and *Prevent* will also "now address radicalisation to all forms of terrorism" (Home Office 2011c, 12). The increase in "dissident" Republican activity is given as the primary reason for this adjustment in focus (Home Office 2011c, 10). While both *CONTEST* and *Prevent* note that they are not designed to deal specifically with "Northern Ireland–related terrorism" (Home Office 2011b, 40; 2011c, 14), this is essentially because responsibility for developing "policies and programmes for tackling terrorism" lies with the Secretary of State for Northern Ireland and the devolved power-sharing Northern Ireland Executive (Home Office2011a, 40). However, both documents also note that many of the issues dealt with by these revised strategies "and the principles it [*Prevent*] sets out are relevant to the attempts to counter the threat from Northern Ireland–related terrorism" (Home Office 2011c, 14). Other recent developments point in a similar direction. These include, for example, an apparent increase in the use of the extended period of pre-charge detention in "dissident"-related cases and the noted use of "stop and search" powers.

Any discussion of police-community engagement in the North should be aware of how potentially damaging and disastrous an attempt to integrate a "counter-terrorism" agenda would be for whatever social and political progress has been made since the signing of the Good Friday Agreement. There may be a greater degree of cross-community consensus in Northern Ireland around many aspects of policing today. However, policing remains a key touchstone of social and political developments, particularly within the Nationalist/Republican community. There are ongoing concerns over the renewed activities of intelligence agencies, failings in dealing with historic truth and justice cases, and the potential loss of life or injury that could result from the use of plastic bullets. Getting policing wrong, most obviously through echoing the failures of the past, still has a capacity to have profound political consequences.

## NOTES

1. *Contest* is the British Government's overall "counter-terrorism" strategy. First introduced in early 2003, an update in July 2006 established four key platforms on which the strategy is based: "Pursue," "Prevent," "Protect," and "Prepare." A revised version of *Contest* was released in March 2009 before *Contest III* appeared in July 2011.
2. As noted, *Prevent* is one of the four key elements of the *Contest* "counter-terror" strategy. Specifically Prevent is the "preventative strand" of the government's strategy. and its self-declared aim is to "stop people becoming terrorists or supporting terrorism" (Home Office 2012).
3. The symposium was organized in collaboration with Relatives for Justice, the Islamic Human Rights Commission, and the Committee on the Administration of Justice.

## REFERENCES

*Belfast Newsletter*. 2010. "PSNI Still Has Power to Stop and Search." July 8, 2010. http://www.newsletter.co.uk/news/local/psni-still-has-power-to-stop-and-search-1-1848875.

Cameron, David. 2011. "PM's Speech at Munich Conference," February 05. http://www.number10.gov.uk/news/pms-speech-at-munich-security-conference/.

Committee on the Administration of Justice. 2008. *Lessons from Ireland*. Belfast: CAJ.

Donohue, Laura. 2007. *Counter-Terrorist Law and Emergency Powers in the United Kingdom, 1922–2000*. Dublin: Irish Academic Press.

Fekete, Liz. 2009. *A Suitable Enemy: Racism, Migration and Islamophobia in Europe*. London: Pluto Press.

Greer, Steven. 1994. "Review of P. Hillyard (1993) *Suspect Community: People's Experience of the Prevention of Terrorism Acts in Britain*, London: Pluto Press." *British Journal of Criminology 34*: 510–511.

———. 2010 "Anti-Terrorist Laws and the United Kingdom's 'Suspect Muslim Community': A Reply to Pantazis and Pemberton." *British Journal of Criminology 50*: 1171–1190.

Hewitt, Steve. 2008. *The British War on Terror: Terrorism and Counter-Terrorism on the Home Front Since 9/11.* London: Continuum.

Hickman, Mary, Lyn Thomas, Sara Silvestri, and Henri Nickels. 2011. *Suspect Communities? Counter-Terrorism Policy, the Press and the Impact on Irish and Muslim Communities: A Report for Policy-Makers and the General Public.* http://www.londonmet.ac.uk/fms/MRSite/Research/iset/Suspect%20Communities%20Findings%20July2011.pdf.

Hillyard, Paddy. 1993. *Suspect Community: People's Experience of the Prevention of Terrorism Acts in Britain.* London: Pluto Press.

———. 2005. "The 'War on Terror': Lessons from Ireland." In *Essays for Civil Liberties and Democracy.* European Civil Liberties Network in Europe. http://www.ecln.org/essays/essay-1.pdf.

Home Office. 2011a. *Review of Counter-Terrorism and Security Measures: Review Findings and Recommendations.* London: TSO. http://www.homeoffice.gov.uk/publications/counter-terrorism/review-of-ct-security-powers/review-findings-and-rec.

———. 2011b. *Contest: The United Kingdom's Strategy for Countering Terrorism.* London: TSO. http://www.homeoffice.gov.uk/publications/counter-terrorism/counter-terrorism-strategy/strategy-contest?view=Binary.

———. 2011c. *Prevent Strategy.* London: TSO. http://www.homeoffice.gov.uk/publications/counter-terrorism/prevent/prevent-strategy/prevent-strategy-review?view=Binary.

Human Rights Watch. 1992. *Children in Northern Ireland: Abused by Security Forces and Paramilitaries.* New York: Human Rights Watch.

Kundnani, Arun. 2007. *The End of Tolerance: Racism in 21st Century Britain.* London: Pluto Press.

———. 2010. *Spooked: How Not to Prevent Violent Extremism.* London: Institute of Race Relations. http://www.irr.org.uk/pdf2/spooked.pdf.

McGhee, Derek. 2008. *The End of Multiculturalism? Terrorism, Integration and Human Rights.* Maidenhead: Open University Press.

McGovern, Mark (with Angela Tobin). 2010a. *Countering Terror or Counter-Productive? Comparing Irish and Muslim Experiences of Counter-Insurgency Law and Policy: Report of a Symposium Held in Cultúrlaan McAdam Ó Fiaich June 2009.* Ormskirk: Edge Hill University.

———. 2010b. "The IRA are not Al-Qaeda: 'New Terrorism' Discourse and Irish Republicanism." In *Political Discourse and Conflict Resolution: Debating Peace in Northern Ireland.* Edited by Katy Hayward and Catherine O'Donnell. 192–208. London: Routledge.

Peirce, Gareth. 2010. "Was It Like This for the Irish?" In *Dispatches from the Dark Side: On Torture and the Death of Justice.* 51–72. London: Verso.

Police Service of Northern Ireland (PSNI). 2012. *PSNI Stop and Search Statistics.* http://www.psni.police.uk/index/updates/updates_statistics/updates_stop_and_search_statistics.htm.

Walsh, Dermot. 2000. *Bloody Sunday and the Rule of Law in Northern Ireland.* London: Palgrave.

# 4

# The Muslim Safety Forum: Senior Police and Muslim Community Engagement during the War on Terror

*Robert Lambert*

In this chapter I will provide a brief, preliminary account of police and Muslim community dialogue at the Muslim Safety Forum (MSF) in London; in doing so I will draw on my experience as a police member of the MSF and later as an academic researcher (Lambert 2011a; 2011b). Between 2001 and 2011, the MSF was home to regular meetings between senior police officers and representatives of Islamic institutions and Muslim community organizations. When the dialogue commenced, there was an expectation on both sides of the table that the forum would provide opportunities to enhance public safety for all London citizens and improve relations between the police and Muslim communities. Ten years later when MSF dialogue ended, there was a mixed record of success and failure.

No doubt, when committed community volunteers meet with police officers to solve problems, success is likely to accrue, but to some degree failures are also to be expected as part of any worthwhile learning experience. However, in one important respect, the efforts of police and Muslim community representatives to succeed were hampered by government policy in regard to the war on terror. That impediment is the thread that runs through this account of the MSF dialogue and that helps explain the most crucial failure: a failure to build adequate trust, which in turn helps explain the forum's eventual demise.

Broadly speaking, throughout the ten-year period, the prime police interest was on the threat of terrorism inspired or directed by the al-Qaeda, and the prime interest of Muslim community organizations was on the community impact of the war on terror and a related increase in anti-Muslim or Islamophobic bigotry and violence. This is not to overlook a common interest in all areas of public safety and community relations more generally, but principally to highlight competing priorities and perspectives. Nor is it intended to reduce the work and significance of the MSF to just these two themes, but rather to highlight their importance.

My aim is to demonstrate how the war on terror had an unintended and unacknowledged adverse impact on MSF business generally, and on engagement in these two key areas—(a) UK counterterrorism policing strategy and (b) Islamophobia, especially anti-Muslim bigotry and violence—in particular. More specifically, in respect of both police and Muslim community priority interests, the war on terror—either expressly by name or indirectly in terms of political and community impact—is shown to have made successes harder to achieve and failures harder to avoid for both parties in the MSF. Success, in this context, represents an ability to develop common goals and priorities and a greater empathy and respect for each other's perspective. To the extent that success remained elusive, the war on terror is shown to have introduced obstacles to progress of this kind for both parties involved in the MSF.

I begin by focusing attention on the war on terror; then I describe my developing focus from practitioner to academic research interest in the topic; followed by a description of the background and role of the MSF; thereafter, I sketch scenarios relating to (a) UK counterterrorism policing strategy and (b) Islamophobia, especially anti-Muslim bigotry and violence, discussed at MSF meetings; and in the conclusion I suggest how the war on terror had an adverse impact on the work of the MSF in relation to these scenarios.

## The War on Terror

Insofar as the war on terror was devised and driven by the US government and had a primary focus in Afghanistan and Iraq, it is not self evident why, and certainly not usual that, a US foreign policy should have any impact at all on domestic police policy in the United Kingdom. It will not be possible to explain how and why the Tony Blair government in the United Kingdom embraced and adopted the war on terror as enthusiastically as it did in this short chapter, still less to give an account of all the ways in which UK foreign and domestic counterterrorism policy was premised on US policy and strategy. Suffice it to say I have written elsewhere about the adverse impact of the Blair government policy on counterterrorism policing more generally and the extent to which it can be explained by a slavish devotion to US war on terror policy during the two Bush administrations (Lambert 2008a; 2008b; 2011a; 2011b).[1] There are three fundamental strands to the war on terror that have each impacted adversely, if at times indirectly, on the MSF. The first has been a dramatic departure from the rule of law that has often rendered investigative and preventative police work redundant. The second has been a wide focus on "radical Islam" or "radical Islamists" rather than a tight focus on al-Qaeda terrorists and terrorist suspects. The third and most crucial is closely related to the second and consists of the delegitimatization of many Muslim community organizations as "extremist."

The war on terror is generally regarded as beginning in the immediate aftermath of 9/11 and having either ended or entered a second less belligerent phase after Barack Obama replaced George Bush in the White House in 2009. Similarly, the United Kingdom is understood to have been the most loyal and the least critical US ally during the Bush phase and to have become rather more independent minded after Gordon Brown replaced Tony Blair in 10 Downing Street in 2007. The war on terror is also generally understood to be principally concerned with military campaigns abroad and not with a national and local initiative like the MSF in London. Both understandings have some justification, but the war on terror cast a long shadow over the MSF, which remained tangible long after George Bush and Tony Blair left office (Lambert 2011). Moreover, as we will see later, it would left to the Cameron government in 2010 to bring the policy to full and final fruition in terms of the delegitimization of mainstream Muslim organizations groups as "extremist" (Oborne 2011, 16).

Most striking about the Blair government's embrace of the war on terror was a significant disregard for the adverse impact it was likely to have, and in the event proved to have, on the ability of police to win proactive support from Muslim community organizations. This was the kind of support the police officers involved in MSF dialogue were aiming to win. Instead, when the Blair government acknowledged a shortfall in proactive support from Muslim community organizations, it was couched in terms that cast doubt on their loyalty and commitment. The Brown government was less wedded to the notion that "radical Islam" was the problem and adopted a more inclusive approach to Muslim community engagement. In contrast, the Cameron government adopted the same hard-line approach as Blair and took it to its logical conclusion (Lambert 2011b).

To be sure, the Muslim community is not the first community to be targeted by the politically expedient "tough" counterterrorism policies in the United Kingdom. Irish communities in London, Birmingham, and other towns and cities have sometimes found themselves treated as "suspect communities" (Hillyard 1993; 2005; Hickman et al. 2011) in ways that often undermine effective counterterrorism (Jackson 2008; Lambert 2012). However, while research shows much in common in the experiences of Irish and Muslim communities during different eras of UK counterterrorism, there are also distinctive features during the war on terror (Hickman et al. 2011). In any event, it is the latter experience of Muslim communities during the war on terror that provides the backdrop to the MSF dialogue discussed next.

## The Muslim Safety Forum

Senior Metropolitan Police Service (MPS) officers in London first met Muslim community leaders in regard to operational policing matters in 1989 during *The Satanic Verses* affair in which a national Muslim demonstration was staged in London for the first time (Ansari 2004; Lambert 2011, 81). Prominent then was the late Zaki Badawi, founder of the Muslim College and former director of the Islamic Cultural Centre and senior Imam at the London Central Mosque, who was described in an obituary in *The Guardian* as ranking "on matters of faith alongside the archbishop of Canterbury and the chief rabbi" (O'Sullivan 2006). Badawi, a Sunni scholar, and Syed Yousif Al-Khoei, director of the Shi'a Al Khoei Foundation in London, subsequently had occasional contact with senior police officers during the 1990s and were among the first to be consulted about the formation of the MSF in 2001. They became two of its first leading members. So too were Dr. Abdul Rahim Khan, a retired consultant surgeon, who was the first MSF representative of the Muslim Council of Britain (MCB) and the late Dr. Syed Aziz Pasha, the founder of the Union of Muslim Organizations (UMO), the first Muslim umbrella organization in the United Kingdom.

Later, the meetings were chaired by an MSF community appointee, the first being Azad Ali, representing Islamic Forum Europe (IFE), and the second (briefly) Raza Kazim of the Islamic Human Rights Commission (IHRC) in 2004. Ali and Kazim, in contrast to Badawi,

Al-Khoei, Khan, and Pasha, were second-generation British-born Muslims who were, broadly speaking, less deferential and more challenging to police perspectives. The change of chairmanship from police to community representatives signaled a change of emphasis from police agendas to community agendas, which included a stronger emphasis on Islamophobia and anti-Muslim hate crimes. It was also during the second half of the decade under review that the MSF formed working groups consisting of police and Muslim community members to examine specific work streams including counterterrorism and Islamophobia.

During the period 2001–2003, MSF meetings were generally chaired by David Veness, Assistant Commissioner Specialist Operations (ACSO), responsible for counterterrorism in the Metropolitan Police, or his deputy. Veness took a keen interest in the MSF, committed time and energy to it, and shared the view of his colleague John Grieve that police benefited from engaging with stern community critics rather than with "nodding dogs," that is to say, overly compliant community representatives (Lambert 2011a, 61). After Veness retired from the MPS in 2005, he was succeeded by senior counterterrorism police officers who did not always share his appetite for robust community engagement at the MSF. Neither did they share Veness's willingness and ability to stay in the same post for over a decade, so that whereas Veness became well known to and trusted by a wide range of community representative groups over a long uninterrupted period, his four successors between 2005 and 2011 were unable to establish the same level of understanding. On a related point, one former MSF community chair described in an interview how Veness would be regularly in contact and available at New Scotland Yard well outside conventional office hours.

Gradually, senior police officers primarily concerned with diversity and community engagement policy took over the lead police role at the MSF from counterterrorism officers such as Veness and his successors and their deputies and staff. Similarly, whereas during the period 2002–2007 when I was head of the counterterrorism-focused Muslim Contact Unit (MCU), colleagues and I were regular attendees at MSF meetings, it subsequently fell from the MPS role. Again whereas Veness emphasized on the small MCU team the importance of investing time at MSF meetings ("be the first to arrive and the last to leave") this level of commitment and interest in community perspectives was less evident in the leaders who succeeded him. A succession of senior police officers attended MSF meetings until the forum closed for business at the end of 2011. In March 2012, the inaugural meeting of the London Muslim Communities Forum (LMCF) signaled an end to an independent MSF and its replacement by a forum managed by the MPS (*MPS News* 2012).

The MSF has sometimes been understood in two slightly different ways. Police officers who had experience or knowledge of it generally regarded it as a forum in which Muslim community representatives met on a regular basis to discuss public safety and community relations issues with senior officers in the Metropolitan Police Serviceand the Association of Chief Police Officers (ACPO), generally once a month commencing at 6 p.m. and finishing between 8 p.m. and 9 p.m. on a Wednesday evening at New Scotland Yard, the iconic headquarters of the MPS situated between Victoria and Westminster in Central London. This is not inaccurate but simply one dimensional. A typical meeting would comprise ten police officers, fifteen Muslim members and associates of the MSF (also representing their respective organizations and institutions),[2] and a single representative from bodies including the Metropolitan Police Authority (MPA), the Crown Prosecution Service (CPS), and the Independent Police Complaints Commission (IPCC). Muslim community representatives who have been involved in the MSF tend to have a greater awareness of its additional work including meetings as a forum independent of the MPS.

So the difference is small but interesting insofar as it denotes both a *forum* for debate between police and Muslim community representatives and a *forum* for discussion simply among those Muslim community representatives who are engaging with police. Very often those MSF meetings away from police would take place in the boardroom of the Islamic Cultural Centre adjacent to the London Central Mosque in Wellington Road, close to Regents Park and between St. John's Wood and Baker Street tube stations. Later, meetings also took place at the London Muslim Centre in Whitechapel, a new purpose-built venue that opened in 2004. At an early stage in the development of the MSF, Muslim participants sought and obtained a degree of independence and came to take ownership of MSF as a body that engaged with police.

Clearly the MSF existed as a forum in both senses, and this is a minor point of difference in terms of perspectives, but it does touch on the issue of ownership and independence that is germane to my account in this chapter. It may also help to put my account into context, based as it is on my police experience and my subsequent academic research work with police and Muslim community members of the MSF.

## THE RESEARCHER

From January 1977 until December 2007, I was employed as an MPS police officer (Jackson 2008; Lambert 2011a). I began the last phase of my police career as head of the MCU in January 2002, and that role brought me into regular contact with the MSF and the representatives of the Muslim community organizations who took part in it. Since January 2008, I have worked as an academic researcher and lecturer spending a considerable amount of time engaged in research with representatives of Muslim community organizations I first met at MSF meetings in London.

Ultimately, I have enough research material to develop a book or a series of articles on the topic of the MSF, but for the purposes of this preliminary analysis I have chosen to foreground the issue of the adverse impact of the war on terror as a theme that best illustrates a recurring tension between Muslim community organizations and senior police officers during the lifetime of the MSF. In doing so I do not overlook the fact that engagement between representatives of Muslim organizations and senior police officers took place elsewhere and under different auspices during the same period. For example in 2001 and 2002, it was not uncommon for the secretary general of the MCB, then Sir Iqbal Sacranie, to attend meetings with the Metropolitan Police Commissioner, then Sir John Stephens, at New Scotland Yard, not independently from the MSF but rather signifying a sense of importance that attached to the MCB role then: that would not last once the MCB fell from government grace (Lambert 2011a).

In this latest development of my research agenda I am indebted to the guidance of Basia Spalek who has attended MSF meetings herself and has played a pivotal role in shaping my research agenda and methodology. When I first met Spalek in 2004 I was immediately struck by her genuine and empathetic interest in offering space to hidden or marginalized voices in the criminal justice system generally and in counterterrorism and community policing in particular. While other academics sought to record the organizational strategies of police services in relation to counterterrorism, community and neighborhood policing, sometimes in research projects sponsored and funded by the ACPO or the Home Office, Spalek was more concerned about raising the profile of less influential voices involved in community policing and in grassroots police and community partnerships at the local level.

I have certainly been a beneficiary of Spalek's bottom-up approach to academic research as this chapter testifies. As a rank and file police officer represented by the Police Federation and not by either ACPO or the Police Superintendents Association (PSA), I was not expected to take part in public debate on the war on terror on counterterrorism policing. Spalek encouraged me to value my own perspective notwithstanding a divergence from organizational policy, and she was the first academic to nurture and encourage it. Later in 2005 I had the good fortune to meet Bill Tupman who had the unique experience of tutoring police officers and expertly guided me through a PhD research program that provides the basis for my book. Tupman's own critique of the war on terror provided the stimulus for my research, and he played a key role in allowing me to develop my own local analysis (Tupman and O'Reilly 2004). In particular, Tupman encouraged me to explore the impact of Washington and Whitehall policy on local policing initiatives. I have received the same encouragement from other academics, most notably Max Taylor and Jonathan Githens-Mazer, and it is no coincidence that other voices in this arena have been encouraged and empowered by them as well.

In all probability I was less wedded to corporate police thinking or organizational policy than my senior colleagues who took center stage when engaging with Muslim communities and the wider public in the wake of 9/11 and throughout the war on terror. To a certain extent, a lower-ranking perspective made it possible to facilitate my role as a participant observer at MSF meetings and in meetings with members and associates of the MSF. In addition, as a specialist detective in charge of the MCU, I often worked away from the day-to-day influence of ACPO and Home Office policy strategy and was often in close touch with Muslim communities where the impact of the war on terror was most keenly felt.

Significantly, after I was asked to write this chapter, my covert role as (a) an undercover police officer in the 1980s and (b) a supervisor of undercover police officers in the 1990s became the subject of media attention (Evans and Lewis 2011). While I do not propose to engage here in the debate about my prior undercover role, it is relevant to this chapter in a way that I should briefly describe. Being an undercover police officer involves using trust-building skills on an instrumental basis—not unlike a police hostage negotiator who seeks to win the trust of a hostage taker for a strictly limited purpose (Lambert 2011c). In contrast, my work on the MCU involved using trust-building skills transparently for a shared partnership purpose (Lambert 2011c). Suffice it to say, media revelations concerning my earlier undercover—"police spy"—role have raised concerns about the authenticity of my subsequent MCU partnership role and highlighted the need to rebuild damaged trust. Writing directly to this concern I pointed to "my willingness to learn from mistakes and to help make improvements in the future" (Lambert 2012b). In the circumstances, I was pleased to be the recipient of an award for my research work from the Muslim Association of Britain (MAB) in June 2012.

## British Muslims Complain of Harassment

In August 2002, Muslim community representatives at the MSF raised concerns about the alleged harassment of British Muslims in circumstances that were directly related to the war on terror. A news report in the *Muslim News* under the banner headline "British Muslims Complain of Harassment" and the strap line "MI5 and Special Branch Officers Have Visited the Homes of over 30 British Muslims since May" fairly record the circumstances as they were presented by Muslim community representatives at the MSF. Described in the paper as "fishing" expeditions that were "part of a new strategy to collect information on possible terrorists" in which "no one was arrested," the home secretary, David Blunkett, was reported to have apologized to some of the Muslims interviewed, "I am sorry" he is quoted as saying, "that anyone interviewed was distressed by the experience." It is instructive to quote further from the *Muslim News* report:

> "We felt intimidated. They alleged that our names and addresses were found in the Tora Bora region of Afghanistan," one Muslim from Blackburn was quoted as saying. Most of those visited preferred not to be identified.... All the Muslims said they co-operated with the security services and answered their questions. Some of them said they reluctantly agreed to talk to the Special Branch as they were "too frightened" to say "no." (Versi 2002)

Coming as it did when the MSF was in its infancy, the issue provided an early opportunity for discussion about the direct impact of the war on terror. Muslim community representatives asked the following questions and made the following observations and suggestions to police at the MSF meeting:

- Were individuals being approached as suspects and potential informants and not as responsible citizens?
- Was the war on terror targeting innocent Muslims rather than being focused on terrorists?
- In future, Muslim community representatives should be notified in advance by police of this kind of operation—on the basis that forewarned was forearmed.

- Allied to the first point was the observation that community representatives would be challenged by communities along the lines—what was the point of attending MSF meetings at New Scotland Yard if they were not going to be briefed about these kinds of operations.
- Again on timing, police were asked to ensure that MSF Muslim community representatives were at least notified as soon as possible after operational police activity and in any event before the media was notified.

These were the kind of areas where police and the MSF could make progress. Indeed, subsequently, notwithstanding many repeat performances some progress was made, especially up to 2005. Here too, MCU work fed into MSF dialogue. Naturally, the report was widely known, and it created fear and suspicion that the MSF and the MCU were actually just an extension of this intrusive approach. Then, and later, the MCU was able to explain its role to the MSF and that at least went some way to reassuring key representative groups that partnership engagement was at least intended to be qualitatively different toward source recruitment (i.e., the recruitment of informants or what is described above as "fishing expeditions"). However, from 2006 onward, even on the relatively straightforward issues of timing and communication, police were hampered by a growing government concern about the suitability of some of the Muslim community participants in the MSF. That growing concern was directly related to the war on terror as will become clear.

Similar incidents were brought to the attention of police at MSF meetings. For example reports of Muslims in Tower Hamlets being approached to work for the Security Service in circumstances that were interpreted by MSF Muslim community representatives as being unfair and coercive. These were clearly sensitive issues that needed to be assessed individually and on their merits. Although the MSF served a valuable purpose in providing an outlet for community concerns, on this kind of issue it was generally less effective at putting policies in place to achieve solutions.

## QUESTIONING OF YUSEF MOTALA

At an emergency MSF meeting held at New Scotland Yard on November 14, 2003, Dr. Khan, the MCB representative, raised an important issue at the outset. He expressed outrage and disbelief that a senior Muslim scholar, Sheikh Yusuf Motala, had been questioned by police at Heathrow airport and consequently missed an important flight taking him on pilgrimage. Why, he asked, was Motala questioned at an airport about his role as principal of the Darul Uloom seminary in Bury when that information was freely available on request at less inopportune moments? When complaining about the indignity caused to Motala, Dr. Khan likened the incident to the archbishop of Canterbury being questioned by police at Heathrow airport about his work. Dr. Khan expressed concerns that were fully articulated in an MCB press release, part of which is reproduced here:

> In a letter to the Home Secretary sent today the MCB Secretary General, Iqbal Sacranie said "No clear explanation has been forthcoming by either the police or the Home Office as to why Shaykh Yusuf Motala was subjected to such unacceptable behavior.... There is a very real concern that Muslims are now being singled out for profiling and discrimination in the name of fighting terrorism."

Significantly, the press release highlights an awareness on the part of the MCB that the government rather more than police themselves had responsibility for policy in relation to counterterrorism and therefore, indirectly, the circumstances that gave rise to Motala's questioning. The press release concludes by linking Motala's experience to the experience of Muslims more generally:

> This case is just one of many that highlights the greatly increased level of suspicion and prejudice that British Muslims now have to encounter almost every day. It is not only demeaning to the community but is eroding their trust in the police and security agencies...we are therefore urging the Home Secretary to investigate this matter thoroughly so that such appalling incidents do not recur. (MCB 2003)

The express connection between counterterrorism policy and Islamophobia was one that would be articulated and recur throughout the history of the MSF. It would also be fair to say that police would at this or any point during the decade of MSF engagement have access to Muslim community voices that did not share the same level of concern expressed by Dr. Khan on behalf of the MCB with regard to the Motala incident. Nonetheless, according to an MSF interviewee, the incident caused real anger around the country:

> Everyone knew [Motala] was a devout and peaceful man. Anger. Phone never stopped ringing. What was going on? What was the point of having an MSF and an MCU if this kind of thing happened? Did the

> Commissioner know how much upset this had caused? The important point is that you can ask the Sheikh anything any time, you don't have to button hole him at the airport.[3]

What then was the reason for Motala's questioning at Heathrow Airport? The following report by Ahmed Versi, editor of the *Muslim News*, fairly represents the MSF Muslim community understanding of the case at the time:

> [Motala] said he was interrogated by three officers, an Immigration officer, an anti-terrorism officer and MI5 officer. Shaykh Motala related that when he was stopped he was [subsequently] asked by an MI5 officer in Urdu why he was being detained, he replied that it was because of his black case which contained his computer. "No, said the MI5 agent, adding in Urdu to me—"aap bahot bade admi ho." (You are a very important person.) I replied, that I wasn't. He replied, "Aap bahu mashhoor aadmi ho, Brtainia aur aqwame alam mee" (You are a well known person in the UK and internationally), the Shaykh said in reference to the initial encounter. (Versi 2003)

A wide range of Muslim community concerns were expressed in the *Muslim News* report by many, including the chairman of the Lancashire Council of Mosques, Ibrahim Master, who knew the Shayk personally and said, "We support the Government's initiative on national security, but not at the hounding of innocent Muslim citizens" (Versi 2003).

After the MSF meeting, the *Muslim News* reported that "the Muslims attending...were told that Shaykh Motala was detained because of 'intelligence information' received by the security forces" but that "the police refused to discuss what this information was but promised to look into the matter further" (Versi 2003). In many respects this was an initial response from the police to allow time to look into the circumstances of the case. Subsequently, it emerged that with better liaison between police and security services, it might well have been possible to avoid the seven-hour delay experienced by Motala at Heathrow airport.

Once all the facts became known, I was one of three police officers who visited Shaykh Motala's home in Bury to apologize for the inconvenience and distress caused by the questioning at Heathrow airport. The visit was also an opportunity to visit staff and pupils at the Darul Aloom school. This in turn allowed police to report favorably to the MSF on the repair of good relations with Motala, his school, and supporters throughout the United Kingdom and the world. However, while the goodwill visit achieved some of its purpose, there was a difficulty translating repair work of this kind into organizational policy to reduce risks in the future.

## *THE SUN* DENOUNCES TARIQ RAMADAN AS TERRORIST SUPPORTER

In the immediate aftermath of the 7/7 London bombings, Muslim community organizations represented at the MSF retained some influence with government and police. This can be seen in a willingness to stand up to a blistering attack from *The Sun* newspaper for inviting "terrorist supporter" Tariq Ramadan to London. Just days after terrorists inspired or directed by al-Qaeda bombed London, *The Sun* explained to its readers how this atrocity was linked to Palestinian resistance by seizing on a planned visit to London by the academic to make its case:

> Extremist Islamic scholar Tariq Ramadan, who backs suicide bombings, is to address a London conference part-funded by police…in our bomb-hit capital he is being given a platform to speak—while the victims of Britain's worst terror atrocity wait to be buried. Ramadan is no ranting Abu Hamza or Omar Bakri. He's more dangerous than that…He is a soft-spoken professor whose moderate tones present an acceptable, "reasonable" face of terror to impressionable young Muslims…In one breath he condemns the horrors in London and Madrid.…The police must pull the plug without delay. And Home Secretary Charles Clarke must move swiftly to ban Professor Ramadan from our shores. (*The Sun* 2005)

Richard Littlejohn's accompanying comment in *The Sun* was aimed fairly and squarely at Sir Ian Blair, the Met Police Commissioner:

> You couldn't make it up. Days after the carnage in London, it is revealed that the police are sponsoring a Muslim extremist who supports terrorism. Between them, the Met and the Association of Chief Police Officers are donating £9,000 to a conference starring Swiss-based fanatic Tariq Ramadan at the Islamic Cultural Centre, near Regent's Park. Ramadan is banned from America by the Homeland Security Agency after a speech in which he justified suicide bombing. (*The Sun* 2005)

*The Sun*'s coverage was condemned by community members of the MSF, notably by Ruhul Tarafder of the 1990 Trust, who issued the following press release:

> *The Sun*'s sensationalist, disgraceful and irresponsible front-page story is simply an attempt to fuel Islamaphobia. Tariq Ramadan is a

> highly respected moderate Muslim scholar and was one of the first to condemn the London bombings, as he has condemned previous outrages. This demonization does nothing but promote hostility towards Muslim communities. At a time of high emotions and the need for strength and unity between all faiths and communities, the inaccuracies and lies in this account only seek to encourage divisions. (Tarafder 2005)

In the circumstances, Blair showed a lot of courage by defending the invitation on the basis that Ramadan's "was an important voice that would be listened to by young radicalised Muslims" (BBC 2005). So too, did Rob Beckley, one of the most successful ACPO officers at building Muslim community trust at the MSF, who was quoted as saying "Like *The Sun*, we believe we shall never be beaten. Part of that response must be open debate" (Islamophobia Watch 2005). However, significantly, police at this point received some political support for their position. For example, despite widespread media pressure to block Ramadan's entry to the United Kingdom, the Home Office was reported to be "unlikely to act in his case, as he is a best-selling author who promotes a progressive Islam" and was "also described by the Foreign Office as 'the leading Muslim leader/speaker in Europe'" (Travis 2005).

In addition to the targeting of specific "extremists" such as Ramadan, Murdoch's newspapers (and often the *Telegraph*, *Mail*, *Express,* and *Star* as well) regularly stigmatized Muslim communities in Britain. According to research published on the sixth anniversary of the London bombings, the *News of the World* and *The Sun* contributed to the creation of "suspect communities" through reporting that fails to distinguish between terrorists and the communities where they live (Hickman et al. 2011).

## MSF Islamophobia Conference

By January 2007 when Sir Ian Blair spoke at the MSF Islamophobia conference, he appeared to have succumbed to political and media pressure on the subject of "getting tough on Muslim extremists," which—on this media account—included getting tough on "extremist" Azad Ali, the former MSF chair (Islamophobia Watch 2009). Only this kind of pressure can help explain the surprising decision by Blair to dismiss Islamophobia, the topic of the conference he was invited to address, and talk about counterterrorism instead. Equally significant, no doubt, the government had toughened its stance against "radical Islam" in the way that Murdoch journalists and others had demanded. I describe elsewhere how this became apparent when government minister Ruth Kelly announced a new program of Muslim community engagement in 2006 that conspicuously excluded leading MSF members (Lambert 2011a, 252; 2011b).

In any event Blair certainly played to a Murdoch media agenda when he surprised the MSF conference organizers and began his keynote address by declaring that he did not think Islamophobia was a significant problem, and that instead he would deliver a speech on the al-Qaeda terrorist threat—a version of a speech, he said, he had delivered in Italy a few days earlier. Interviewed in 2010, MSF volunteers recalled their disappointment with this unexpected and unannounced turn of events:

> [Blair] came onto the stage and he actually decided he didn't want to talk about Islamophobia... he said it doesn't actually exist, it's not really a problem, and what he wanted to talk about was counter-terrorism. And most of the people there, especially from the community were a bit outraged. Loads of people commented they felt sorry, but this wasn't what the actual conference was about, so to come on for an actual conference on Islamophobia to completely disregard it, showed that the chief of police is not even interested, and doesn't see it as a problem, so where do we go from there, and I think we were quite shocked, because we actually set the speeches.[4]

To better appreciate this sense of surprise, it will help to read this extract from the MSF press release that advertised the event:

> The issues of Islamophobia and hate crimes against Muslims have increased particularly since September 11th 2001, and many members of the Muslim community live in fear of being subjected to such incidents. The MSF is seeking to find ways to address these issues in co-operation with the police and government bodies.[5]

For the MSF community volunteers who organized the Islamophobia conference, Ian Blair's opening statement sent out a negative signal above and beyond the topic subject of the conference:

> When that happened, that really did dumb down all of us, because.... that's the chief of police basically coming to a conference on Islamophobia, choosing obviously, made a conscious decision that he's not going to talk about Islamophobia—the conference was entitled Islamophobia—not to talk about Islamophobia and talk about counter-terrorism, so what... what message does that send out, and it

> sent out a clear message to all of us that look, this guy doesn't want to engage.[6]

From an organizer's perspective, Blair's approach to the event also caused problems for their fragile community credibility and legitimacy:

> I think our point from that conference is what we wanted was to broker that relationship between community and police, and I think he completely threw that out, and instead of brokering that, it made us the organizers—yeah, I think it's quite demoralizing to have spoken to [the police] extensively, just as I had spoken to all the key speakers that came on the day,...to reassure communities, and then to have him come on and completely disregard everything.[7]

On more than one occasion, Azad Ali, former MSF chair, explained to ACPO officers at the MSF how he sometimes needed to demonstrate to angry youth on the streets of Tower Hamlets that there was some tangible benefit in engaging with police at the MSF. At times like the Forest Gate raid in 2006, it became very difficult for MSF volunteers like Ali to convince local youth that police were listening to their concerns. Trust building becomes fraught in such a situation:

> And it does compromise our situation as an organization, because here's us trying to liaise with the police and the community, as realistically it is difficult ground, and then when something like that happens, it's very much people who are anti-engagement, it's very easy to say well what's the point, because look what's happened. So Ian Blair in that instance did hand people.[8]

In the event Blair's speech led to expressions of complaint:

> I think for the chief of police to come in and do that was just not on. And we said as much, I think we sent letters out as well, we said as much. We were not impressed.[9]

Although it was a big story on Islam Channel TV, Blair's performance did also receive some media coverage:

> We had Islam Channel, lots of people—heads of community, and just individuals that came on the day, they came because of the conference, because it was on Islamophobia, to see it being addressed and having key speakers from both government side; government, police and

> community. It was not done before, especially in a Muslim institution. They were quite shocked, and I think loads of them commented on it, and I saw quite a few in the BBC clips, of people that were there on the day saying that was just completely disrespectful of him to come in, we didn't agree with what he said, we didn't like what he said, and he should have just not bothered turning up then.[10]

I was not the only police officer in the audience who was surprised and disappointed at this turn of events. It seemed to me that Ian Blair had missed a golden opportunity to support a reasonable and important MSF initiative that would have gone a long way to building trust and serving both police and community aims well. Yet, the writing was on the wall. The change in Ian Blair's tone and direction marked a victory for a new phase in the war on terror that was now strongly focused on a wide target of "radical Islam" and driven by an agenda not set or shared by the MSF Muslim community leadership. In truth the war on terror—as conceived by its neo-Conservative architects—always had been aimed equally at Muslim supporters or sympathizers of Palestinian resistance, as it was concerned with al-Qaeda. It had simply taken additional pressure from neo-Conservative politicians, think tanks, and Murdoch's papers in particular in the wake of 7/7 to bring civil servants and police fully into line (Lambert 2011a; 2011b).

Further evidence for the significance of 7/7 in the neo-Conservative agenda can be found in a Hudson Institute report in the series *Current Trends in Islamist Ideology* (Fradkin, Haqqani, and Brown 2005). In the preface, Fradkin notes approvingly that "there has been a dramatic increase in the appreciation of the importance of the ideological dimensions of Islamism and radical Islam." "This is", he suggests, "in large measure a result of the London bombings of July 7, 2005 and the attempted bombings of July 21, 2005." "In response to those attacks," Fradkin observes, "Prime Minister Tony Blair announced that the ideological component of the struggle with radical Islam was as important as the military and operational aspects—if not more so" (2005, 1). This was the turning point in the UK's policy in relation to the war on terror that was marked by Tony Blair's memorable phrase, "the rules of the game have changed" (Wintour 2005).

## Coming to the End of the Road

Another significant political development that marked a downturn in MSF fortunes was the election of Boris Johnson as mayor of London in place of Ken Livingstone in 2008. Whereas Livingstone was an outspoken supporter of "radical Islamists," he assessed instead to be mainstream, Johnson was far more in tune with the thinking of his Conservative colleague Michael Gove who wrote a withering attack on Islamists and political Islam after 7/7 (Gove 2006). It therefore came as no surprise when Johnson announced that he was cutting funding to the MSF because of his disapproval of Azad Ali, the former MSF chair. Johnson's decision was reported to follow revelations in the *Evening Standard* that City Hall was funding the MSF "despite the fact that one of its founding members is Azad Ali." Ali had already hit the headlines "when he was suspended from his civil service job at the Treasury over a blog attack on the government's policy towards 'the Zionist terrorist state of Israel'" (Islamophobia Watch 2009b).

Once Johnson's Conservative colleagues came to power in Westminster in 2010, it was probably only a matter of time before the MSF would be wound up. On February 5, 2011, the UK prime minister, David Cameron, addressed a security conference in Berlin and signaled that the UK government would come down hard on "non violent extremism," and this was clearly intended to include groups and individuals represented at the MSF (Lambert 2011b, 215). It was this political imperative that made it impossible for police to engage freely with many of the groups and individuals who attended and took part in the MSF during its ten-year existence. This is not to suggest that all of the Muslim organizations and Islamic institutions under the MSF umbrella were deemed uncongenial partners by the yardstick of government policy, far from it. But a significant number almost certainly were, and it was one of the strengths of the MSF that it brought police into contact with vocal critics as well as enthusiastic supporters in the community. The replacement model would be carefully managed by the police instead—under the watchful eye of the mayor of London.

Were it not for this political imperative derived from the war on terror, the MSF might well have flourished. In and of themselves, the day-to-day issues discussed in this brief overview did not amount to insurmountable hurdles to effective partnership engagement and trust building at the MSF. Throughout the ten years, individual police officers and individual Muslim community representatives worked extremely well together in respect of a shared goal of enhanced public safety and community relations. The failure of police and Muslim community leaders to find common cause on the issue of Islamophobia serves to identify an important sense in which the war on terror had the unintended and undeclared consequence of undermining positive engagement between senior police officers and Muslim community leaders. Ultimately the failure was the result of the pressure of dogmatic government policy that was wedded to the war on terror and its defining insistence that "radical Islam" or "radical Muslims" were as much a threat as al-Qaeda terrorists. This, Peter Oborne reminds us, was "the neoconservative analysis," "open to scrutiny through the writing of Michael Gove, Melanie Phillips, Nick Cohen and many, many others. . . . " where "political Islam is a mortal enemy which the West must confront." Critics of this analysis, Oborne notes, "argue that political Islam, far from being an escalator to terrorist violence, plays an important role in preventing it" (2011, 16). Regrettably, that valid argument can no longer be made on behalf of MSF Muslim community representatives.

## NOTES

1. To better grasp the rationale of the Blair government's enthusiastic support for the war on terror, I have found three texts especially helpful: Blair's own *A Journey* (2010, 2011); David Owen's *The Hubris Syndrome: Bush, Blair and the Intoxication of Power on Blair's Susceptibility to Powerful Washington Influence* (2007), and Peter Oborne's *The Use and Abuse of Terror: The Construction of a False Narrative on the Domestic Terror Threat on Blair's Expedient Approach to the Facts of Counter-Terrorism Investigations* (2006).
2. Organizations and institutions that have been represented at the MSF throughout or for the main part of the period 2001–2011 include the Muslim Council of Britain (MCB); the Al-Khoei Centre; Islamic Forum Europe (IFE); the Muslim Association of Britain (MAB); the Muslim Welfare House (MWH); the Mosques and Imams National Advisory Board (MINAB); and the Islamic Cultural Centre (ICC).
3. Interview ref. MSF/12.
4. EMRC/MSF interview record.
5. MSF archive.
6. Ibid.
7. MSF interview record.
8. Ibid.
9. Ibid.
10. Ibid.

## REFERENCES

Ansari, Humayan. 2004. *"The Infidel Within": Muslims In Britain since 1800*. London: Hurst.

Balloch, Susan, and Marilyn Taylor. Eds. 2001. *Partnership Working: Policy and Practice*. Bristol: The Policy Press.

BBC News. 2005. Muslim Scholar's Invite Defended. July 12. http://news.bbc.co.uk/1/hi/uk/4675335.stm.

Blair, Tony. 2010. *A Journey*. London: Random House.

———. 2011. *A Journey*. London: Arrow. Paperback edition: new introduction.

Evans, Rob, and Paul Lewis. 2011. "Progressive Academic Bob Lambert Is Former Police Spy." *The Guardian*, October 16. http://www.guardian.co.uk/uk/2011/oct/16/academic-bob-lambert-former-police-spy.

Fradkin, Hillel. 2005. "Preface." In *Current Trends in Islamist Ideology*. Vol. 2. Edited by Hillel Fradkin, Husain Haqqani, and Eric Brown. 1–3. Washington, DC: The Hudson Institute.

Githens-Mazer, Jonathan and Robert Lambert. 2010. *Islamophobia and Anti-Muslim Hate Crime: London Case Study*. Exeter: University of Exeter.

Gove, Michael. 2006. *Celsius 7/7*. London: Weidenfield & Nicholson.

Hillyard, Paddy. 1993. *Suspect Community: People's Experience of the Prevention of Terrorism Acts in Britain*. London: Pluto Press.

———. 2005. "The 'War on Terror': Lessons from Northern Ireland." *Essays for Civil Liberties and Democracy in Europe*. London: ECLN. http://www.ecln.org/essays/essay-1.pdf.

Hickam, Mary, Lyn Thomas, Sara Silvestri, and Henri Nickels. 2011. *A Comparative Study of the Representations of "Suspect" Communities in Multi-Ethnic Britain and of Their Impact on Muslim and Irish Communities*. London: London Metropolitan University. http://www.londonmet.ac.uk/research-units/iset/projects/esrc-suspect-communities.cfm.

Islamophobia Watch. 2005. "Sun Denounces Tariq Ramadan as Terrorist Supporter." July 12. http://www.islamophobia-watch.com/islamophobia-watch/2005/7/12/sun-denounces-tariq-ramadan-as-terrorist-supporter.html.

———. 2009a. "Witch-Hunt of Azad Ali Continues, Courtesy of Andrew Gilligan." March 12. http://www.islamophobia-watch.com/islamophobia-watch/2009/3/12/witch-hunt-of-azad-ali-continues-courtesy-of-andrew-gilligan.html.

———. 2009b. "Boris Capitulates to *Evening Standard* Witch-Hunt of Azad Ali." March 13. http://islamophobia-watch.squarespace.com/islamophobia-watch/2009/3/13/boris-capitulates-to-evening-standard-witch-hunt-of-azad-ali.html.

Jackson, Richard. 2008. "Counter-Terrorism and Communities: An Interview with Robert Lambert." *Critical Studies on Terrorism*. August: 293–308.

Lambert, Robert. 2008a. "Empowering Salafis and Islamists against Al-Qaeda: A London Counter-Terrorism Case Study." *Political Science and Politics 41*(1): 31–35.

———. 2008b. "Salafi and Islamist Londoners: Stigmatised Minority Faith Communities Countering al-Qaida," *Crime Law and Social Change*. Special Issue *50*: 73–89.

———. 2011a. *Countering Al Qaeda in London: Police and Muslims in Partnership*. London: Hurst.
———. 2011b. "Competing Counter-Terrorism Models in the UK." In *Jihadi Terrorism and the Radicalisation Challenge*. Edited by Rik Coolsaet. Farnham: Ashgate.
———. 2011c. "Community Intervention as an Engagement Strategy—al-Qaeda in London." In *Engaging Extremists: Trade-offs, Timing and Diplomacy*. Edited by W. Zartman and G. O. Faure. 81–105. Washington DC: United States Institute of Peace.
———. 2012a. "Counter-Terrorism and Its Effectiveness in the UK since 1969: Does It Pay to Be Tough on Terrorism? In *Ashgate Research Companion to Political Violence*. Edited by Marie Breen-Smyth. 728–754. Ashgate: Aldershot.
———. 2012b. *Rebuilding Trust and Credibility*. CSTPV staff webpage. http://www.st-andrews.ac.uk/~cstpv/staff/staff.html.
Lambert, Robert, and Jonathan Githens-Mazer. 2010. *Islamophobia and Anti-Muslim Hate Crime: UK Case Studies*. Exeter: University of Exeter.
*Metropolitan Police News*. 2012. "London Muslim Communities Forum Launched." March 27. http://content.met.police.uk/News/London-Muslim-Communities-Forum-launched/1400007687255/1257246745756.
Muslim Council of Britain. 2003. "Police Harassment of Leading British Muslim Scholar"—press release. November 15. http://www.mcb.org.uk/media/presstext.php?ann_id=53.
Oborne, Peter. 2006. *The Use and Abuse of Terror: The Construction of a False Narrative on the Domestic Terror Threat*. London: Centre for Policy Studies.
———. 2011. "Where's the Divide?" *The Spectator*, January 29.
O'Sullivan, Jack. 2006. "Visionary Arab Scholar Who Helped British Islam Make Peace with Modernity: An Obituary." *The Guardian*, January 25. http://www.guardian.co.uk/news/2006/jan/25/guardianobituaries.religion.
Owen, David. 2007. *The Hubris Syndrome: Bush, Blair and the Intoxication of Power*. London: Politicos.
Spalek, Basia. 2002. Religious Diversity, British Muslims, Crime and Victimisation. In *Islam, Crime and Criminal Justice*. Edited by Basia Spalek. 50–71. Cullompton: Devon.
———. 2005. "British Muslims and Community Safety Post-September 11th." *Community Safety Journal 4*(2): 12–20.
Spalek, Basia, and Robert Lambert. 2008. "Muslim Communities, Counter-Terrorism and Counter-Radicalisation: A Critically Reflective Approach to Engagement." *International Journal of Law, Crime and Justice 36* (4): 257–270.
———. 2010. "Policing within a Counter-Terrorism Context Post-7/7." In *The New Extremism in 21st Century Britain*. Edited by Roger Eatwell, Matthew Goodwin. Oxon, UK: Routledge.

The Sun. 2005. "Meet Islamic Militant Professor." July 12, via Islamophobia Watch. http://www.islamophobia-watch.com/islamophobia-watch/2005/7/12/sun-denounces-tariq-ramadan-as-terrorist-supporter.html.

Tarafder, Ruhul. 2005. "1990 Trust / Blink press release: *The Sun's* Irresponsible Front Page. July 13, via Islamophobia Watch. http://www.islamophobia-watch.com/islamophobia-watch/category/tariq-ramadan?currentPage=11.

Travis, Alan. 2005. "Ministers Seek Assurance on Treatment of Deportees." *The Guardian*, July 15 http://www.guardian.co.uk/politics/2005/jul/15/july7.immigrationandpublicservices.

Tupman, W. A. and C. O'Reilly. 2004. "Terrorism, Hegemony and Legitimacy: Evaluating Success and Failure in the War on Terror." Political Studies Association Conference, Lincoln, August 3, 2004. http://www.psa.ac.uk/cps/2004/tupman.pdf accessed 4.8.12.

Versi, Ahmed J. 2002. "British Muslims Complain of Harassment by Security Services." *Muslim News*, August 24. http://www.muslimnews.co.uk/index/press.php?pr=152.

———. 2003. "Muslim Leader's Detention Condemned. *Muslim News*, November 28. http://www.muslimnews.co.uk/paper/index.php?article=1359.

Wintour, Patrick. 2005. "Blair Vows to Root out Extremism." *The Guardian*, August6.http://www.guardian.co.uk/politics/2005/aug/06/terrorism.july7.

# Part III

# 5

# Communities and Policing in Transition: The Northern Ireland Experience

*Noel Rooney and Liam Maskey*

## Historical Background

The uneasy balance between the Protestant and Catholic communities in Northern Ireland, mediated through and impacted by state attitudes and responses to civil unrest, has lasted since the partition of Ireland in 1921. This has resulted in periods of violent political conflict, most notably in the period 1969–1994, known as "The Troubles." In April 1994, a multiparty peace agreement was signed recognizing parity of esteem between and beyond the two communities, and establishing shared organs of governance as a means of furthering political and social agendas by exclusively peaceful means.

Within the context of both the period of "The Troubles" in Northern Ireland and the ensuing peace process, policing and security has loomed large as a major factor to be addressed. Relations between communities and policing have been deemed pivotal in the context of broader peace-building reforms taking place, yet often macrolevel change does not translate easily or visibly to a local level.

One of the main rationales for the Independent Commission on Policing (ICP 1999), set up on foot of the multiparty peace agreement, was to address the severe legitimacy deficit between the police and the working-class Republican, and to a lesser extent, working-class Loyalist communities. Recent research conducted within Loyalist and Republican communities suggests that deep-rooted sensitivities continue to surround the area of policing (Byrne and Monaghan 2008), and that the Police Service of Northern Ireland (PSNI) has been unable to foster the trust of those communities traditionally most alienated from the police in the past.

It is against this backdrop that the Communities and Policing in Transition (CAPT) program, as an initiative of the community organization, Intercomm, and a range of civil society and policing partners, was developed.

## Intercomm Model for Community Transformation: A Paradigm Shift?

*We are going nowhere without each other.*

Intercomm, the lead partner in this initiative, was founded in 1995 against the backdrop of a fragile and contested peace process. The organization was born from grassroots community concerns to address intercommunity conflict and social deprivation in North Belfast, in a local, visible, and practical way. Intercomm saw the need to "*assist in combating the social, economic and political problems created by 40 years of conflict and help construct a concrete and viable peace*".

This was not just a question of getting people into a room together or arranging monthly meetings. Engagement had to be meaningful, to facilitate and encourage unpalatable conversations, and to recognize that not everyone was starting from the same page or with the same destination in mind. Nor did all people, many of whose life experiences up to this point had been brutalized and brutalizing, have the same capacity to make their voices heard in a way that would allow others of differing viewpoints to listen, understand, and empathize. Among a range of other capacity-building activities, Intercomm saw the importance of developing and helping to maintain structures for effective dialogue between a range of key stakeholders in North Belfast, coming from a range of different political persuasions. It also recognized the need to bring these and other local community activists into practical and informed contact with government departments, key statutory bodies, such as the police, and academics working in relevant areas.

From experience of this kind of working, Intercomm developed a number of core principles that it sees as the bedrock for any community transformation process. These are viewed, by those who operate them, as transferable to many societies dealing with issues of racism, xenophobia, knife crime, bullying, gangs, or political conflict. They are focused around empowering communities to take responsibility for their own safety through meaningful engagement with others they might previously have seen as enemies or "other":

- A critical element in any community envisioning process must be the empowerment of local communities to shape and inform an agreed analysis of issues currently dividing them, so that collectively they can start to plan how to address them. From the outset, there must be an acknowledgment of what barriers prevent the resolution of present issues that prevent all of us thinking about the future. Until local people have the ability to envision a way forward, that is mutually acceptable to diverse interests within and across all communities, there is not much chance of enhancing community cohesion. In reality, what we have found is that it is highly problematic to address the contentious and difficult issues unless the communal fear, which is either perceived, contrived, or real, is acknowledged from the outset.
- Part of taking responsibility for creating a new and better future is coming to terms with the reality that we must live side by side with people that we distrust and fear. In reality there is no option but to shape an integrated and inclusive process that involves all stakeholders. In reality this will involve communities realizing that we are only going to get what we can build together, and to engage in this, we all need both strong partners and strong partnerships.
- Given this, the purpose of a confidence-building process must be twofold. First, it must assist local communities in thinking through how their goals and aspirations must be modified in light of the fact that they need the cooperation of "the other side" to have any realistic possibility of achieving them. Second, it is to explore ways of achieving these goals and aspirations that does not disempower the other community at the same time. This last point can be put stronger: it is to recognize that your own empowerment depends on the empowerment of the other community.
- Participants need to come to processes as individuals with a stake in their community, not as representatives of groups. They must commit to work together as individuals and give leadership toward the goal of creating a better future that appreciates all diversity and difference.
- The emphasis on a collaborative problem-solving approach has to meet certain prerequisites. First, there needs to be general agreement about what people want the future to look like. No problem-solving approach will overcome radically different views of where we want

to go. It can be general, like living with our differences, but then there must be agreement about what living with differences actually entails. Second, the people involved need to think of themselves as a single group. Problem solving is not two groups seeking common ground, but one group using common ground as a basis for transforming conflict into a puzzle to be solved.

- Collectively, we all need to see the future as an agreed vision that *we* have and that we want to realize. We must also be conscious that there are very real barriers that prevent *us* from getting from here to where *we* want to be. Even in a problem-solving approach, no one is going to get everything he or she wants. If communities assess outcomes only on the basis of what advances their self-interest, there will be little success.

Problem solving requires a willingness to respect the legitimacy of something that runs counter to what you see as your immediate/short/medium/long-term self-interest. One key measure of this is the degree to which one is willing to place his or her preferred outcomes within a framework that appeals to the goals and aspirations of the other side. One has a right to expect reciprocity from the other side. Still, people who refuse to countenance this will probably not reach accommodation to any significant degree.

The Intercomm peace-building model for conflict transformation and peace building went on to develop three pillars for engagement:

- *Practical interventions*: Intercomm's raison d'être is to devise workable and useful ideas for intervention. While it is important to be strategic, it is also essential to be relevant to emerging needs and problems. Experience has shown that, in reality, local credibility is key to problem-solving (local policing and community safety) issues. In addition, it is critical to build group and community capacity to generate and produce imaginative proposals that can both contribute to the lessening of tensions and the development of alternative ways of doing business.
- *Collaborative Problem Solving*: Solutions in the longer term involve the establishment of a level of trust and understanding between power brokers, community leaders, policy makers, and facilitators. This requires investment in the generation of a context in which "real talking" can happen. Collaborative problem solving is both a short-term strategy and a long-term investment in a new way of dealing with problems in divided [and contested/otherwise conflicted] societies.

- *Big Picture Thinking*: In order to make meaningful interventions in highly fragile situations, it is essential that the nature of intervention moves from "panic and escape" to the generation of a learning and changing society. Intercomm has demonstrated that critical to this project is the connection of local experience to external support in a way that recognizes the essential contribution of both.

## COMMUNITIES AND POLICING IN TRANSITION

The CAPT program developed directly from these foundations as a consequence of the overall Northern Ireland peace process. It linked specifically into the reconstruction and development of civic society, in the context of major political and structural changes. The focus was broader than some previous initiatives in being deliberately cross-border as well as cross-community, and addressing rural, as well as urban, concerns.

The CAPT program represented a concrete attempt to impact on the consolidation of civic society, and prevent a return to the politics of violence, in terms of both community and state actors.

While the program rolled out, significant changes were taking place in the policing and justice environment in Northern Ireland, most notably the devolution of policing and justice powers from Westminster to Northern Ireland in 2010. At the same time as local accountability in this arena was increasing, these years also witnessed an upsurge in paramilitary activity.

While security-related incidents had decreased significantly over the previous ten years, the years from 2008/9 were characterized by a marked increase in paramilitary- and terrorism-related incidents. For instance, in 2010/11 there were 99 bombing incidents and nearly 200 arrests under the Terrorism Act (PSNI 2011).

The key driving agenda throughout all of this was around creating and developing ownership, engagement, and buy-in to changes by both key community influencers and police at a senior level. Part of the premise was to develop the necessary skill sets within both the community and policing institutions, to facilitate constructive and respectful engagement on contentious and sensitive local policing issues. The basis of the model was, therefore, the engagement of key community activists, from both sides of the conflict, alongside the senior police in the new setup. The project aimed to involve these actors, and others, in exploring often contentious and difficult issues in a safe environment. As part of the process, training programs and other activities were specifically designed to equip participants with enhanced knowledge and understanding, both of each other and of community safety issues, as perceived by constituencies different from their own. All of this involved a lot of explaining in its initial phases as to what exactly the project was about, why it would be useful, and how it would fit in with other agendas and initiatives being pursued at a party, community, and/or policing level. Setting it up as a training and development program allowed it not to be seen as some new operational initiative being parachuted into areas where work was already being done/or deliberately not being done on the ground.

## Aims and Objectives of CAPT

The overall aim of the CAPT project was:

> To facilitate structured and meaningful engagement between communities and policing (on a local, cross community and cross border basis) to assist the development of a safer and more peaceful society.

The project was explicitly concerned to work with previously alienated or devalued constituencies, so as to enhance their experience of engagement in this arena.

The regional objectives of the CAPT project were as follows:

- to formulate a model for reconciliation and transition in relationships between policing and communities;
- to provide an integrated and structured approach to reduce sectarianism and racism in organizations and workplaces;
- to build on knowledge and operational requirements for relationship building between policing and communities;
- to improve trust and tolerance among participants culturally and political diverse;
- to enhance community policing by fostering interaction and engagement between PSNI and Garda Siochana;
- to create a better understanding of the impact of beliefs and identity upon individuals and organizational culture;
- to enhance knowledge of effective and efficient community/policing mechanisms for preventative, support, and safety measures to deal with community policing issues; and
- to strengthen cross-border relationships among and between communities and policing.

Those at the hard edges of the conflict were deemed necessary participants in terms of articulating often marginalized and highly challenging viewpoints; equally the project aimed for a broader mix of participants and, for instance, found the Rural Community Network particularly helpful in this respect, in terms of getting inputs about different experiences from rural and urban constituencies.

Top level buy-in was deemed crucial, so senior police and former paramilitary commanders were identified as important to speak to, and involve, in the initial phases and training events. These people were deemed best placed to bring their constituencies forward. Without their engagement and sign-off, middle-ranking officers, or those working directly at the coalface, would not have sufficient resources, support, or influence to drive the learning from the program forward in a sustainable and holistic way. In hindsight, the investment of time and strategies to ensure high-level buy-in could be even further improved in the early stages of an initiative like this, as it is so vital to the success of the project as a whole.

One of the unique, and not easily transferable aspects, of the CAPT program is that it was funded to the tune of over £1million by the European Regional Development Fund[1], to provide a strategic focus for collaboration between the policing services on the island of Ireland and communities and key social partners as represented through Intercomm, Irish Congress of Trade Unions (ICTU), and the Tyrone Donegal (a cross-border) Partnership. The fact that the project was a bottom-up, independently funded training and development initiative allowed the program to be shaped in particular ways to achieve buy-in from constituencies who would historically be suspicious of state-funded or police-led initiatives. A funding stream independent of the police and government also, importantly, permitted more equality in the power relationships among participants.

## Background to Project Partners

The *PSNI* and *An Garda Síochàna* represent the two official state policing organizations on the island of Ireland, north and south: The two police forces are separate entities in separate political and legislative jurisdictions. They share commonalities, but also very different histories, experience, and contexts. For instance, AGS is by and large an unarmed police organization, whereas the PSNI carry personal issue weapons as standard. Both organizations engage in covert operations and have had their share of controversies in terms of intelligence and the running of informants, but both also point to their community commitment and operate a number of schemes in this regard.

The *Tyrone Donegal Partnership* is an established cross-border development agency, whose aim is to act as a catalyst for the identification, development, and implementation of innovative cross-border initiatives in the communities of West Tyrone and Donegal. The organization has experience in cross-community development, facilitating greater understanding of heritage and cultural traditions. They have implemented a number of Building Futures Programs that have developed and delivered training on conflict, peace, and reconciliation and provided a safe opportunity for people from diverse backgrounds and divergent opinions to explore their individual, community, and institutional experiences of sectarianism resulting in prejudice and disadvantage.

*The Irish Congress of Trade Unions (ICTU)* strives to achieve economic development, social cohesion, and justice by upholding the values of solidarity, fairness, and equality. The ICTU is an umbrella organization that represents workers in unions. The ICTU is also a social partners grouping that constructs and advocates for a platform of policies capable of delivering a just society. They engage with government, employers, civil society organizations, voluntary groups, and international bodies to promote social inclusion. ICTU supports unions in their efforts to secure a fairer distribution of the wealth their members create.

*International Conflict Research (INCORE)* is a joint project of the United Nations University and the University of Ulster. INCORE was established in 1993 and combines research, education, and comparative analysis to address the causes and consequences of conflict in Northern Ireland and internationally. It also promotes conflict resolution management strategies. INCORE aims to influence policy makers and practitioners involved in peace, conflict, and reconciliation issues, while enhancing the nature of international conflict research. They work with a wide range of organizations internationally, and within Northern Ireland. State bodies, NGOs, think tanks, community and voluntary groups, academic and research institutes, and the media all have worked with INCORE on various projects relating to peace and conflict research.

As the project developed, the benefit of widening the participant base to include statutory agencies other than the police became apparent.

## THE PROGRAM

The project was designed to target interface (where Protestant/Catholic residential areas border each other) and disadvantaged areas in Belfast and Derry City Council areas and the Tyrone and Donegal border region.

It sought explicitly to enhance the peace-building skills of community workers and senior police officers through informed discussion and debate, assessment of good practices, and exposure to and training in conflict resolution. It was an innovative venture combining workshops, seminars, skills training, and best practice visits, with a vision to build capacity within the community for conflicts to be managed and resolved without violence and within universally agreed standards and practices. In addition, the project conducted action research identifying trends in violence/crime in Northern Ireland and the border region. This research, some of which is still currently underway, will be used in the future to identify barriers to and opportunities for conflict resolution, transformation, and prevention.

The core constructs of the framework, and thus the model, were:

- bringing together key people who would otherwise be in conflict;
- creating a safe environment to discuss uncomfortable issues;
- providing neutral facilitation; and
- providing and co-creating a practical and learning model that could be applied back in communities and in policing institutions.

It was not necessarily easy to achieve buy-in. Certain of those approached within the Loyalist community were suspicious of the endeavor as being an All Ireland initiative, involving a police force from what they would consider to be a separate country. Certain people from the Republican community hesitated in giving credence to the PSNI, when historically they had been viewed as the enemy. The project activities were deliberately designed to address just these kinds of individual and group lifelong held views and opinions, cultural and institutional values, and perceptions. As such, CAPT was intended to be a meaningful vehicle to establish cross-border and cross-community healthy relationships to create connections, to improve trust and tolerance, and to reduce levels of sectarianism and racism.

Early in the process, it was recognized that good practices needed in terms of policing and community safety required to be developed on a multiagency basis. Many issues were not simply a matter for the police and/or community representatives. Many problems required the participation and buy-in of other statutory agencies such as the Housing Executive and local government councils. As such these stakeholders needed to be factored into any engagement process and be provided with the same opportunities for making connections, identifying issues, and developing skill sets as other participants. Broadening the base for partnership also had the effect of diluting concerns some stakeholders may have had about interfacing specifically and only with the police. It also helped "sell" the project to traditionally alienated communities as an appropriate program in which to invest time and resources.

## The CAPT Training Program

Each training program consisted of eight days training, including a two-day residential, rolled out over three months. The training program was accredited by the University of Ulster and the Institute of Leadership and Management.

The training program was made up of six modules, delivered over eight sessions:

- Understanding Cultural Competence
- Leadership Skills and Behaviors
- Understanding Violence
- Change and Peace Building
- Transformation in a Time of Postconflict Transition
- Building Peace

All participants were asked to complete an evaluation questionnaire at the beginning and on completion of their training, and these were drawn on as part of the overall evaluation strategy.

## International Best Practice Visits

Six international best practice visits were organized to be undertaken over the three years of the project, and a number of the participants, who had completed training programs and maintained engagement, were invited to attend, with an eye toward an appropriate mix of participants along constituency, gender lines etc. These visits were designed to provide the participants with a sense of what is unique to, and what is generalizable from, their particular experience in strengthening police-community relations. By comparing experiences, it was hoped they may develop a better sense of what has worked elsewhere and why, and what has worked in their case, and why.

## Research

The CAPT project also involved the delivery of a series of innovative and strategic action research publications regarding the changing nature of violence in Northern Ireland. These were to include action research reports as well as a series of action plans agreed jointly between communities and the police during CAPT project activities.

## Measurable Outputs of the CAPT Program

The project delivered and developed, among other things:

- A comprehensive training manual.
- 15 accredited training programs to 324 participants, in Belfast, Derry, and the Border Region.
- Training was intended to be rolled out in groups of 24 (4 PSNI officers, 4 An Garda Siochana officers, 12 community leaders, and 4 other professional staff from other relevant statutory agencies).
- 9 policing and community workshops with approximately 240 participants delivered in Belfast, Derry, and the Border Region and 3 joint action plans agreed and published.
- 3 dissemination seminars delivered in Belfast, Derry, and the Border Region.
- 6 international best practice visits for 24 participants to places as diverse as Kosovo, Cyprus, South Africa, and Manchester.
- An annotated bibliography on policing research with two further research papers in the process of being finalized and disseminated.
- A range of promotional activities.
- A CAPT website to be used by local, regional, and global beneficiaries.
- A Training the Trainers event with approximately 12 participants from communities and policing.
- An exit plan.
- A feasibility study in terms of the sustainability of the learning going forward.

The project was recently evaluated by an independent evaluator (KPMG 2012) as having successfully achieved the vast majority of indicators it set itself over the three years of the project. Behavioral and attitudinal change was indicated in important respects, and understanding of and between other communities and the police appeared to be demonstrably improved.

A small number of participants went on to be successfully appointed to new government-sponsored policing and community safety partnerships—and each attributed their move in this direction to participation in the CAPT program. Another participant spoke of now being able to see the person not just the uniform and, while distrust still lingers, CAPT has better equipped them to hold police to account. One police officer indicated that while he was "instructed to go on the course," it ended up being the most valuable course he had ever participated in.

*Postscript: CAPT was extended for a further three months in 2012 to facilitate transferring learning into a similar initiative being designed for young people (aged 18–25) along similar lines to CAPT. This future project is also funded by the European Peace initiative.*

## Note

1. The project obtained extensive funding from the European Union's Peace III Program and was managed by the Special European Union Programs Body. The EU's special funding program for peace and reconciliation (PEACE), (which started back in 1995), has been utilized in such a way to have a direct impact on postconflict peace building in Northern Ireland and the border region for almost 15 years. The current peace program runs from 2007 to 2013, to the value of $333 million, and is in addition to a level of investment (in excess of a billion Euros) made available in the previous programing period. Its support for cross-community and cross-border initiatives aimed at realizing (broadly framed) goals of peace and reconciliation has enhanced the opportunities for and capacities of community-led initiatives such as the CAPT project for peace building at "grassroots" level. Furthermore, as a consequence of the conditions placed on PEACE funding, the EU has a unique capacity to enable cooperation at various levels between different actors on a cross-community and cross-border basis and the potential for a lasting legacy for peace building both North and South of the Border (Accord 2011, 33).

## References

Byrne, Jonny, and Lisa Monaghan. 2008. *Understanding Key Issues for Local Communities and PSNI.* Coleraine: Institute for Conflict Research.

Independent Commission on Policing (Patten Commission). 1999. *A New Beginning for Policing: Northern Ireland: Report of the Independent Commission on Policing for Northern Ireland* Belfast: HMSO. http://www.nio.gov.uk/a_new_beginning_in_policing_in_northern_ireland.pdf.

KPMG. 2012. *Intercomm Evaluation of the Communities and Policing in Transition Project Final Evaluation Report.* Belfast: Intercomm.

PSNI. 2011. *Police Recorded Security Situation Statistics Annual Report.* http://www.psni.police.uk/index/updates/updates_statistics/updates_security_situation_and_public_order_statistics/updates_security_situation_and_public_order_statistics_archive.htm.

# 6

# Making Sense of Models of Community-Police Engagements in North Belfast

*John Loughran*

## Introduction*

In this chapter I will draw on my professional experience as someone who has worked in peace building from 1996 and who lives in the community from which I have drawn the case studies, detailed here. The chapter will seek to: (a) discuss some of the practices and models that have sought to build community-police relations in the post-Patten era, (b) investigate models of practice developing separately within two Republican and Loyalist communities in North Belfast, (c) examine shared models of community-police relations at the sectarian interface of these communities, and (iv) identify lessons that may have resonance elsewhere.

## Historical Overview

As a state police force, the Royal Ulster Constabulary (RUC) was unquestionably a combatant in the conflict. Indeed, implementing repressive legislation, in an overly exclusive fashion, against one particular community, ensured that the RUC symbolized, in a very public way, much that was wrong with the law and legal processes (O'Rawe 2007, 9). The police acted in an operational environment within which "normal" constraints were suspended to deal with those expressing unacceptable political dissent (Smyth 1999). This point provides a baseline insight into how far attitudes to and working relationships between Republican communities and the police have progressed in the last five to six years—particularly since 2007 when Sinn Féin endorsed the new policing arrangements.

Loyalist communities have had their own share of disaffection with the police, most notably since 1985, when the policing of the Anglo-Irish Agreement was seen as evidence of a sellout by a 92 percent Protestant police force that Unionists had traditionally thought of as their own. (See also Chapter Seven in this book).

## Policing and the Peace Process

The success of the peace process in the North of Ireland was inextricably linked to the attainment of a transformation in policing (O'Rawe 2003). For many, particularly in Republican communities, the reform of policing was the touchstone issue.

What passed for community policing in North Belfast before the 1994 ceasefires was the flak jacketed and armed RUC, supported by heavily armed British soldiers, moving in convoy in armored Landrovers to bring "policing" to the host community. Years later, it is now defined by unaccompanied PSNI officers sitting at community tables, developing agreed solutions to identified problems.

Only by understanding the dynamic of the conflict, and the political role of the RUC, is it possible to fully appreciate the seismic changes that communities have shaped and created, with respect to embracing models of community policing—the effectiveness of which is now dependent on their participation and consent.

In any transition, the degree of success of a peace process is the extent to which it delivers locally and is understood by local people. The constitutional, historical, and political divisions have been left largely intact by the new dispensation in the North of Ireland, but what is significant in North Belfast is that specific communities, from very different political, religious and cultural backgrounds, are clearly embracing and committing to a new order—an order where there is growing confidence in, and respect for, the rule of law. This demonstrates that progress can be made from very difficult and volatile circumstances.

In part, the sea change, in terms of willingness to work with the police, has to do with state-led reforms that took place as a result of the Patten Commission on Policing in 1999. These have been geared toward changing the face, structures, and symbols of policing over the past 15 years. Concrete changes in terms of these indicators have assisted in the creation of a new reference framework for community-police relations. A new social and political space has evolved that is no longer preoccupied with the safety of the nation so much as the safety of communities. There are still, however, serious risks and challenges that will potentially unravel the community-police relations model that has been evolving as a vehicle for building safer communities.

For instance, the Patten recommendations were forward-looking; the new processes of engagement within communities did not grapple head-on with the kinds of broader conflict legacy issues exercising Loyalist and Republican communities. The reforms were not designed to place the police in a role to deal with the past—arguably this political reality, which leaves the PSNI still charged to address over 3000 unsolved conflict-related deaths, could potentially jeopardize confidence in the "policing with the community" model envisaged by Patten.

The community policing models that have developed in North Belfast have walked a tightrope between past and present. They have tried to focus attention on what needs to be done, here and now, to create safer societies. Macrolevel political conversations, (albeit with a very personal content for some families), tend to be left to more high-level strategic engagement or communities pursuing them separately from the police. This does not mean these issues cannot form part of conversations with police at a local level, but there is a recognition that engagement to create safer societies needs to happen now, and quality-of-life issues cannot be put on hold till the more contentious aspects of the conflict have been accomodated. On the contrary, the possibility of any such accommodation might arguably be improved, or brought nearer, by time spent focusing on quality-of-life issues stemming from communal needs and shared agendas. The key seems to be that, while recognizing that broader issues exist, and require to be dealt with, engagement proceeds on the basis of identified concerns at a more local level.

It was recognized by community leaders on the ground in North Belfast that, regardless of any government-sponsored policing reforms, if real changes were wanted on the ground, people in local communities would need to take an active role in owning, reshaping, and embedding them. That is not to say that there is a consistent quality of engagement in all communities (even in Belfast), but the evidence in this chapter, and elsewhere, shows that effective community-police engagements are possible in the most challenging of environments. Republicans, in particular, have moved from a policy of total non-cooperation with state authorities to actually encouraging people to engage in a proactive way in shaping a community safety agenda, with police as key partners. The context of deep distrust and total alienation from the "forces of law and order" in North Belfast makes it a particularly significant area with respect to drawing examples of positive practice. This was an area that suffered disproportionately as a result of the political conflict—one that witnessed almost 23 percent of all conflict-related deaths, many of which were of a sectarian nature, and a number of which were carried out by, or with the collusion of, state security forces.

Given this backdrop, and the huge levels of fear and distrust still apparent, it is encouraging that community-police engagement has proceeded so positively at a local level. Relationships between communities, and between communities and the police, have flourished, based on an agreed need for safer communities, as defined by communities themselves, in partnership with others. Joint collaborative working with the police defines progress in terms of the visible delivery of a palpable and enhanced degree of safety being felt in local communities.

While this chapter focuses primarily on two different communities in one small geographic area, their practice does have a resonance beyond the immediate area. More importantly, it demonstrates what can be achieved when the will exists to work together to improve the quality of community life.

## Understanding the Environment: Introduction to Case Studies

In this section, by drawing on personal experience, local materials, and a working knowledge of the processes, I want to give an insight into two different approaches to building new relations with the police, one set happening within a single community perspective and the other where Republican and Loyalist communities are working in collaboration and partnership to address issues of interface violence and economic regeneration.

## Security and Political Environment

North Belfast has a population of 83,500 people[1] and, at the height of the conflict, attracted notoriety as "the murder triangle," not least because more than one-fifth of all those murdered in over 35 years of violence died within the area. Although containing only 5 percent of Northern Ireland's population, North Belfast has suffered over 20 percent of all deaths associated with the "Troubles" (Hamilton et al. 2008) Proportionately, more murders were committed in North Belfast than in any other part of Northern Ireland.

North Belfast is a patchwork of small Protestant and Catholic enclaves where the proximity of the two communities in largely segregated living environments inevitably leads to tensions and, in some cases, violence. Ardoyne, for example, is an interface area that has witnessed some of the worst violence in Northern Ireland including mass movement of people, open street fighting, clashes with the police, shootings, and intimidation.

Over the last few years, North Belfast has also become a target for dissident Republican activity. This is illustrated by the disruption caused by bombings and an upsurge in paramilitary shootings. The most significant driver of fear is demographic change. The Protestant community has declined in North Belfast as the Catholic community has grown. Twenty years ago, the broader Protestant-Unionist population had approximately 20,000 more voters than the Catholic community at general elections. Today, the numbers are drifting in the Nationalist community's favor. In the May 2011 Northern Ireland Assembly Elections, the Unionist/Loyalist vote was 15,170 and the Nationalist/Republican vote 14,696.[2]

## Social and Economic Environment

North Belfast is the most mixed segment of the city in terms of religious composition. However, each segment of North Belfast is highly segregated into either majority Catholic or Protestant populations. Statistics show, for example, that more than 90 percent of the New Lodge population is from a Catholic background while over 90 percent of the neighboring Tiger's Bay community is from a Protestant background.

North Belfast is recognized as an area suffering from multiple deprivation. The Northern Ireland multiple deprivation measures (NISRA, 2010)[3] show the North Belfast Assembly area as the second most deprived in Northern Ireland. There are 47 super output areas[4] in North Belfast, of which 21 are ranked in the top 100. In North Belfast the most deprived super output area is New Lodge (ranked 5th out of 890), with the least deprived, Cavehill, only a mile or so up the road (ranked 835th out of 890; see table 6.1).

In these difficult economic circumstances, a vicious circle developed: areas of traditional high unemployment experienced much conflict, which in turn meant that more jobs were lost and deprivation deepened. As the more violent areas acquired increasing notoriety, few new companies/enterprises could be persuaded, despite sizeable government grants, to locate there, and, therefore, unemployment

**Table 6.1** North Belfast Multiple Deprivation Measures (2010).

| Indicator | North Belfast value | North Belfast rank[a] | Northern Ireland value |
|---|---|---|---|
| Population (2008) | 83,500 | | |
| Extent[b] | 59% | 2 | 18% |
| Number of people income deprived[b] | 34,825 | 3 | |
| Percentage of population income deprived | 42% | 2 | 25% |
| Number of people employment deprived[c] | 9,283 | 4 | |
| Percentage of working-age population employment deprived | 20% | 2 | 13% |

[a] There are 18 Assembly areas in Northern Ireland. For each measure, a rank of 1 indicates the most deprived according to the measure, and 18 is the least deprived.
[b] "Extent" measures the percentage of the Assembly population living within 30 percent most deprived super output areas. In other words, 59 percent of the North Belfast people live in the most deprived super output areas in Northern Ireland.
[c] The income scale shows that there are 34,825 people in North Belfast with income deprivation, and the employment scale shows that 9,283 people with employment deprivation. North Belfast is ranked third most deprived out of the 18 Assembly areas in terms of the number of people who are income deprived and fourth in terms of people who are employment deprived.
*Source*: Northern Ireland Statistics and Research Agency (NISRA) http://www.nisra.gov.uk/.

got worse. This was classically the case in North Belfast where jobs drained away from both Ardoyne and the adjoining Shankill district. The two districts remain separated by some of the city's highest peace walls, concrete physical structures that define and separate areas of different religion but similar deprivation.

## Enhancing Community Policing from the Bottom Up

In 2008, the Greater New Lodge Community Empowerment Partnership commissioned a study by local academics, Drs. Pete Shirlow and Graham Ellison, seeking the attitudes of local residents toward policing, community relationships with the PSNI, and experiences of crime and antisocial behavior. Some of the findings will have resonance in similar urban working-class communities, but are overlaid with further layers of complexity relating to the impact of the communal trauma of violent conflict and its ongoing legacy.

The report was designed, not only to raise awareness about residents' expectations of policing, but also to deal with some of the hearsay negativity around attitudes to policing.

These were some of the findings:

- 51.9 percent stated that they *would* now contact the PSNI directly about crime or antisocial activity; 22.7 percent stated that they would not.
- 35.1 percent felt that policing was changing in a positive way in the Greater New Lodge area compared to 24.2 percent of respondents who felt it was not; 25.3 percent were undecided.
- 52.6 percent rated the PSNI's response to crime in the Greater New Lodge area as very poor or fairly poor; 12.6 percent felt the PSNI were doing a very good or fairly good job.
- 54.3 percent felt the PSNI were not effective in tackling the issue of antisocial behavior in the Greater New Lodge; 15.5 percent felt the PSNI were effective in this role.
- 81.2 percent felt that tackling the issue of "illegal drugs" should be an urgent priority for police, followed by under-age drinking (77.9 percent), physical assaults (73.2 percent), interface/sectarian violence (71.1 percent), and car theft (71.1percent).
- 76.09 percent agreed that the police need to liaise with community groups to learn more about the policing needs of the community.
- 82.9 percent agreed that local community groups should engage on the community's behalf with the PSNI to tackle crime and antisocial behavior.
- 79.5 percent of respondents stated they were more cautious than they were two years previously when leaving their home at night, and 62.4 percent were more aware of rowdy behavior in the streets compared to two years earlier.
- 58.2 percent felt that the Greater New Lodge was a less desirable place to live in as compared to two years back, and 8.2 percent thought the area was more desirable.

Should this survey be conducted now, dissident Republican activity is also likely to feature highly as a further concern.

Ellison and Shirlow (2008) make the point that the difficult relationship between the Nationalist New Lodge community and the police had manifested itself in a lack of confidence in the police's ability to tackle crime, which in turn leads to high levels of nonreporting. While a considerable number of respondents had been the victims of crime, many did not report it to the police. Those taking part in the survey recalled 413 incidences of crime in the previous three years, but 55.69 percent (230) of these were not reported to the PSNI. Indeed, the report highlighted that the police response to crime and antisocial activity was seen as inadequate,[5] and local priorities were not being efficiently tackled.

In addition, the Ellison/Shirlow (2008) report provided clarity, and an evidence base, to the community sector on what their role and responsibility should be in relation to engagement with the police. It also placed an obligation on police to discuss with the community how a genuinely effective and accountable service could be developed. Developing a policing service that is genuinely accountable to the community was never going to be an easy project, though communities and the PSNI are finding ways (and a maturity) to juxtapose past and contested experiences of policing with the current imperative of creating safer communities in the present.

This participatory bottom-up approach to policing and community safety is not exclusive to Republican communities. Loyalist communities, too, are working collaboratively to shape better policing and deliver safer and vibrant neighborhoods, while at the same time tackling the sensitive issue of paramilitarism. Participating in this work, while living in the same community, is not risk free. For example, one community leader had his home attacked consistently over a period of a couple of years to intimidate him from working with the police, and death threats have been issued to a number of people to dissuade them from collaborating with, what are still deemed in certain quarters, as the forces of oppression. However, the various initiatives embarked upon began to reveal that the police were not a monolith, and that good could come from working with them as strategic partners in conjunction with other agencies. This, coupled with political endorsement that such work was needed, helped in the growth of a critical mass of people who were prepared to work with police in an overt way.

## Case Study 1: Single Identity–Based Initiatives

### The Greater New Lodge Safer Streets Committee and The North Belfast Community Development and Transition Group[6]

*This illustration focuses on the creation of a community structure to deliver a safer community. This work has involved working collaboratively with the PSNI within a wider multi-agency framework.*

The New Lodge community is a proud Republican community that has experienced great loss as a result of the political conflict in the north of Ireland. Historically, members of this community were deeply suspicious of the police—in part some of this suspicion and fear still remains.

Despite this, the Greater New Lodge Safer Streets Committee, made up of residents, community workers, and political activists, has been working hard to develop effective strategies in relation to issues of community safety. These include combating the use and sale of drugs, whose trade, in Northern Ireland, is enmeshed with, and tends to be run by, certain paramilitary groupings. The group engages with a range of statutory and other agencies including: the Northern Ireland Housing Executive, Housing Associations, the Police Service for Northern Ireland, Belfast City Council, Youth Justice Agency, Social Services, and Community Restorative Justice Ireland.

The increasing drug culture across many working-class communities has led to the exacerbation of other problems as well, including domestic violence, loan-sharking, burglaries, and general antisocial behavior, all of which contribute to a sense of community insecurity. The Greater New Lodge Safer Streets Committee is designed to give local people hope that they do not have to live with high levels of crime. In many ways they are defining and refining how their community is policed.

Their engagement with the PSNI (taking into consideration the political environment and their communities' past relationship with the RUC) was initially a huge step. The committee is a vehicle to build collaborative working practices and relationships with the PSNI to deliver a safer community. Their strength is their collective approach, working as a single entity, in the name of all residents. It is with this unity of purpose that they hold public agencies accountable as they work toward building a safer community.

The level of engagement with the PSNI and the Greater New Lodge Safer Streets Committee is such that the community has now requested that the local police provide regular information updates to residents on their performance in the Greater New Lodge area. With access to direct information through the community magazine, local residents can judge for themselves the quality of the policing service in their community. The symbolic significance of printing a PSNI report in a local community magazine is an indication of distance travelled in terms of delivering effective and accountable community policing.

The PSNI report of Friday June 10, 2011, details a decrease in burglaries while also encouraging residents to be vigilant with regard to home safety. The report also detailed that a number of drug searches were carried out, and that arrests were made and drugs and money seized. The PSNI also requests residents to report any suspicious activity. On the issue of youths causing annoyance, the PSNI identified 10 youths involved in activities of a harmful nature. This level of concrete detail is helpful in assessing just what is happening and assists in dealing with safety issues on the ground.

It is significant that the PSNI share all information with statutory partners, and they pledge themselves to joint action if required. The honesty[7] and the lack of conditionality in the PSNI report is a further indicator of how robust the community-police partnership has become. Offering support to parents and detailing personal contact (including cell phone) numbers for the Neighbourhood Team, the PSNI states: "We do not want to see young people enter the criminal justice system, but we have a responsibility to protect residents and ensure that their quality of life is not affected by this activity."

Again, the community has extended and grown in its approach to building a safer society. The New Lodge Safer Streets has developed a multiagency, problem-solving approach to tackle issues of social complaints, contributing to and locating its work within this framework: this approach ensures that all public agencies, are engaged in resolving a particular issue. Nothing is simply a police matter—the policing of poverty and social deprivation requires a more sophisticated analysis and response system.

Drawing on evidence around housing allocation policy, where tenants are involved in drug and alcohol abuse, the New Lodge approach is to involve (and hold accountable to their statutory obligations) the Northern Ireland Housing Executive. One example cited in the community magazine involved a person housed in a flat after his release on parole after being convicted and serving a sentence for a serious offense. His behavior included constant drunkenness, loud noise, verbal threats and abuse, public urinating, and general annoyance. The approach adopted by the Greater New Lodge Safer Streets Committee was to engage with the PSNI, Belfast City Council, and the Northern Ireland Housing Executive. The lesson here again is that community safety is a key strategic priority for all residents. Through the established community vehicle, other agencies are engaged and, as an action, the community has identified and requested that the PSNI monitor the designated area.

These engagements and models demonstrate that, at the local level, communities do have the capacity and commitment to identify problems and work collaboratively with the PSNI and other agencies. The PSNI equally appears up for the challenge of policing with the community.

The North Belfast Community Development and Transition Group provides an example within the Loyalist Community in North Belfast of working strategically and practically to build confidence, responsibilize individuals and organizations and create an environment free of "negative paramilitary influence or criminality." Paramilitarism was rife in this area of Belfast during the Troubles, and indeed beyond. The police were either unwilling or unable to break the stranglehold of the local paramilitary godfathers.

The significance of the work of the NBCDTG has been to create a positive environment wherein there is no need for paramilitary groups. This has not been an easy or risk-free process. Within their literature, the NBCDTG state they are committed to addressing the "legacy of fear and criminality associated with previous North Belfast paramilitary regimes."

The work of the NBCDTG has been to micromanage peace process issues, such as decommissioning, demilitarization, negative paramilitary influence, and criminality at the local level. The internal process of discussion, debate, and reflection has facilitated the NBCDTG in constructing a working principle of "law before violence" and, as an outcome, it encourages everyone to contact the PSNI to report criminality, illegal drug activity, and suspicious behavior.

The NBCDTG has a forward-looking vision that incorporates their responsibilities to their own constituency, community, and also to neighboring Republican and other communities. Their assessment is that despite powers being available to the PSNI, drug dealing, drug abuse, and criminality persist. The response of the NBCDTG is to mobilize the community through area-based policing and community safety partnerships, and for the community to take ownership of these issues in a collaborative and "law abiding" manner.

## Case Study 2: Cross-Community Initiatives

### The Cityside Model

*Drawing on the work of Claire Pierson (2011), this illustration details how the identification of a key conflict issue, and the formation and facilitation of meaningful partnerships can concurrently resolve the issue and create the platform for sustainable change. CITYSIDE is a cross-interface initiative that comprises community leaders, from different religious and political communities, working collaboratively with the PSNI and local retailers.*

The CITYSIDE complex (formerly Yorkgate) is a retail park neighbored by the New Lodge and Tigers Bay communities, which are to either side of the main throughway and the buffering zone of Duncairn Gardens.

Duncairn Gardens serves as the interface between the New Lodge and Tigers Bay. The road has been subject to extensive regeneration through the development of a business center and voluntary and community organizations. This road and North Queen Street were subject to outbreaks of violence at various times of the year, triggered by certain events (parades, football matches, Gaelic matches, bonfires, and Halloween) and sparked by a variety of factors (alcohol and drug use, flying of flags, political events, night-time economy, etc.). Although this violence was of a sectarian nature, in terms of the events and times when these outbreaks occur, most interface workers point out that it is linked to antisocial behavior more generally.

Because of the levels of violence, public disorder, and criminality, the previously named YORKGATE complex, was failing to deliver on the economic targets that were required to sustain major shops and other retail units. The complex provided significant local employment, leisure and retail outlets, all of which contributed to a more vibrant local community. Issues were identified that restricted YORKGATE expansion and the future viability of the site, intercommunity violence being chief among these, having spilled over from the streets and into the YORKGATE complex itself. The consequence was twofold: (a) a reduction in footfall, primarily from the Unionist community and (b) a reduction in YORKGATE's ability to attract shoppers/moviegoers from beyond local communities.

## The Intervention "from Below"

A number of community partners that primarily included the North Belfast Interface Network (NBIN), the North Belfast Community Development and Transition Group (NBCDTG), and INTERCOMM, working with the PSNI, have transformed this situation through a number of interlinked interventions:

- INTERCOMM, NBIN, and NBCDTG in the first instance engaged with local community representatives and local residents. They recognized that they would need to work in partnership with all the key stakeholders to create an action plan and an agreed upon way forward to respond to the deteriorating situation. Most important was the explicit recognition that communities from both major traditions needed to be involved in the design of the intervention process.

- This resulted in a series of meetings that, in the first instance, identified the range of stakeholders and their specific roles in developing an action plan to deal with a deteriorating situation.
- For example, community representatives played a key role in promoting early response and antisectarian strategies within their own respective communities. The PSNI recognized that they had to change their style and direction of policing and be more responsive to community needs. The retail outlets realized that close partnership and interaction with the other key stakeholders would lead to a win-win situation.

As a consequence of this partnership, the following key outputs have been achieved:

- YORKGATE (now CITYSIDE) has increased its footfall dramatically and is now seen as an attractive retail outlet complex. This is demonstrated by an increased number of retail outlets in the complex. For example, four new retail outlets subsequently opened over a 12-month period, leaving no empty units. The irony now is that car parking space, which was previously a venue for intercommunity confrontation and rioting, is now so safe that it is impossible, at peak times, to locate parking spaces.
- The increased footfall is partially from the wider community, but significantly includes both traditions from across North Belfast. This, in turn, leads to other positive outcomes for the local community. Economic regeneration leads potentially to more jobs and, thus, informs education and training.
- In addition, economic regeneration provides opportunities for health. Local people (a) become more economically active and (b) the wider population has access to cheaper, healthier food on its doorstep, which impacts on the poorest families in the community.
- In addition, there has also been a substantial focus on targeting criminal elements in the community who would have been at the forefront of sectarian confrontation and other antisocial activity in the area. This has helped to target antisocial behavior and address it at source through innovative partnership approaches.

All of this has contributed to the creation of a safer and more vibrant community. The outcome has been a reduction in sectarian attacks and the creation of solution-focused innovative working practices:

- The decreases in antisocial behavior are evidenced and indicated by a reduction from 66 nights of sustained violence over a 3-month period in 2006 to 6 nights of violence in 2008. This transformation has now freed up police resources to address other issues being faced by the local community, such as burglary and drug crimes.
- The consequence of this activity is that police detection rates in criminal activity have increased and, as a result, community confidence in the PSNI to provide an effective policing service has increased, as has community safety.

A further outcome of this intervention has been an improvement in overall relationships between all of the key stakeholders. This is captured in the following comment by a PSNI officer on the merit of the CITYSIDE process: "*People can bring issues to us and discuss them openly and hold us to account, this way it's easier to get things done and we have a better opportunity to engage with people that we couldn't have met before.*"

- Two examples of this are: (a) INTERCOMM with NBIN and NBCDTG are now delivering front-line training to response officers in North Belfast and are also the first port of call for the police in the area to ensure that local community sensitivities are assessed and addressed before the police can carry out their role in protecting the public and (b) the partnership has now begun proactively to discuss other key local contentious issues.
- Tangible outcomes have been agreement at a local level on the relocation of a contentious July 12 bonfire, and subsequently wider community dialogue about bands marching and related activity around "The Tour of the North" has taken place.
- Taken collectively, all of this work has contributed to the reimaging and rebranding of YORKGATE to CITYSIDE. This name change offers a fresh start. The CITYSIDE model can be replicated in other commercial areas to address local sensitivities and divisions that currently exist.

The CITYSIDE process has a number of distinct features and lessons:

- Communication between police and interface workers was one of the most important measures in reducing violence.
- Face-to-face meetings replaced dialogue by phone.

- There were intensive meetings during the peak of rioting, held up to two or three times a week. During calmer periods, these were held on a monthly basis.
- Interface workers were present during riots and kept a record of incidents to minimize "the blame game."
- Community representatives accepted much of the violence was simply antisocial behavior and worked to dispel the myth that rioters were "defending" their area.
- Local residents worked with police to patrol streets and prevent violence erupting.
- A more neutral environment was created by reimaging murals (which had previously been paramilitary in focus) and relocating bonfires.
- Longer-term initiatives of creating diversionary activities for young people were developed, such as fun days and football tournaments.
- Community workers talked to young people in schools and youth groups.

The trust and generosity generated in the CITYSIDE process, among key partners, is now defined as an effective engagement model in the promotion of community-police relations. It is the investment in relationship building, dialogue, and cooperation at the point of need that has laid the foundations of establishing new norms and protocols to deal collaboratively with issues on the location of bonfires, community safety, the potential for interface conflict, and parades.

In essence, measures developed through the CITYSIDE process, and implemented to manage the potential for interface violence, have had a significant impact. Incidences of rioting and violent behavior have, by and large, dramatically reduced: for example, December 2010 saw the lowest number of recorded incidents since 2008 (25 in total), and events, such as the Tour of the North parade, passed off peacefully in 2010.[8] Again the progress is captured in a comment by a PSNI Officer: "*We had the quietest Tour of the North here that we've ever had... I policed on the Nationalist side which I wouldn't have done before as it would have caused trouble... but being there this year I could see people I knew and they were helping.*"

Although there have been points of disturbance over the past year or two, these, with the notable exception of disruption generated in late December 2012 and continuing into 2013 around the flying of the Union Jack flag at Belfast City Hall, are much less visible than in previous years and, in the vast majority of cases, violence is greatly reduced by the presence and work of community activists. There is now a forum where discussion can take place which allows for preempting and planning for potential problems associated with contentious events. One of the key successes has been in communicating with the PSNI, which enables interface workers, with local knowledge of the community, to identify offenders and provide key knowledge to police officers, and perhaps intervene before more official action has to be taken. The police also acknowledge that the link with local community workers has been a learning curve for them and has improved their ability to do their job.

The PSNI are now actively directing resources at hotspots and targeting those involved in antisocial behavior. All of this is evidencing a qualitative change in the policing service delivered. There is a growing effort to operationally improve the quality of policing delivered. The mood music is beginning to change. These small incremental steps are taking us further down the road of delivering policing with the consent of the community.

These indigenous models of community-policing engagements are proof positive that there is a new chapter being written that is delivering a new "bottom-up" beginning to policing. The concept and practice of locally envisioned community policing is now firmly embedded; the next phase is to allow it to gain momentum and enhance the community policing project to the extent it continues to deliver concrete results in terms of safer communities. While still at an early stage, there is evidence, through the CITYSIDE process and other initiatives, outlined earlier, that community leaders are now increasingly focusing on a common set of community safety engagement processes and outcomes that transcend traditional sectarian boundaries.

Indeed, it is this working toward a common set of outcomes that is opening up new and shared possibilities. Defined by community participation and ownership, evolving working practices in North Belfast are practically demonstrating how genuine community, police, and other agencies working together can deliver safer communities.

The only caveat to continued confidence in the community policing model is the lack of shared analysis, consensus or generosity pertaining to the role of the police when it comes to discussing the violence of the past and its implications and resonances for the present.[9] This, alongside an increased dissident Republican threat, and high levels of Loyalist insecurity, if these variables are aligned, could potentially undermine progress in community-police relations.—Revelations around the "investigative bias" of historic investigations into past atrocities, and more particularly any suspicion of continued state cover-up in this regard or suggestion that any such bias continues to taint present-day investigations,[10] may also impact detrimentally. Also, if the PSNI adopts a much more traditional national security response to policing in response to the dissident threat, this, too, will have the capacity to undermine all the progress made to date.

## Challenges to Community Policing

Communities are currently well aware of the issues over which they have influence and agency. In many ways the community rebuttal of the PSNI chief constable's position on the Police Ombudsman's report into the bombing of McGurk's Bar in December 1971 (OPONI 2011) not only demonstrates the distance traveled but also gives an insight into how the community is attempting to juggle past memories and open wounds alongside the hope that the future policing models can be different.

In reality, it is the everyday practice of policing within local communities that will determine whether public confidence has been achieved in policing. However, it does not take a lot for communities to fall back on their default positions on policing. What is different now is possibly a greater degree of political maturity that facilitates a remodeling of new attitudes toward the PSNI exclusively around quality-of-life issues, no matter the strength of feeling in terms of conflict legacy issues.

The key lesson is that the past, and policing practices in the past, should not and cannot be allowed to contaminate community-based policing, which is now forward looking: the real challenge is how this tension is managed in the transition forward toward a much better society.

## "Policing with the Community": Capturing the Learning

In summary, the delivery of policing in urban areas is adapting to the changing political environment—local communities and indeed the PSNI are central to this improvement process. The PSNI is being tested and held accountable to communities on its approach to tackling drug dealing, criminality, and antisocial behavior. Communities are asking questions and engaging, to varying degrees, within government-sponsored policing and community safety partnerships: Meanwhile authentic community voices are most evident and effective within their own localized community structures.

In the postconflict period, the outcome of community-policing engagements has been to open minds to the possibility that the PSNI has changed in ethos and intent from its predecessor, the RUC. While the initial engagements were tentative, they are now clearly much more affirmative and positive. Confidence and trust now define the nature of many relationships. It is the personal commitment of those involved that has defined the quality of community-policing relationships and engagements: it is this investment in relationships and the co-creation of effective and inclusive working practices that will make this work sustainable in the long term.

In pursuit of safer communities, local people, are courageously and innovatively pioneering models of engagement with the PSNI, from which key learning points have been identified and actioned. These can be taken as characterizing effective community-police relations in this particular location at this particular time.

Key learning points for others might be summarized as follows:

- The need for local ownership of the community safety agenda (including access to and influence over budget allocation and implementation).
- The need for credible and sustained community leadership.
- The need for political support.
- A need to progress at a pace that does not hold back collaborative community-policing working, but that is equally sensitive to historical sensitivities and hurts.
- An effective communication strategy that promotes the positive outcomes of community-police engagements to the wider community.
- The need to position local engagement processes within wider, though complementary, processes engaging a range of other statutory and nonstatutory agencies.

Every positive result is a building block for the next engagement—community-police engagements that are dynamic and seen to deliver are likely to self-perpetuate and open the way to positive working possibilities on even the most contentious of issues. Table 6.2 illustrates the key learning from experience to date.

**Table 6.2** Key Learning from Community-Police Engagements.

| | |
|---|---|
| Values | Underpinning any process on community-police engagement should be an understanding that there exist different memories of past policing practices. The purpose of present engagements is to deliver safer communities, improve quality of life for all, and deliver a shared and better future where rights are respected and upheld. |
| Ownership | From the outset of any community-police engagement process, it is crucial that communities feel both acknowledged and involved as an equal partner in the collaborative relationship. Therefore, it is important that the police are responsive to community needs and concerns and seek to integrate them into forward planning processes at the local level. |
| Knowledge | The community-police engagement process must account for differentials in community capacity, competency, and wider level of endorsement—an effective communications strategy is vital. |
| Relationships | Personal and organizational relationships are core to the sustainability of local engagement processes. The ability of individuals to shape, grow, and maximize wider participation in processes cannot be underestimated. The reality is that community people will first relate to an individual before they relate to an institution—there is also a responsibility on all involved to be innovative and entrepreneurial to grow practice and participation. |
| Oversight | An engagement forum that pulls together all stakeholders in a sustained dialogue and planning process is vital. Regular meetings and engagements are critical to meaningfully embed models of engagement—that forum should itself be accessible and transparent. |
| Systemic | Review, reflection, and documentation should be the foundation of any community-police engagement process. Equally, the practice should seek to connect with formal policing and community safety structures. |

## NOTES

*This paper draws on the practise and publications of the Greater New Lodge CEP, North Belfast Community Development and Transition Group, INTERCOMM and the CITYSIDE initiative. The author would also like to acknowledge the research of Professor Colin Knox and Drs Pete Shirlow and Graham Ellison in shaping arguments, and the input of Brian Caskey, Conor Maskey, Gerard O'Reilly, Liam Maskey, Dr Jonny Byrne and Dr Mary O'Rawe. The views articulated are, however, solely those of the author.

1. The population of 83,500 is based on the Belfast North Assembly area boundary at 2008 (Northern Ireland Statistics and Research Agency, 2011).
2. Election statistics sourced from Electoral Office for Northern Ireland: http://www.eoni.org.uk/
3. The Multiple Deprivation Measure is based on levels of levels of employment, dependence on welfare, levels of crime, levels of educational attainment and training, health and care and housing, the environment, and transport.
4. Super Output Areas (SOAs) are a new geography, which are being developed by Northern Ireland Statistics and Research Agency (NISRA) to improve the reporting of small area statistics.
5. This report is now more than four years old. My own assessment is that a similar poll, carried out now, would see higher levels of satisfaction.
6. The NBCDTG is strategically focused on assisting the UDA complete local transition from a paramilitary group into a community development based organization to support and develop Loyalist areas of North Belfast and ensure continued conflict-resolution work through cross-community engagement and dialogue in partnership with other community and statutory partners.
7. It is well recognized that the personality and integrity of each member of the PSNI Neighborhood Team has made a significant difference. Equally, the North Belfast district commander and district commanders have been firm advocates for community policing approaches—not as an optional add-on but as a core principle of policing practice.
8. http://www.belfasttelegraph.co.uk/news/local-national/hopes-for-calm-at-tour-of-the-north-march-14844875.html.
9. In reality it is the failure to politically address the past that has now placed the PSNI center stage in dealing with unsolved killings through the work of the PSNI Historical Enquiries Team (HET). Coupled with the most recent allegations around the Office of the Police Ombudsman for Northern Ireland (OPONI) about its independence, there is a risk that these outstanding issues could dilute the huge progress that communities and the PSNI are making to deliver safer communities and a more accountable and transparent approach to policing with the community.
10. Examples include the Police Ombudsman Operation Ballast report 2007 and controversy surrounding the 2012 De Silva report about state collusion in the murder of solicitor Pat Finucane.

## REFERENCES

Ellison, Graham, and Pete Shirlow. 2008. *Community Attitudes to Crime, Anti-Social Behaviour and Policing in the Greater New Lodge*. Belfast: Greater New Lodge Safer Streets Committee.

Hamilton, J., J. Bell, U. Hanson, and S. Toucas. 2008. *Segregated Lives: Social Division, Sectarianism and Everyday Life in Northern Ireland*. Belfast: Institute for Conflict Research.

Office of Police Ombudsman for Northern Ireland (OPONI) 2011. "Report into the McGurk Bar Bombing That Claimed the Lives of 15 People in 1971." http://www.bbc.co.uk/news/uk-northern-ireland-12521952.

O'Rawe, Mary. 2003. "Transitional Policing Arrangements in Northern Ireland: The Can't and Won't of the Change Dialectic." *Fordham International Law Journal 22*(4): 1015.

———. 2007. "Human Rights, Transitional Societies and Police Training: Legitimating Strategies and Delegitimating Legacies." *St. John's Journal of International Law*.

Pierson, Claire. 2011. *An Evaluation of the CITYSIDE Initiative*.

Smyth, Jim. 1999. "Policing Ireland." *Capital and Class 69*.

# 7

# Lessons Learned from Loyalist-Police Engagement in Northern Ireland: The Connect Program

*Winston Irvine*

## Introduction

The issue of policing remains one of the most contested aspects of Northern Ireland's peace process. The legacy of the conflict has left building relations between the police and the two main communities, one of the thorniest issues in the ongoing transformation process. Violent actions and events during the conflict and the subsequent circumstances surrounding them, involving all protagonists, have informed and conditioned mind-sets, both consciously and unconsciously in terms of how the conflict is perceived by all sides.

Over the years, the relationship between the police and large sections of the two main communities has been characterized by animosity, distrust, and violence. This has been reinforced due to the absence of any structured substantial grassroots dialogue. Within this context it is recognized that dialogue does occur. However, it has tended to be at the highest levels between the police and civic society, and generally mediated through and by politicians. Meanwhile, the people who live in the most economically and socially deprived areas, and suffer from some of the highest crime rates, have been largely absent from the discussion table.

From a Unionist perspective, this is, in part, due to the disconnection between political Unionism and working-class Unionist communities and, in particular, those who identify themselves as

Loyalists. Overall, there is a strong sense of underrepresentation politically within those areas, and a belief that Loyalist neighborhoods are experiencing problems relating to civic exclusion. This is evidenced in terms of the lack of representation on the District Policing Partnerships that were set up in the wake of the Patten Commission. Although one could argue that the reason for this lack of representation is due to the absence of a political mandate for Loyalism, that argument, on its own, seems somewhat churlish, and even, to a degree, superficial, given that there is positive bias shown toward other socially underrepresented classifications within society. Add to this, that since the peace process began in the early 1990s, beginning with the ceasefires and followed by the signing of the Good Friday Agreement and subsequent devolved government, Loyalism has played a pivotal role in *winning the peace.* Furthermore, the present role of Loyalist community representatives continues to be hugely undervalued in terms of the work that they do in preventing and reducing conflict at interfaces, not to mention their critical contribution during loyal order parades, very often in a voluntary capacity. All of this, quite frankly, begs the question, why are Loyalists not being regarded as key resources and stakeholders in strengthening the transformation process?

Viewed in this way and within this wider context, it was evident that the current situation in regard to relations between the police and Loyalist communities was unsatisfactory. The fact that there was a greater emphasis being placed on building a rapport between the police and the Nationalist/Republican community reaffirmed the belief that there was a problem in creating a level playing field in terms of the police engaging with communities.

## Addressing the Democratic Deficit: Bringing Loyalists in from the Cold

In this regard, necessary steps were taken to address the situation. Drawing on the analysis outlined, a mandate was secured to support a practical police and Loyalist community engagement program with the aim of developing durable relationships between them.

The desired impact of the program was to create an effective engagement structure that would help address problems that threatened the safety and security of the public. From the outset, a key component in the process was acquiring the support of people living in the local community who were viewed as role models and who were well respected by their peers.

## IDENTIFYING COMMUNITY LEADERSHIP

A critical factor in this approach was identifying people who were capable of and prepared to demonstrate leadership, without wanting to become leader. In other words, leadership needed to be seen as a process of actions, displayed by a range of actors, in different settings, in a manner that would allow people involved to feel valued and seen as an important part of the process.

While recognizing there are times that call for individuals to exercise leadership, it has, however, to be said that it is much more transformative and strategic in nature, if leadership can be internalized as a behavior that is to be expressed in various forms by a variety of people. In my view, this kind of communal working embodies a genuine transformation ideal in the sense that leadership ought to be about increasing the ability of others in order to drive forward positive change, and not the exclusive preserve of any one person or group.

## SECURING HIGH-LEVEL POLICE BUY-IN

One of the key ingredients during the process was securing high-level support within the police for the initiative. In doing so, the engagement carried with it an element of authority that not only countered the perceived exclusionary nature of the civic structures for police engagement, but also sent out a clear message down the chain of command that this issue mattered. In turn, this instilled legitimacy into the program and solidified the commitment to establish an effective concept and construct for engagement.

It was also recognized that, in order for this program to have a positive impact, it had to convince and make visible the potential benefits to the police who were working on the ground, and those members of the public who lived in the area that was identified. The means by which this was done was to have the mandated community representatives and police representatives respectively articulate to each of their constituencies the fundamental benefits that participation in the program could offer. This was done based on the rationale that by working closely with each other, there would be an enhanced delivery of service to the local community. Conversely, an effective partnership with communities would assist not only in combating crime but would also be a vital factor in mitigating against, and challenging those who are prepared to commit, extreme acts of violence.

## Ensuring Symmetry in Power Relations and Complementarity of Approch

Selecting the right approach to the process was significant for a number of reasons. First, it was to ensure that there was symmetry within the project. By this we meant that whatever approaches were adopted by the police to address an issue needed to be as similar as possible to, and supportive of, the kinds of intervention being undertaken by the community.

This was particularly important in terms of the coordination and coherence of the necessary preparatory work required in the pre-development stage of the project. This was to ensure that there was sequencing and a coalescing of the briefing meetings to each constituency in terms of the overall process. People, from the community and the police alike, needed to find out the information they needed at the right time and be involved as equally valued members of the process. It could not look like some were more in the know than others, or that the police were in control or privy to information that wasn't being more widely disseminated.

Second, because of the imbalance in the relations between police and community members, again it was important that the approach addressed concerns relating to implied inequities that arose from the initial political analysis, specifically around the issue of polarization. In this respect, it was agreed that the program design, development, and implementation would be carried out from start to finish on a joint basis with each decision being taken collectively. In doing so, this had a hugely positive localized effect that instilled confidence and an authenticity into the relationship. Furthermore, agreeing to work collectively on an equal basis imbued a sense of joint ownership in a way that enhanced the autonomy and self-respect of the people involved, and created a mutual sense of responsibility and accountability to one another.

In order to build on this progress, it was felt that there needed to be a more formal approach to this phase of the development process, and so a formal working group was established that reflected both the police and the community partners. Following this, another formality was agreed and the project was given the working title the *Connect Program*.

One of the first tasks of the working group was to identify the key objectives that would meet the overall stated aims of the program. The main objectives set out within the program were:

- to increase understanding between the two constituencies and to create a learning environment that would enable that to happen;
- improve communication between police and local community;

- assist the community and the police in appreciating how their behavior affects others;
- promote the value and benefits of working in partnership and develop working relationships; and
- raise community awareness of the limitations and constraints that can apply in delivery of service.

## The Connect Training Program

It was decided a training program would be the best way to increase mutual understanding between the two sets of constituencies. The duration of the training program was a full day operating over a six-week period and running twice a week, with over ninety members of the community taking part and nearly two hundred police officers from a variety of ranks, including senior officers. The type of officers involved in the program included response officers, TSG, neighborhood, CID, and other specialized officers from the rank of constable up to superintendent. From a community perspective, the participants ranged from people involved in youth work, residents' associations, senior citizens' forums, interface workers, restorative justice practitioners, local business owners, ex-prisoners, and representatives from religious organizations.

It was decided that the best means to achieve the project's objectives was to use a variety of techniques and methodologies and original ideas that included the use of individual pre-recorded video testimonies. Using both positive and negative experiences recorded by members of the police and the local community of real-life encounters in terms of community/policing experiences, participants were encouraged to discuss and debate the issues in a constructive and honest manner and feed back their findings. The training approach also consisted of a series of scenarios whereby the participants were mixed into small groups and shown CCTV footage or video clips, and asked to critique the recording and come up with reflective learning points, which were then fed back in a plenary. This approach involved *role plays* in which members of the public were asked to explain and justify the police's handling of a difficult policing situation involving the community and vice versa. In mixed small groups, the role play involved members of the police articulating concerns from a community perspective in relation to a negative policing operation. Other resources were also used to highlight assumptions and perceptions that show how often people jump to wrong conclusions about others. The use of personal- and real-life experiences ensured that participants were active and lively, and that field-based realities were being discussed as opposed to abstract theories. Moreover, the training served to demonstrate what difficult community policing situations are like from the other person's perspective.

There are a number of important factors to highlight in this phase of the process. Beginning with how the training was delivered, it was important that each session was co-facilitated by a community trainer working alongside the district policing trainer. Second, at the beginning of each day, a high-ranking police officer and well-respected community leader made a joint address to the participants to highlight the importance of the program and to encourage participants to engage personally, corporately, positively, and without fear.

There is a subtle but significant nuance in this respect, particularly from a policing perspective, given the code of ethics and risk-averse nature of the working environment in which they work. It is not very often that police officers feel comfortable enough to speak from a personal perspective in relation to some of the community policing problems. It is easy to overlook the fact that police officers are also members of a community in their own right. Hearing their viewpoint and experiences outside of their working environment was extremely refreshing and, in many ways, a humanizing experience for the participants. It helped move the situation onto a human level that enabled people to see past the uniform on the one hand and the stereotypes that are sometimes portrayed of community representatives by some elements in the media. This experience proved to be an extremely effective dynamic in terms of the relationship-building aspect of the process.

By carefully choosing the training program format and content, we were able to locate the participants' discussions and engagement with one another within the overall context of peace building. In addition to this, we believed that the project would be more effective if located within the broader understanding of what are believed to be the present and future problems in terms of policing and community issues. Some of those challenges identified for discussion included the reintegration of ex-prisoners and former paramilitaries into civil society, conflict legacy issues relating to addressing the issue of victims, the issue of sectarianism and intolerance, police and community relations, and issues relating to social and economic development.

However, while setting out a clear strategy for the engagement project, we realized that we needed to be flexible enough to allow participants to raise and discuss issues that mattered to them personally and not expect our direction of thinking to fit neatly into everyone else's idea of what might be called a worthwhile conversation. This was especially relevant given the assortment and vast array of participants who came from a wide range of community backgrounds.

## LEARNING FROM THE TRAINING

After completing the training workshops, the participants' critical awareness had been raised and they had a better understanding of each other's views and issues. Utilizing concrete, real-life experiences in a safe learning environment enabled participants to reflect personally on past experiences and on their own set of values and belief systems. In doing so, they were able to focus on the issues from the opposing viewpoint and adjust their frame of reference when analyzing past and existing situations. This type of participation not only promoted mutual learning but also raised the levels of empathy within the group and deepened the engagement between community and police. This style of action learning ensured that participants were active in their participation and, by combining the knowledge, experience, empathy, and expertise of those involved in handling conflict-related scenarios, it positively supported the personal, professional, and social capacity of those involved in the program.

It also has to be said that there were limitations that existed within the process. In particular, it should be noted that there are fundamentally different reasons as to why participants decide to come round the table to dialogue. Of course it is obvious to suggest that you should not expect people to share the exact same set of motivations. Instead it is quite natural for that to be the case. However, there is an assumption that for some of those who participated in the experience, it was just part of the daily ups and downs of their job. Indeed, from a policing perspective you could argue that police participants were directed to attend as opposed to members of the public who chose to go to the training of their own free will. This, then raises a question of how this affects the quality of the dialogue and the authenticity of the proposed relationship-building element of the process.

Realistically, the question is probably more important than the answer at this stage, not least of all because of the goodwill that is currently emanating from the police in regards to community engagement. Nonetheless it is an important assumption that needs to be tested over time.

There is also the common problem within the police in terms of the high turnover of officers who move from one district or department to another. This was widely accepted as an issue that not only restricts the ability to build relationships with police officers but also seriously hinders the chances of developing effective partnerships in the longer term.

Unfortunately, this appears to be an issue that is going to continue to challenge and limit the extent to which durable working relationships can be created between police and communities. This is also compounded by the changes in community representation within the voluntary sector.

In addition to this, there is also the issue of providing the opportunity to develop the relationship beyond the training environment. One of the biggest challenges going forward is being able to maintain the links that are established in the initial stages and perpetuate motivation among the participants outside of the learning setting. Perversely, the main opportunities for sustaining and developing the relationships are predicated mainly around issues of conflict or citizens having negative experiences. The challenge, therefore, must be to continue to create positive and mutually beneficial experiences that facilitate and foster relationships and strengthen partnership working while at the same time reducing levels of conflict.

## Conclusion

Overall, there is a paradox in the concept of community policing especially in conflict-related regions such as Northern Ireland. The necessity to transform relations between the police and community into strong effective partnerships that build mutual confidence and trust appears to be at odds with the context in which the police operate. Any policy framework that allows systems and/or agendas to operate, albeit under the auspices of ***national security,*** without any real or robust civic accountability mechanism, will invariably prove to be problematic in restoring confidence and trust with communities, especially those that are historically and traditionally suspicious of policing agendas. While there has been a lot of discussion and debate around the structural reform of policing, this is a major issue that requires much more consideration.

There are still extremists within communities who want to drag us back into violent conflict and will use any means at their disposal to do so. In violent political conflict, this usually means exploiting future generations of impressionable young people and manipulating those who feel socially economically and politically disenfranchised. While poverty and social deprivation does not automatically lead to conflict, it remains a pervasive source for malcontents. Within the du jour economic climate, it is, therefore, imperative that politics is seen to be working and delivering on the ground. Furthermore, any effective police service has to have the consent of the communities that they are policing. In practical terms this means tackling the issues that are relevant on the ground and involving indigenous people in shaping the policing plans and priorities for their neighborhoods in a way that goes beyond previous political rhetoric.

Meaningful community engagement that relates to where communities are at in relation to policing, and, in particular, addresses the needs and experiences of young people, is crucial in preventing extremist elements gaining any further traction. Providing holistic, local and strategically effective responses that address root causes of conflict and having these, insofar as possible, structurally inclusive, will, in effect, stand as a bulwark against violent extremism.

# 8

# Prevent and Police-Community Partnerships in Birmingham

*Zubeda Limbada*

In the United Kingdom, the city of Birmingham has long held to a tradition of police-community partnership working when it comes to tackling difficult issues, although old challenges and new problems continue to evolve. The city's rich history and its young and diverse million-strong population—with just fewer than 15 percent being resident Muslim communities recorded in the 2001 Census—provide a fascinating insight into multicultural community dynamics.

In 2007, Birmingham was selected by the UK government to be a "pathfinder" "Prevent" city, and in 2008–11 the city received additional funding to implement Prevent counterterrorism projects. Government agencies encouraged partners from West Midlands Police, Birmingham City Council, prisons, probation, and other agencies to work alongside communities to deliver partnership projects. The investment was used to address community vulnerabilities to extremism and to create stronger, more resilient communities as a result. There was never a doubt that Prevent's focus would principally target the British Muslim communities; the challenge for the local police force lay in building a meaningful relationship with a faith group about whom little was known, and which had not previously been active on the radar.

For the purposes of this chapter, I will attempt to provide a practitioner perspective on community-police partnership based on my various experiences in Birmingham, noting both positive and negative experiences and solutions utilized to overcome the barriers to engagement. I hope my contribution may be of value to other communities and police departments working in a similar area.

## PARTNERSHIP PERSPECTIVES

While everyone belongs to one or more communities—even members of the police force consider themselves part of a "policing family"—my involvement in the delivery of Prevent projects as a local government practitioner since 2007, one who happened to be Muslim female and wearing a headscarf, placed me in a visibly ambiguous and challenging role within this kaleidoscope of community-police partnership working, especially since I had never worked with the police before and had had minimal interaction with law enforcement officials.

As it happened, at that time I was already working in a nonpolicing-related Prevent practitioner role. This involved creating and delivering two community-based arts and media projects, working alongside Muslim communities in Birmingham. In 2009, however, I began a second, more substantial Prevent project due to being seconded to West Midlands Police Counter Terrorism Unit (CTU) as a project manager to design and deliver two outcomes with other strategic public bodies: (a) to select a diverse group of community-based mentors addressing al-Qaeda–inspired (and later, extreme far right and animal rights) extremisms and (b) to create processes, tools, and a six-day accredited training program, which could be used to train mentors around the intervention arena in the wider West Midlands area.

## WHAT MADE A COMMUNITY-POLICE PARTNERSHIP NECESSARY?

For those individuals who decided to work with the police—myself included—there were practical factors to consider, such as why a partnership approach with the police was required, as well as fear of the unknown in terms of taking the risk to work with police officers who were collectively seen as being part of the problem rather than the solution. These perceptions were based on the following observations, which were prominent issues at the time:

*The police and the policed.* The short-term requirement to talk, explore, and work with the police was important in addressing a developing "us vs. them" situation that was not healthy within a local policing context. Trust between the police and the Muslim community seemed to be at an all-time low. Global events were very much intertwined with local dynamics, and the introduction of Prevent complicated a policing relationship that was borne out of necessity and that gave the impression that Muslim community relations were securitized from the outset, an impression that had been given yet more steam under the revised 2006 Terrorism Act, which extended police detention powers. The perception was that the government and the police were only now interested in working with the Muslim community in order to stop terrorism associated with those belonging to that faith group. Conflated events such as Operation Gamble, the 2007 attempt by a local Muslim man to behead a Birmingham Muslim soldier; the undercover documentary ("Dispatches Undercover Mosque" 2007) filmed in a local, Birmingham mosque in 2007 by a national TV channel; and continued high-profile terrorism arrests leading to tensions confirmed the necessity for partnership. Individuals from both sides came to recognize that unless a space for dialogue was opened, vulnerabilities could be exploited, risking an alternative narrative that played on people's fears, suspicions, and mistrust. While mistrust of the police remained, by this stage most community individuals were prepared to at least listen.

*The police and foreign policy.* My first memory of interacting with the local police was at a local community "Prevent" event in which the foreign minister of the UK government of the time—David Miliband—was due to speak and take questions from the local Muslim community regarding Palestine, Israel, Pakistan, Somalia, and British foreign policy in general. Such events were critical in terms of authorities and the government engaging, debating, and exchanging opinions. While foreign policy discussions were always significant and heated events, they were also reminder that only politicians could engage with the community on this issue, and not the police; and that, for most people, law enforcement was previously only visible when maintaining law and order at protests or stopping and searching people on the streets. By openly attending these events, and being exposed to such community feelings, the police found a better way of understanding community anger as well as the impact and significance of the words "foreign policy" when used in the context of radicalization. The lesson learned during this period was that policing could not take place in isolation, and that events such as these, which were held regularly at community venues and mosques across the city, could act as a gauge to measure—not monitor—local attitudes.

*Establishing visibility and trust.* By 2007, at many of these events, two to three discrete but uniformed police officers, identifying themselves as West Midlands CTU officers, were present. While some in the Muslim community saw this visibility as a provocation, or viewed police officers with suspicion and wondered if they were spying on community voices and leaders, on reflection, I feel that these feelings demonstrated how little both sides knew one another. While most people identified the police with solving "normal" crime, the lack of knowledge and lack of a sustained relationship was obvious. Some police officers themselves struggled with community-policing approaches that required a certain set of skills and a "softly-softly approach" involving lots of meetings, teas, and honest dialogue in new places with a community that was seen as being distant, angry, and having too many self-professed leaders.

*Barriers to effective community-police engagement.* In most Western democracies, individuals often have limited interaction with the police until a "key critical event" occurs (see the related discussion in Silk and Limbada 2012). Key events are commonly perceived by the public as negative interactions due to a crime being committed or a perceived miscarriage of justice having taken place, which may adversely target a specific group. In the case of Prevent, many UK Muslim communities felt the government was policing their faith and convictions and that a set of double standards was being applied. I would argue that while the emotion and the political intensity of the early stages of Prevent have diminished, some of these detrimental feelings still hold true today despite relationships with the police having considerably improved.

The London Forestgate incident in July 2006 was such a key event. It involved two Muslim brothers who had been shot by the Metropolitan police at their East London homes after the latter were alleged to have received terrorism-related intelligence. Police later released the men due to lack of evidence; however, the incident was a national game changer in terms of how the arrests played out, when due processes seemed to be substandard, thus exacerbating simmering tensions.

Another key event, this time in Birmingham, was *Project Champion*—a £3 million government-funded scheme earmarked for tackling terrorism by installing more than 200 covert and overt surveillance cameras, described as a "ring of steel," in mostly Muslim areas of east Birmingham. This had to be dismantled following a local outcry that threatened to undermine partnership trust and confidence. Details later emerged that the West Midlands Police CTU-led police partnership team had sold the scheme to local individuals as a crime safety issue, rather than declaring the counterterrorism link. While the project was conceived in 2007/8, it was not until 2010 that details of the project began to emerge into the public domain, and various angry, public meetings expressing concern about "spying" through hidden cameras prompted an external investigation (Thornton 2010) and a subsequent public apology from the assistant chief constable of West Midlands Police (Ferguson 2010).

Using the key events as case studies, the points mentioned next provide insight into what I feel were some of the barriers to effective engagement:

*Organizational changes.* In 2007, West Midlands Police—like most UK police forces—were undergoing organizational change. Regional policing units were being restructured by the government, and dedicated counterterrorism units with trained personnel to address all aspects of the national counterterrorism strategy were being established.

Although these changes were occurring, the community as a whole would not really have been in a position to understand the dynamics and ideological significance of the police approach shifting from one that relied on covert special branch tactics to overt community policing partnership work. It would be fair to say that the police force as a whole was still seen as being the enforcing arm of government policy and local police officers as having little contact with their Muslim communities. With community tensions already on the rise, I remember being wary of being approached by friendly police officers who suddenly were saying "*salaams,*" who were smiling and engaging, but who still wore a uniform and were talking about a government program called Prevent. Suspicions multiplied as these police officers were now present at local events—perhaps attending an *iftaar* in the local mosque they had been invited to, but whose purpose was never fully explored in different communities. Many did not feel confident having public conversations or taking an ideological position for fear of being seen as endorsing a government strategy, or indeed attracting the attention of the very few, but very vocal, Muslim individuals who would condemn them for working with the "authorities" and giving license to those in government to spy on Muslims.

Meanwhile, some police officers did make efforts to gain deeper understanding about Islam; for example, I remember one police officer saying he been learning about the basic importance of the five pillars of Islam, removal of one's shoes when entering a mosque, how to read a mosque prayer timetable, and the centrality of Friday *Jum'aa* prayers, as well as the many different structural power dynamics of the newly arrived Somali communities compared to the more established majority, Pakistani communities. In the mixed training events I held in a few different mosques in Birmingham, common questions from police officers centered on whether men were able to shake women's hands, about wearing shoes in mosques, and about the differences between *Shia, Salaf,* and *Sunni* Muslims, while others were intrigued that a single leadership figure did not exist within Islam.

*Media.* For many Birmingham Muslim communities, one of the earliest incidents reflecting the tense climate of 2007 was the impact national media coverage was having directly in the homes and areas of people, and how they perceived police collusion within this role. On the one hand, some Muslims felt they were receiving mixed messages from the government—nationally, ministers were urging "moderates" to speak out and to help the police in rooting out extremists, while various government road shows were arranged to challenge Islamophobia. Locally, while all this was happening, there was a feeling that the government and the police were keen to send a strong message of wanting to arrest and disrupt individuals on terrorism offences, but these individuals were not always charged,[1] which added to a sense of unease and misgiving.

More specifically, such strong, visible messages were reflected in how the police would carry out raids on houses in full glare of pre-arranged publicity; for example, leaks of the imminent arrests were allegedly provided in the aforementioned Birmingham *Operation Gamble* case by the Home Office[2] and police to media outlets, who then broadcast these police arrests live regardless of personal or community safety or innocence. Quite often, such national media stories presented a significant barrier to cooperation in terms of how they forced local communities to react angrily to the mixed messages they were getting from the police, while in reality there seemed to be a disregard for the widespread feeling of whole areas being tarred with the "hotbed of radicalism" brush.

With doors being knocked down in early morning while residents looked on in fear and vanloads of police officers filled the streets, neighbors spoke fearfully of media images of their communities harboring rows upon rows of terrorists. The damaging effect of this was recognized when deputy assistant commissioner Peter Clarke of the Metropolitan Police, a former, senior counterterrorism officer, said to politicians in his testimony of the Birmingham antiterror operation:

> On the morning of the arrests, almost before the detainees had arrived at the police stations...it was clear that key details of the investigation and the evidence had been leaked. This damaged the interview strategy...and undoubtedly raised community tensions.

He added:

> Off-the-record press briefings also have the very practical effect of interfering with ongoing police investigations, possibly even increasing the chances of suspects evading arrest. Once the media have been tipped off about the potential location of a terror rated arrest, the press inevitably "arrive" in the area for "breaking news" (with the) arrival of numerous TV crews, journalists and equipment. (House of Commons: Home Affairs Committee 2009, 18)[1]

*Leadership and the impact of government monies on cultural dynamics.* One challenge to community-partnership work has always been that of trying to identity just who is a Muslim community "leader." While British Muslims represent a diversity of communities, cultures, religious leaderships, and faith identities, the media and politicians have sometimes dealt with this group as though it were a singular cultural community that tends to cause problems. This can alienate people and reduce the willingness of stakeholders to work in partnership with police.

One Muslim community individual publicly stated that his view should be sought by the police, since he "knew what was best for his community" and, as a qualified scholar, understood it better than the police, who he warned would scare the community. Unqualified opinions like these led to the creation of new gatekeepers who spoke on behalf of whole communities without their consent, but whose prestige was raised by being invited and included on government and policing community events as speakers and leaders.

The wariness of engaging with the police and government was further compounded by the huge sums of money that were suddenly poured into local community groups in order to deliver Prevent partnership–led work. Birmingham was the largest recipient of Prevent money, receiving £2.4 million from 2008 to 2011, which led to further suspicion about whether this was a government sweetener, and created resentment on the part of other faith and minority groups such as the Sikh community. Some individuals felt that offering sums of money to one particular faith group was not just morally wrong but created visible community divisions and created new power dynamics.

On the whole, the views expressed in community meetings across the country at the time were that having access to financial grants paradoxically encouraged the worst community instincts, as it propelled some individuals and groups to classify themselves as experts on extremism narratives, radicalization processes, and community vulnerabilities, as the government and the police themselves lacked any tangible expertise or authority.

In essence, there were two key problems. The first was that the Prevent strategy was never sold to the wider Muslim community as a legitimate need, and so that void was filled by those who—rightly or wrongly—emphasized the negative aspects. Second, while high numbers of individuals engaged with Prevent projects, the short-term pressure for the police to engage with communities led to an internal joke that there were only ever "50 key Muslims in Birmingham" present at events. These were often the well-connected, third generation, politically savvy, articulate men and women, and this highlighted the disconnect between the traditional community-based leaders and the younger nonelected leaders more at ease with navigating through national and local power structures.

## Solutions for Barriers to Engagement

Addressing barriers and community fears required vision and good leadership from public authorities as well as sustained and genuine engagement-based approaches. This type of approach worked on the premise that unless local police consistently involved the public in "peace time"—that is, when a crisis or incident is not happening—communities and stakeholders would be less willing to collaborate when incidents do occur, due to relationships and structures not being in place. I found that sustained relationships consistently built in this way opened channels of communication and reduced the role of gatekeepers—on both sides—thereby allowing connections to be more direct. Over time and even today this is an important factor, because the Muslim community continues to feel disproportionately affected and targeted on policing matters. However, through heightened awareness around the solutions listed here, knowledge of accountability structures has increased.

Structures and techniques have been refined over time. In the beginning, softer engagement and less structured consultations and meetings did occur but were of limited value and did not allow wider engagement with communities who, as described above, were wary and suspicious, or not interested in working with the Prevent agenda or police officers. Listed here are some key examples of engagement solutions used in Birmingham to address the trust and confidence gaps arising from earlier experiences.

## OVERT AND VISIBLE POLICING

Compared to other major police forces, a key principle that has defined the "West Midlands approach" over the last four years has been that counterterrorism officers have continued to operate on a "visible, transparent and accountable" model. This means that CTU police officers have to be in uniform at all times when meeting the public and doing outreach work in order to reduce suspicion that the police could be conducting covert surveillance and community engagement at the same time. Examples of covert surveillance by undercover police in mosques by other UK police forces, or allegations that undercover police officers were trying to access community information, caused paranoia and mistrust leading some people to reject talking to the police altogether (see, e.g., Bano 2011). I believe this type of visible policing approach in Birmingham has demonstrated real results.

*Channel panels.* Channel is a controversial (Kundnani 2009) nationwide Home Office scheme established as a harder-edged intervention tool that has been chiefly created to support those individuals who are assessed as being particularly vulnerable to recruitment by violent extremists. Local professionals from public bodies such as police, social services, health, youth offending team workers and community individuals meet to provide professional judgment on vulnerable individuals to decide collectively if a person should be monitored under Channel or not.

*Independent advisory groups (IAG).* The primary role of the IAG is to function as a consultative forum between police and community groups using the expertise of key local individuals around specific topics. The groups are convened when community tensions start to occur, enabling them to work in dynamic environments. Recent examples of group sessions have been around the Schedule 7 airport stop-and-search trust and confidence group (Dodd 2011), and airport scanners. Within the counterterrorism realm, IAGs have been established in order to address those topics in which communities feel the policing relationship is being affected. Community buy-in and senior officer involvement in these groups have been significant factors in making such groups work.

*Community events.* These are both formal and informal events that local people (including myself) have organized monthly or annually, be it at local mosques or community centers, in order to break boundaries and connect individuals. Numbers can range from 5 to 500, with a mix of stakeholders, communities, CTU police officers, and so forth to listen to or deliver community and police presentations and conduct activities with the idea of creating networks and dialogue.

*Targeted community—police sessions.* These are police-led, three-hour interactive consequence management exercises, such as *Operation Archer*, utilized as a soft engagement tool between police and stakeholder communities. Being inexpensive, the primary purpose of these sessions is to enable community groups to learn about the decision-making processes often faced by the police in crisis situations in counterterrorism cases by asking what decisions the stakeholders would take in these roles. The purpose is to provide community partners with an insight into the difficulties around CTU police decision making, while facilitating community discussions based on real experiences.

*Key information network (KIN).* KINs are mass-collated names of local people, constituency based, who are seen as key active individuals. Their details are stored on a police database with the idea that if local events or arrests are taking place, or community information needs to be disseminated by the police, then the KINs will be made aware via e-mails or text messages. The KIN's primary role is to help communicate with communities, advise, and support by providing reassurance, and act as "critical friends" to help tailor responses to community needs.

To summarize, I feel that the range of consultation tools described here shows that no one formula can or should be used to engage communities; some exist to gauge views or measure opinions, while some aim for different outcomes such as to reassure, to consult, to partner, or to emphasize a set of required values. The key point here is that solutions must be reflective of the requirements of a particular community, and that both sides must listen, share, and learn.

## Key Characteristics of Success

When the "Preventing Violent Extremism" agenda was nationally launched in 2007, £63 million of national monies was set aside for "Prevent" projects over the course of three years; locating credible local community voices was sometimes a challenge for local government officials, and police officers were tasked with creating a partnership-based approach to tackling violent extremism in their communities. In 2011, the government re-adjusted Prevent to reflect some of the underlying concerns by splitting counterterrorism work from the broader integration work, and by focusing priorities on the *3 Is*, namely ideology, individuals, and institutions (HM Government 2011).

And so, with over five years of experience and reflection, I believe the following key points should be observed in order to create successful outcomes:

- Differentiating between covert and overt activities and assessing their impact on projects and communities from the outset.
- Understanding that good CT work is a 24-hour-a-day activity.
- Creating localized solutions that better reflect the needs of local communities.
- Stronger understanding of the community and its stakeholders. This includes better utilization of the skills and expertise of women and young people, whose involvement currently tends to be restricted to consultation groups rather than in key decision-making bodies.
- Making partnerships the critical factor for success in the community-policing arena.

To complement this, the three points outlined next are to be borne in mind by communities and police departments in order to build on the successes already achieved:

*Leadership and connectors.* A good police force that wants to embed community partnerships as a core value will work hard to address organizational change and values within itself first, without always putting the onus on "the community." Additionally, finding out who the diverse community leaders and stakeholders are, even if they do not like the police or are challenging personalities, should not impede this process. Locating the community "connectors" (Spalek and McDonald 2012), that is, those individuals who are able to negotiate and navigate the intricacies of community memberships, would indicate success in terms of partnership work.

One important point I learned was that good CTU police personnel—and especially visionary police officers—tend to be moved very quickly within their wider organization, and this can impact on building sustained community relationships and retaining the vision and expertise. How can this creative leadership ethos be maintained organizationally by senior officers?

*Transparency and accountability.* Overt terrorism measures have to remain consistent in order for trust to be built, especially since Muslim communities believe they are a targeted community. Fundamentally, having CT police officers in uniform encourages better community confidence compared to police forces that have not adopted this measure; over time communities do feel comfortable in approaching police officers not only for CT-related issues but for a wider policing relationship as well. In the West Midlands, the police have recognized that unless key community individuals remain interested in engaging with the police and are prepared to talk to the police, they will undoubtedly be fighting a losing battle trying to win the "hearts and minds" of the communities whose trust and consent they require. Likewise, communities feel that unless they are able to constructively air their grievances, their avenue to raise issues directly with law enforcement officials is hindered, making them feel further disempowered and detached.

*Good usage of external research and evaluation to further transparency.* While numerous consultative mechanisms exist and extensive counterterrorism research has been conducted, which together have informed the CTU work for West Midlands police in general, in-depth external research needs to be built to further refine the available analyses. I believe that year on year, independent research using robust qualitative and quantitative methodologies that monitor trust and confidence measures of both communities and police are a worthwhile endeavor. Placed alongside hard statistical data on the challenging topics of stop and search, Schedule 7 arrests, Channel referrals, community events, and so forth, this would contextualize the rhetoric of trust into an accountability mechanism. While there is considerable open-source data and quality research that is already publicly available, I think this approach would provide a new benchmark in terms of what successful partnerships can offer in tackling equality and addressing all forms of extremism.

Even now—in late 2012—with just under five years of Prevent experiences, key critical events continue to occur demonstrating that relationships should never be taken for granted. My own experience too in the Muslim community was that they believed that those talking to police officers—let alone working with themwere suspect themselves, which made wagging tongues and undermining of personal reputation a key job hazard. My personal feeling was that, overall, most people wanted to work with the police, but that unless regular events took place, the process of humanizing one another and establishing an informal process to build trust and confidence would not occur. After all, both the US and UK police subscribe to a community-policing model, and while ordinary community members may not always be familiar with the model and its principles, they do recognize the long-term value of cooperation and partnership.

## Notes

1. This is one attempt by a UK Muslim organization logging terrorism-related arrests and outcomes, and available on the web. The article is called "Muslims in Britain." http://www.salaam.co.uk/themeofthemonth/september03_index.php?l=48
2. Cobain, Ian, Vikram Dodd, and Will Woodward. 2007. "Terror Leaks: Both Home Office and Police implicated." *The Guardian*, April 26. http://www.guardian.co.uk/politics/2007/apr/26/uk.terrorism (accessed September 30, 2012).

## References


Bano, Rahila. 2011. "Community Rift over Undercover Police in Mosques." *BBC News*, November 24. http://www.bbc.co.uk/news/uk-england-15840339.

"Dispatches Undercover Mosque." 2007. Channel 4. http://www.channel4.com/programmes/dispatches/episode-guide/series-19/episode-1.

Dodd, Vickram. 2011. "Asian People 42 Yimes More Likely to Be Held under Anti-Terror Law." *The Guardian*, May 23. http://www.guardian.co.uk/uk/2011/may/23/counter-terror-stop-search-minorities.

Ferguson, Corinna, 2010. "Why Is Birmingham's CCTV Scheme 'Unlawful'?" *The Guardian*, July 2010. http://www.guardian.co.uk/commentisfree/libertycentral/2010/jul/06/birmingham-cctv-unlawful-liberty.

HM Government. 2011. *Prevent Strategy*. Norwich, UK: The Stationery Office.

House of Commons: Home Affairs Committee. 2009. *Police and the Media 2008/9 HC 75*. Norwich, UK: The Stationery Office. http://books.google.co.uk/books?id=q0-qOChrXm4C&pg=PA18-IA16&lpg=PA18-IA16&dq=terrorism+arrest+in+Birmingham+media+2007&source=bl&ots=Oo4qNLoqVw&sig=IE5U-BqETMpk2WPm6xrWyE4iofU&hl=en&sa=X&ei=jdpdUPudGqeb1AXA3oGIDQ&ved=0CDUQ6AEwAg#v=onepage&q=terrorism%20arrest%20in%20Birmingham%20media%20 2007&f=false.

Kundnani, Arun. 2009. *Spooked! How Not to Prevent Violent Extremism*. London: Institute of Race Relations. http://www.irr.org.uk/pdf2/spooked.pdf.

Silk, P. Daniel, and Zubeda Limbada. 2012. "Trust in Dialogue." *Police Professional 319*, August 30: 22–24.

Spalek, Basia, and Laura Zahra McDonald. 2012. *Conflict with and between communities: Exploring the Role of Communities in Helping to Defeat and/or Endorse Terrorism and the Interface with Policing Efforts to Counter*

*Terrorism*. AHRC Connected Communities. http://www.ahrc.ac.uk/Funding-Opportunities/Research-funding/Connected-Communities/Scoping-studies-and-reviews/Documents/Conflict%20with%20and%20between%20communities.pdf.

Thornton, Sara, 2010. *Project Champion Review*. http://www.west-midlands.police.uk/latest-news/docs/Champion_Review_FINAL_30_09_10.pdf.

# 9

# Community Partnerships Thwart Terrorism

*Deborah Ramirez, Tara Lai Quinlan, Sean P. Malloy, and Taylor Shutt*

## Introduction

In an October 2010 address, FBI director Robert Mueller identified homegrown terrorism as a growing concern to the US national security community (Mueller 2010). Mueller said the threat from homegrown extremists, meaning those born or residing within the United States and targeting US interests, is challenging given its "quickly evolving" nature and the lack of a "typical" homegrown terrorist profile (Mueller 2010).

Because law enforcement is focused on the terrorism threat from Muslim communities, this chapter focuses on this community, arguing that accurately addressing this issue requires creating and fortifying long-term, bona fide partnerships between law enforcement and Muslim communities. We argue this goal is achievable using lessons learned from US community policing. To illustrate the compelling need to integrate the community policing model with counterterrorism policy, we identify three categories of incidents involving al-Qaeda–inspired extremists and voluntary community assistance. First, we examine incidents where Muslim community members provided tips to law enforcement to prevent a terrorist incident; second, incidents where individuals provided information that law enforcement failed to act on to prevent an attack; and third, events that may have been prevented had law enforcement worked collaboratively with the Muslim community earlier on. While partnerships have proven successful in terrorism prevention in the decade since 9/11, they remain underutilized to our collective disadvantage.

## Community Policing and Engagement

Any successful counterterrorism strategy requires efficient gathering and distilling of reliable intelligence (Adams, Nordhaus, and Shellenberger 2011, 14–15; Huq, Tyler, and Schulhofer 2011, 728–729). Obtaining valuable counterterrorism information is readily achievable by applying community engagement techniques to post-9/11 terror policing. Al-Qaeda–inspired violent extremists might reside within American Muslim communities, or might consist of outsiders attempting to blend into these communities to avoid law enforcement attention.[1] Successfully addressing the threat of homegrown terrorism requires bona fide trust relationships between law enforcement and the communities where homegrown terrorists might attempt to reside. While American Muslim communities have very clearly established their overwhelming commitment to combating terrorism, law enforcement has repeatedly failed to employ community partnerships, thereby omitting this essential terrorism-prevention tool from the national counterterrorism toolbox.

## The Modern US Policing Model

In the contemporary US policing model, first implemented by the 1950s and 1960s (Newburn 2011, 90), officers patrol in cars and respond to radio calls reporting crimes or requesting assistance (Erickson and Haggerty 1992, 19). This reactive, "professional policing" model (Braga 2002, 6; Dobrin 2006, 20; Stone and Travis 2011) removes police from daily interactions with community members that once characterized policing (Goldstein 1979, 238; Understanding Community Policing, 1994; Braga 2002, 6; Stone and Travis 2011). This model means that police generally engage with the community in response to public reports of crime or nuisances, or when police observe suspicious activity (Erickson and Haggerty 1992). In this model, officers' primary responsibility is to quickly respond to and "clear" calls, then get back out on patrol (Erickson and Haggerty 1992, 19). Due to the prevalence of this policing model, today, local police typically have minimal interaction with community members (Goldstein 1979, 238; Braga 2002, 8).

## Community Policing

While the reactive policing model dominates US policing, the community policing model developed in the 1970s offers an alternative

(Manning 1984, 207–209; Forman 2004, 4; Stone and Travis 2011). Community policing means that police depend on the public "as co-producers of public safety, rather than hostile antagonists" (Forman 2004, 6; Eck and Spelman 2005, 412) and provide a strategy to balance against the reactive policing model. The significant policing research of the 1970s laid the groundwork for the implementation of the community policing model, as criminologists argued that traditional reactive policing was seriously inadequate, and had caused police-community relations to deteriorate to unsustainable levels (Understanding Community Policing 1994; Eck and Spelman 2005, 412; Forman 2004, 7). Early community policing projects in Los Angeles and Flint, Michigan, sought to enhance officers' contact with the community through "innovative use of a relatively small proportion of the force" (Kennedy 1993, 5; Interrupting Violence 2011). The 1980s saw an increase in community-oriented policing projects in US police departments (Kennedy 1993, 5; Eck and Spelman 2005, 412). By the 1990s, several large police departments had begun implementing community policing principles to the large-scale policing of cities (Kennedy 1993, 5; Lurigio and Skogan 1994, 315; Pate and Shtull 1994, 384).

But what is "community policing" today? The Department of Justice defines community policing as the "systematic use of partnerships and problem-solving techniques, to proactively address the immediate conditions that give rise to public safety issues such as crime, social disorder, and fear of crime" (Community Policing Defined 2012). Community policing thus emphasizes proactive (versus reactive) crime reduction, and the need for joint efforts by both police and the community (Tilley 2011, 373). This model recognizes that community members are often better equipped and more likely than the police to identify potential threats to community security (Eck and Spelman 2005, 412).

The modern community policing model has two core characteristics—community partnership and problem solving (Flynn 1998, 1; Forman 2004, 7; Community Policing Defined 2012, 13). First, communities actively partner with law enforcement, meaning regular meetings between community members and police to jointly define neighborhood problems and set law enforcement priorities (Forman 2004, 7). This allows community members to express concerns and needs, gives police a forum to educate community members about neighborhood issues, allows community members to assert complaints about the police, and gives police the opportunity to report actions undertaken, successes and failures (Forman 2004, 7–8). Second, communities engage in problem solving with police, in which communities work with police to address problems of mutual concern (Skogan and Hartnett et al. 1998, 3; Forman 2004, 8).

## COMMUNITY POLICING AND COUNTERTERRORISM

In the post-9/11 world, the changing nature of terrorism makes adopting alternatives to traditional reactive policing strategies vital. Given some long-term successes in community policing over the years (Skogan 1997), and some current examples of small-scale community policing in terrorism prevention, the United States must urgently implement a nationally coordinated community policing strategy in its national terrorism prevention plan (Braga 2002, 12). In countries like the United Kingdom, police and policy makers have already adopted a national community policing strategy for counterterrorism, and the United States must follow suit.

This chapter highlights examples illustrating how Muslim communities, as key stakeholders in the fight against violent extremism, have played essential roles in fighting terrorism. Muslim Americans have demonstrated very strong commitment, if not more so than other communities, to drive out extremism (Beutel 2010, 10; Goodstein 2011). Moreover, the unique linguistic, cultural, and analytical capabilities of Muslim communities cannot be overlooked, as community members possess the ability to detect unusual occurrences, suspicious newcomers, or those espousing violence that police might (and frequently do) miss (Ramirez and Quinlan 2008, 42; Harris 2010, 125). American Muslim communities not only are ideologically committed to rooting out extremism and ensuring collective safety, but are also valuable resources upon which law enforcement can, and must, rely to prevent extremist attacks.

Despite Muslim Americans' role as stakeholders and resources in fighting terrorism, US law enforcement has largely foregone opportunities to build authentic community partnerships in post-9/11 national counterterrorism strategy. Faced with significant community monitoring, curtailment of their civil liberties and a rise in hate violence, many US Muslims feel unfairly targeted by law enforcement, but are nonetheless committed to fighting extremism (Harris 2010, 125; Beutel 2010, 27–28; Pew Research Center 2011, 43–47; Muslim Public Affairs Council 2012).

Developing and implementing a national community policing infrastructure in US counterterrorism policy is essential, and can be achieved by modeling existing ad hoc community policing programs in communities like Los Angeles, Dearborn, and Northern Virginia. Not only would implementing authentic community policing partnerships illustrate that Muslim communities are trusted law enforcement partners, but it would operationally facilitate positive information flow about suspicious persons or events from community members. Illogically, US law enforcement has disproportionately focused efforts on covert surveillance and infiltration of Muslim communities rather than partnerships, which have not only created civil liberties issues, but also been operationally counterproductive in the long -term (Spalek, El Awa, and McDonald 2008, 12).

## Case Studies in Terrorism Response

It is well documented that Muslim American communities have been the largest source of tips for US terror plots since 9/11 (Kurzman 2011; Kurzman, Schanzer and Moosa 2011; Peter King's Obsession 2011). According to a 2010 study, tips from Muslim American communities helped thwart terrorist plots in 48 of 120 cases involving Muslim Americans, meaning over 40 percent of foiled domestic terror plots were thwarted with help from Muslim Americans (Kurzman 2011; Kurzman, Schanzer and Moosa 2011; Stolberg and Goodstein 2011). The examples listed nextillustrate the potential of community–law enforcement partnerships to significantly increase the likelihood of stopping a potential attack and recognize the valuable role of Muslim communities in counterterrorism.

## Muslim Community Helps Authorities Prevent Attack in Tampa

In January 2012, Muslim community members helped apprehend Kosovo immigrant and US citizen Sami Osmakac, who allegedly planned to attack the Tampa area nightclubs and a sheriff's office with bombs and an assault rifle motivated by a desire to avenge perceived affronts to Muslims (Brown 2012; Collette and Johnson 2012; Kosovo Native Plotted Bombings, Bloodshed in Tampa 2012; Levesque and Thalji 2012; Stacy and Lush 2012). Osmakac had repeatedly raised suspicions in the Muslim community before his arrest, like when Tampa attorney and executive director of the Tampa Chapter of the Council on American-Islamic Relations (CAIR) Hassan Shibly met Osmakac in summer 2011 and noted him behaving in an odd manner (Alleged Extremist Terror Plot Foiled in Tampa

2012; Muslim Man Charged in Bomb Plot 2012; Stacy and Lush 2012). Osmakac had already been banned from two area mosques after filming an inflammatory YouTube video on mosque property (Levesque and Thalji 2012a; 2012b). The CAIR office had also received calls from Muslim community members about Osmakac's extremist views, about which Shibly urged community members to immediately contact law enforcement (Alleged Extremist Terror Plot Foiled in Tampa 2012; Muslim Man Charged in Bomb Plot 2012; Stacy and Lush 2012). One community member thereafter contacted federal officials in September 2011 after Osmakac came to his business "looking for al-Qaida flags" (Stacy and Lush 2012). With law enforcement help, the tipster hired Osmakac and recorded their conversations, including Osmakac allegedly identifying potential Tampa targets, and asking the tipster for help obtaining weapons (Levesque and Thalji 2012; Stacy and Lush 2012). The tipster later met with an undercover FBI agent, and later gave him a $500 down payment to buy several high-power weapons (Brown 2012; FBI Foils Suspected Tampa Bomb Plot 2012; Levesque and Thalji 2012; Stacy and Lush 2012). Officials arrested Osmakac on the day he allegedly planned to initiate his attack (Curtis 2012; Stacy and Lush 2012).

Osmakac had allegedly recorded an eight-minute video before his arrest seeking "payback" for injustices committed against Muslims (Alleged Extremist Terror Plot Foiled in Tampa 2012; Stacy and Lush 2012). Both the special agent in charge of the FBI's Tampa division and the US attorney acknowledged that the Muslim community provided authorities with significant information leading to the prevention of the attack (Stacy and Lush 2012). US magistrate judge Anthony Porcelli ordered Osmakac held without bail, and he faces life imprisonment if convicted on the single count of attempted use of a weapon of mass destruction (Kosovo Native Plotted Bombings, Bloodshed in Tampa 2012; Stacy and Lush 2012).

## Tip Prevents Oregon Ceremony Attack

In November 2010, Mohamed Osman Mohamud was arrested for allegedly attempting to bomb a Christmas tree-lighting ceremony in Portland, Oregon, and charged with attempting to use a weapon of mass destruction (US Attorney's Office 2010). Acting alone, Mohamud allegedly intended to detonate what he believed was an explosives-laden van parked near the tree-lighting ceremony in Portland's Pioneer Courthouse Square (Somali-American Accused of Plotting to Bomb Oregon Tree-Lighting Event 2010; US Attorney's Office 2010). He had allegedly expressed a desire to wage a violent "jihad," selected a target, and mailed bomb parts to individuals he believed were assembling an explosive (Denson 2010; Markon 2010; Miner, Robbins, and Eckholm 2010). Federal officials said that a tip from a Muslim community member concerned about Mohamud's increasing radicalism was instrumental in alerting the FBI to Mohamud's activities (Denson 2010; Markon 2010; Robbins and Wyatt 2010). In conversations with undercover FBI agents, Mohamud said he was committed to serving his "cause" and becoming "operational," meaning his desire to carry out an attack (Robbins and Wyatt 2010). Mohamud allegedly told an undercover FBI agent that he wanted to kill a large number of people "in their own element with their families celebrating the holidays" (Denson 2010; Markon 2010; Robbins and Wyatt 2010). Without the voluntarily assistance from the community, Mohamud may not have been discovered, and he may have succeeded.

## Washington DC Area Students Arrested in Pakistan

On December 7, 2009, Pakistani authorities arrested five Muslim American students from the Washington DC area after tips from their worried families alerted law enforcement to their potentially terrorism-related intentions (Hussain, Gorman, and King 2009; Meyer 2009; Five DC-Area Men Held in Pakistan 2010). The families initially reported them missing, fearing that they had traveled to Pakistan for suspicious reasons (Hussain, Gorman, and King 2009; Khan and Barrett 2009). Before arriving in Pakistan, the five men were allegedly in contact with Pakistani militants with connections to al-Qaeda through Internet chat rooms and YouTube (Gillani and Perlez 2009; Perlez, Masood, and Gillani 2009). The Pakistani militants allegedly instructed the students to travel to Pakistan from where they would get to Afghanistan to participate in "jihad" (Gillani and Perlez 2009).

The concerned families first approached the Council on Islamic Relations (CAIR), who immediately contacted the FBI (Meyer 2009; Khan and Barrett 2009). The parents showed the FBI and Muslim community leaders a video left behind by one of the men that "quoted Koranic verses, cited conflicts between Western and Muslim nations and showed wartime footage" (Markon 2009). Authorities then conducted an investigation with extensive help from the families, who turned over the men's writings and computer files (Markon 2009). Around the same time, in Sargodha, Pakistan, a man alerted Pakistani authorities that a neighbor told him that the neighbor's nephew and four friends had voiced intentions to commit terrorism (Hussain, Gorman, and King 2009).

Officials then observed the American students, Ramy Zamzam, Umar Farooq, Aman Hasan Yemer, Waqar Hussain Khan, and Ahmed Abdullah Minni, in Pakistan for two days before arresting them (FBI: Five Missing from Washington Area in Custody in Pakistan 2009; Hussain, Gorman, and King 2009; Pakistan Reportedly Detains Five DC-Area Muslims 2009). When authorities searched the house where the men had been staying, they allegedly found "jihadist" literature and maps of cities and installations (Hussain, Gorman, and King 2009; Meyer 2009). Evidence also suggested that some of the men wanted to fight US soldiers in Afghanistan (Hussain, Gorman, and King 2009).

As a result of the initial tip and ongoing cooperation of the families, US law enforcement and Pakistani authorities arrested the men before any plan was carried out. CAIR initiated and facilitated ongoing communication between the families and the FBI, who then worked in conjunction with Pakistani officials. Without the existing relationship of trust between CAIR and an FBI field office, it is unlikely that law enforcement would have known of the men or the plot before an attack had been initiated.

## Missed Opportunities: Community Tips Warned of Attacks

Poor law enforcement–community relationships can be detrimental to the shared safety concerns of Muslim communities, law enforcement, and the general public. Fractured or nonexistent partnerships render communities hesitant or unable to report suspicious activity to law enforcement, resulting in potential attacks going undetected. Indeed, since 9/11 there have been numerous instances in the United States where law enforcement could likely have intervened sooner to prevent terrorism plots had it incorporated community policing strategies. In the following examples, communities alerted law enforcement to suspicious behavior, but the information failed to yield timely and effective law enforcement responses.

### Intelligence Failure Leads to Close Call on Christmas Day

On December 25, 2009, Umar Farouk Abdulmutallab flew from Nigeria to Amsterdam, where he boarded Northwest Airlines Flight 253 to Detroit, Michigan, with 90 gm of highly explosive chemicals on his inner thigh (Chang 2009; Goldman and Khan 2009; O'Connor and Schmitt 2009). As the plane approached Detroit, he tried and failed to ignite the chemicals but set his pants afire, and was ultimately subdued by fellow passengers (Chang 2009; Federal Bureau of Investigations 2010; Goldman and Khan 2009; O'Connor and Schmitt 2009). In January 2010, Abdulmutallab was indicted on six counts including attempted murder and attempted use of a weapon of mass destruction (Federal Bureau of Investigations 2010; United States *v.* Abdulmutallab 2010).

Several red flags viewed together should have alarmed officials prior to Abdulmutallab's bombing attempt. While a student at University College London, Abdulmutallab had multiple contacts with individuals under surveillance by MI5, but was not deemed a terrorism risk (UK Intelligence on Detroit Bomb Suspect 2010). Abdulmutallab later obtained a multiple-year, multiple-entry tourist visa at the US Embassy in London in June 2008, but the United Kingdom denied his student visa renewal because he listed a false college on his application (Source: Terror Suspect's Father Tried to Warn Authorities 2009; Eggen, DeYoung, and Hsu 2009). Abdulmutallab then traveled to Yemen, where he was granted entry because he had a valid US visa, and where he allegedly stayed and trained with an al-Qaeda leader (Goldman and Khan 2009).

Most significantly, in November 2009, Abdulmutallab called his father, Alhaji Umaru Mutallab, telling him it would be their last contact, and that his Yemeni associates would destroy his telephone (Goldman and Khan 2009). After the call, an alarmed Mutallab alerted Nigerian officials, who brought him to speak with a CIA agent at the US Embassy in Nigeria (Goldman and Khan 2009; MacAskill, Black, and Norton-Taylor 2010; Profile: Umar Farouk Abdulmutallab 2011). Mutallab told the agent about his son's "radicalization and associations," and that he feared his son was preparing for a suicide mission or "some kind of jihad" in Yemen (Eggen, DeYoung, and Hsu 2009; Goldman and Khan 2009; Profile: Umar Farouk Abdulmutallab 2011). The CIA agent passed the information to the National Counterterrorism Center, and Abdulmutallab was added to the Terrorist Identities Datamart Environment, a security watch-list (Father Alerted US about Nigerian Plane Bomb Suspect 2009; MacAskill, Black, and Norton-Taylor 2010). Abdulmutallab was not, however, added to the "Do Not Fly" list, and Yemeni officials were not alerted (Goldman and Khan 2009). At minimum, the tip from Abdulmutallab's father was a missed opportunity that, if promptly and appropriately handled, could have prevented Abdulmutallab from boarding the plane and nearly succeeding.

After Abdulmutallab's arrest, he met with his family, and was eventually persuaded to cooperate with investigators (Bombing Suspect Provided "Actionable Intelligence" 2010; Detroit Terror Plot 2010; Detroit Bomber "Providing Intelligence about al-Qaida" 2010). An official stated that "the intelligence gained has been disseminated throughout the intelligence community," and "the best way to get [Abdulmutallab] to talk was working with his family." (Zeleny and Savage 2010). Officials including FBI director Robert Mueller confirmed that Abdulmutallab provided them with "valuable intelligence" including information about people he interacted with in Yemen (Zeleny and Savage 2010; Umar Farouk Abdulmutallab Sentenced 2012). Abdulmutallab pleaded guilty to all counts including attempted use of a weapon of mass destruction, conspiracy to commit an act of terrorism, and possession of a firearm or destructive device in furtherance of an act of violence, and was sentenced to life imprisonment (Dolan 2011; Umar Farouk Abdulmutallab Sentenced 2012; Underwear Bomber Abdulmutallab Sentenced To Life 2012). The case illustrates that community tips like the one from Abdulmutallab's father must be promptly and properly reviewed, analyzed, and acted upon, and a protocol for handling credible community tips established.

## Missed Opportunities: Community Should Have Been Trained on Important Warning Signs

Beginning in 2007, reports began surfacing about young Somali American men traveling to Somalia "to enlist in the Shabaab, an Islamist group battling the country's government" (Elliot 2010; Yuen 2009; Yuen and Aslanian 2009; Joseph and Mackey 2012). Two Somali men, Shirwa Ahmed and Zakaria Maruf, had allegedly begun recruiting Somali Americans to travel to Somalia to assist terrorist efforts (Elliot 2009a; Shah, Walsh, and Meryhew 2009; Walsh 2009). Maruf himself was well known in the Minneapolis Muslim community, and regularly engaged large audiences of young, Muslim men in their twenties and thirties through listservs and conference calls to discuss the need to help Somalia (Elliot 2009a; Shah, Walsh, and Meryhew 2009). By late 2007, approximately seven Somali American men who disappeared from the Minneapolis area were believed to have gone to Somalia (Elliot 2009a).

In 2008, a second wave of young Somali American men began disappearing from around Minneapolis (Elliot 2009a; 2009b; Yuen

2009; Yuen and Aslanian 2009; Elliot 2010). In contrast to the first wave, the second group was primarily Somali American teenagers raised in the United States attending high school or college (Elliot 2009a; 2009b). They began dropping out of school between August and November of 2008 to travel to Somalia (Elliot 2009a; 2009b). Between 2007 and 2009, it is believed that al-Shabaab recruited approximately 20 young Somali American Muslims from the Minneapolis area to fight in Somalia (Walsh 2009; Yuen 2009; Yuen and Aslanian 2009; Elliot 2010; Smith 2011).

As word of the disappearances spread in the Somali American community, members were concerned and began to act (Elliot 2009a). Some Somali parents began hiding their sons' passports (Elliot 2009a). Some, like community member Abia Ali, observed two Somali boys from her mosque at her travel agency making travel plans to follow Zakaria Maruf to Somalia, so she alerted mosque leaders, who alerted the boys' parents (Elliot 2009a). Mosque leaders also took action and convened meetings of young mosque members, telling them to focus on their futures in the United States and forget the talk of fighting in Somalia (Elliot 2009a). These dedicated parents and community leaders were an important line of defense in the battle against extremism in their community, and had a reliable channel of communication been open and protocol been established with law enforcement, joint community and law enforcement might have halted the disappearances sooner and expelled the extremist influences from the community more quickly.

## Looking Forward

These case studies illustrate the potential counterterrorism successes achievable if a national community policing model is implemented into national counterterrorism strategy. Such an organized partnership program requires following a number of steps, and must be situated within a framework of dialogue that enables both law enforcement and community to acknowledge their concerns and grievances, and agree on a joint commitment to establishing and maintaining a bona fide relationship with the mutual goal of preventing violence (Spalek, El Awa, and McDonald 2008, 12–13).

## Infrastructure and Training

Police must first establish an infrastructure to work with communities in the long term on community problems like neighborhood blight, drug dealing, youth truancy, gang activity, and slow police response times, in addition to terrorism and radicalization issues. Police must therefore be trained both on the importance of partnering with the community, and the logistics of executing long-term partnership strategies.

Once the partnership infrastructure has been established, the second step is mutual education. On the one hand, law enforcement must train community members to look for unusual occurrences, odd behavior, or out of place newcomers that could indicate terrorist actors hiding in the community. Community members are uniquely situated to serve this function, as they possess the "linguistic, cultural, and analytical skills" necessary to assess the anomalies within their community—abnormalities that law enforcement, as outside observers, might miss altogether (Ramirez and Quinlan 2008, 42). On the other hand, law enforcement must also become well acquainted with the linguistic, cultural, and religious practices of the communities with which they are working. The mutual benefits of training serve important community building functions.

Third, law enforcement must establish clear lines of communication with the community, and protocols for responding to community tips. This chapter highlights multiple instances where law enforcement's failure to properly handle community tips resulted in missed opportunities to avoid terrorist incidents. Law enforcement must not only provide the community with telephone numbers and direct access to operations officials prepared to receive tips 24 hours a day, but must also establish procedures for a community-generated tip to be assessed by counterterrorism officials for actual value. While community tips have often been relegated to non-operations staff, this model requires that operations staff be involved in community tip assessment. Moreover, law enforcement must work with the community to establish a protocol for following up on tips in a way that treats the community respectfully.

These steps are crucial to establishing bona fide law enforcement–community partnerships in a post-9/11 world. While many officials might prefer to rely on covert surveillance, confidential informants, and undercover operatives to infiltrate Muslim communities, relying exclusively on these approaches will not prevent terrorist incidents. Not only are such tactics operationally limited, but they also foster significant distrust, fear, and anger in Muslim communities. Rather than alienating Muslim communities by relying on covert tactics, law enforcement must learn to rely on voluntary partnerships with Muslim communities to address extremism and potential terrorist actors.

## CONCLUSION

Voluntary community tips, when paired with prompt police engagement, can thwart potential terrorist attacks and prevent loss of life in the post-9/11 world. The United States has a Muslim population committed to combating terrorism. While homegrown al-Qaeda–inspired violent extremists are rare, they may also attempt to reside in Muslim communities to avoid detection. While many plots have been thwarted with the help of American Muslims, significant work must to be done to educate US law enforcement about the value of collaborative community work and establishing appropriate protocols for handling community tips. In addition, communities must be trained to recognize suspicious activities, and to understand how to, timely, bring these activities to the law enforcement's attention.

The best way to obtain voluntary tips and to improve relations with Muslim communities is the adoption of established community policing techniques in counterterrorism. The examples highlighted in this chapter demonstrate the importance of creating systems for effectively receiving and evaluating information voluntarily provided by Muslim communities. Law enforcement–Muslim community partnerships are not only essential to preventing radicalization and terrorist attacks, but also to creating long-standing bonds of trust between law enforcement and Muslim communities, which are needed now more than ever, in the post-9/11 world.

## NOTE

1. For purposes of brevity, Arab, Muslim, and Sikh communities will be collectively referred to as "Muslim" communities from hereafter.

## REFERENCES

Adams, Nick, Ted Nordhaus, and Michael Shellenberger. 2011. "Counterterrorism Since 9/11: Evaluating the Efficacy of Controversial Tactics." *The Breakthrough Institute.* http://thescienceofsecurity.org/blog/CT%20Since%209–11_by_Breakthrough.pdf.

"Alleged Extremist Terror Plot Foiled in Tampa." 2012. *CBS News*, January 9. http://www.cbsnews.com/8301–201_162–57355150/alleged-extremist-terror-plot-foiled-in-tampa/.

Beutel, Alejandro. 2010. "Building Bridges to Strengthen America: Forging and Effective Counterterrorism Enterprise between Muslim Americans and Law Enforcement." *Muslim Public Affairs Council.* http://www.

mpac.org/assets/docs/publications/building-bridges/MPAC-Building-Bridges – Complete_Unabridged_Paper.pdf.

"Bombing Suspect Provided 'Actionable Intelligence,' White House says." 2010. *CNN News*, January 5. http://articles.cnn.com/2010-01-05/justice/terror.suspect_1_umar-farouk-abdulmutallab-no-fly-list-actionable?_s=PM:CRIME.

Braga, Anthony. 2002. "Problem-Oriented Policing and Crime Prevention." *Center for Problem-Oriented Policing.* http://www.popcenter.org/library/reading/PDFs/braga1.pdf.

Brown, Robbie. 2012. "Florida Man Charged with Plotting Terror Campaign in Name of Islam." *New York Times*, January 9. http://www.nytimes.com/2012/01/10/us/florida-man-charged-with-plotting-strikes-in-name-of-islam.html.

Chang, Kenneth. 2009. "Explosive on Flight 253 Is among Most Powerful." *New York Times*, December 27. http://www.nytimes.com/2009/12/28/us/28explosives.html.

Collette, Chris, and Kevin Johnson. 2012. "Man Accused of Plotting Fla. Bombings." *USA Today*, January 9. http://www.usatoday.com/news/nation/story/2012-01-09/florida-bomb-plot/52466292/1

"Community Policing Defined." 2012. *United States Department of Justice, Office of Community Oriented Policing Services.* http://www.cops.usdoj.gov/files/RIC/Publications/e030917193-CP-Defined.pdf.

Curtis, Henry Pierson. 2012. "Tampa Bomb Plot Foiled by FBI." *Orlando Sentinel*, January 9. http://articles.orlandosentinel.com/2012-01-09/news/os-tampa-bomb-plot-foiled-20120109_1_undercover-fbi-agent-muslim-community-affidavit.

Denson, Bryan. 2010. "FBI Thwarts Terrorist Bombing Attempt at Portland Holiday Tree Lighting, Authorities Say." *The Oregonian*, November 26. http://www.oregonlive.com/portland/index.ssf/2010/11/fbi_thwarts_terrorist_bombing.html.

"Detroit Bomber 'Providing Intelligence about al-Qaida.'" 2010. *Associated Press,* February 3. http://www.guardian.co.uk/world/2010/feb/03/detroit-bomber-adbulmutallab-evidence-alqaeda.

"Detroit Terror Plot: Suspect Has Provided 'Useful' Intelligence to US Authorities." 2010. *The Telegraph*, February 3. http://www.telegraph.co.uk/news/worldnews/northamerica/usa/7142761/Detroit-terror-plot-suspect-has-provided-useful-intelligence-to-US-authorities.html.

Dobrin, Adam. 2006. "Professional and Community Oriented Policing: The Mayberry Model." *Journal of Criminal Justice & Popular Culture 13*(1): 19–28.

Dolan, Laura. 2011. "Accused Christmas Day Bomber Pleads Guilty to All Counts." *CNN.com.*, October 12. http://articles.cnn.com/2011-10-12/us/michigan.underwear.bomber_1_umar-farouk-abdulmutallab-bombing-attempt-explosive-device?_s=PM:US.

Eck, John, and William Spelman. 1987. "Who Ya Gonna Call? The Police as Problem-Busters." *Crime & Delinquency 33*(1): 31–52.

Eggen, Dan, Karen DeYoung, and Spencer Hsu. 2009. "Plane Suspect Was Listed in Terror Database after Father Alerted U.S. officials." *Washington Post*, December 27. http://www.washingtonpost.com/wp-dyn/content/article/2009/12/25/AR2009122501355.html.

Elliott, Andrea. 2009a. "A Call to Jihad, Answered in America." *New York Times*, July 11. http://www.nytimes.com/2009/07/12/us/12somalis.html?pagewanted=all.

———. 2009b. "Joining the Fight in Somalia." *New York Times*, July 12. http://www.nytimes.com/interactive/2009/07/12/us/20090712-somalia-timeline.html.

———. 2010. "The Jihadist Next Door." *New York Times*, January 27. http://www.nytimes.com/2010/01/31/magazine/31Jihadist-t.html.

Erickson, Richard, and Kevin Haggerty. 1992. *Policing the Risk Society*. Toronto: University of Toronto Press.

"Father Alerted US about Nigerian Plane Bomb Suspect." 2009. *BBC News*, December 27. http://news.bbc.co.uk/2/hi/americas/8431470.stm.

"FBI: Five Missing from Washington Area in Custody in Pakistan." 2009. *CNN News*, December 10. http://articles.cnn.com/2009–12–10/world/pakistan.arrests_1_usman-anwar-pakistani-police-fbi?_s=PM:WORLD.

"FBI Foils Suspected Tampa Bomb Plot." 2012. *CBS Miami*, January 9. http://miami.cbslocal.com/2012/01/09/fbi-foils-suspected-tampa-bomb-plot/.

Federal Bureau of Investigations. 2010. "Umar Farouk Abdulmutallab Indicted for Attempted Bombing of Flight 253 on Christmas Day, Press Release." Federal Bureau of Investigations, January 6. http://www.fbi.gov/detroit/press-releases/2010/de010610.htm.

" Five DC-Area Men Held in Pakistan." 2010. *CBS News*, October 3. http://www.cbsnews.com/stories/2009/12/09/world/main5951110.shtml.

Flynn, D. 1998. "Defining the 'Community' In Community Policing." *Police Executive Research Forum*. http://www.policeforum.org/library/community-policing/cp.pdf.

Forman, James. 2004. "Community Policing and Youth as Assets." *Journal of Criminal Law & Criminology* 95(1): 1–48.

Gillani, Waqar, and Jane Perlez. 2009. "Pakistan Police Say 5 Detained Americans Intended to Fight U.S. in Afghanistan." *New York Times*, December 11. http://query.nytimes.com/gst/fullpage.html?res=9E07E7D6143FF932A25751C1A96F9C8B63.

Goldman, Russell, and Huma Khan. 2009. "Timeline of Terror: Clues in Bomber Umar Farouk Abdulmutallab's Past." *ABC News*, December 30. http://abcnews.go.com/US/timeline-terror-clues-bomber-umar-farouk-abdulmutallabs-past/story?id=9449255.

Goldstein, Herman. 1979. "Improving Policing, A Problem-Oriented Approach." *Crime & Delinquency* 25(2): 236–258.

Goodstein, Laurie. 2011. "Muslims Are Loyal to U.S. and Hopeful, Poll Finds." *New York Times*, August 2. http://www.nytimes.com/2011/08/03/us/03muslims.html.

"UK Intelligence on Detroit Bomb Suspect Was Passed on to Americans." 2010. *The Guardian*, January 4. http://www.guardian.co.uk/world/2010/jan/04/intelligence-detroit-bomb-suspect-passed-to-americans.

Harris, David. 2010. "Law Enforcement and Intelligence Gathering in Muslim and Immigrant Communities after 9/11." *New York University Review of Law & Social Change 34*: 123–190. http://www.law.nyu.edu/ecm_dlv2/groups/public/@nyu_law_website__journals__review_of_law_and_social_change/documents/documents/ecm_pro_068611.pdf.

Huq, Aziz, Tom Tyler, and Stephen Schulhofer. 2011. "Mechanisms for Eliciting Cooperation in Counterterrorism Policing: Evidence from the United Kingdom." *Journal of Empirical Legal Studies 8*(4): 728–761.

Hussain, Zahid, Siobhan Gorman, and Neil King, Jr. 2009. "Students Linked to al Qaeda." *Wall Street Journal*, December 11. http://online.wsj.com/article/SB126045800896585617.html.

"Interrupting Violence with the Message 'Don't Shoot.'" 2011. *NPR.org*, November 1. http://www.npr.org/2011/11/01/141803766/interrupting-violence-with-the-message-dont-shoot.

Joseph, Channing, and Robert Mackey. 2012. "An American Jihadist in Somalia Claims His Colleagues Want to Kill Him." *New York Times*, March 20. http://thelede.blogs.nytimes.com/2012/03/20/an-american-jihadist-in-somalia-claims-his-colleagues-want-to-kill-him/.

Kennedy, David. 1993. *The Strategic Management of Police Resources*, Perspectives on Policing, Nat'l Inst. of Justice, Office of Justice Programs, United States Department of Justice. https://www.ncjrs.gov/pdffiles1/nij/139565.pdf.

Khan, Zarar, and Devlin Barrett. 2009. "Five Arrested in Pakistan May Be Missing DC Students." *NBC Washington*, December 9. http://www.nbcwashington.com/news/local/5-Americans-Arrested-in-Pakistan-Believed-Missing-From-DC-Area-78889822.html.

"Kosovo Native Plotted Bombings, Bloodshed in Tampa, Feds Say." 2012. *CNN News*, January 9. http://articles.cnn.com/2012-01-09/justice/justice_florida-terror-arrest_1_muslim-community-explosives-fbi-employee?_s=PM:JUSTICE.

Kurzman, Charles. 2011. "Muslim-American Terrorism Since 9/11: An Accounting." *Triangle Center on Terrorism and Homeland Security.* http://tcths.sanford.duke.edu/about/documents/Kurzman_Muslim-American_Terrorism_Since_911_An_Accounting.pdf.

Kurzman, Charles, David Schanzer, and Ebrahim Moosa. 2011. "Muslim American Terrorism Since 9/11: Why so Rare." *The Muslim World 101*(3): 464–483.

Levesque, William, and Jamal Thalji. 2012a. "Alleged Terror Plot Targeted Tampa." *Miami Herald*, January 9. http://www.miamiherald.com/2012/01/09/2581898/alleged-terror-plot-targeted-tampa.html.

———. 2012b. "Feds Accuse Man of Planning Bomb and Gun Attacks in South Tampa and Ybor City." *Tampa Bay Times*, January 10. http://www.tampabay.com/news/courts/criminal/man-arrested-in-tampa-bomb-plot/1209814.

Lurigio, Arthur, and Wesley Skogan. 1994. "Winning the Hearts and Minds of Police Officers: An Assessment of Staff Perceptions of Community Policing in Chicago." *Crime & Delinquency 40*(3): 315–330.

MacAskill, Ewen, Iam Black, and Richard Norton-Taylor. 2010. "Airline Bomb Plot Security Review Finds Key Failings by CIA and Terror Agency." *The Guardian*, January 7. http://www.guardian.co.uk/world/2010/jan/07/barack-obama-airline-bombing-plot.

Manning, Peter. 1984. "Community Policing." *American Journal of Police* 3(2): 205–227.

Markon, Jerry. 2009. "Pakistan Arrests 5 North Virginia Men, Probes Possible Jihadist Ties." *Washington Post*, December 10. http://www.washingtonpost.com/wp-dyn/content/article/2009/12/09/AR2009120901884.html.

———. 2010. "FBI Foils Elaborate Bomb Plot in Oregon." *Washington Post*. November 28. http://www.washingtonpost.com/wp-dyn/content/article/2010/11/27/AR2010112700546.html.

Meyer, Josh. 2009. "Five Young Americans Arrested in Pakistan." *Los Angeles Times*, December 9. http://articles.latimes.com/2009/dec/09/world/la-fg-pakistan-arrests10-2009dec10.

Miner, Colin, Liz Robbins, and Erik Eckholm. 2010. "F.B.I. Says Oregon Suspect Planned 'Grand' Attack." *New York Times*, January 27. http://www.nytimes.com/2010/11/28/us/28portland.html?pagewanted=all.

Mueller, Robert. 2010. Director, Fed. Bureau of Investigation, Preparedness Group Conference in Washington, D.C., October 6. http://www.fbi.gov/news/speeches/countering-the-terrorism-threat.

"Muslim Man Charged in Bomb Plot." 2012. *The Oracle*, January 10. http://www.usforacle.com/news/around-the-world/muslim-man-charged-in-bomb-plot-1.2684217.

Muslim Public Affairs Council. 2012. "Statistics: What You Need to Know." Muslim Public Affairs Council. http://www.mpac.org/programs/hate-crime-prevention/statistics.php.

Newburn, Tim. 2011. "Policing Since 1945." In *Handbook of Policing, Second Edition*. Edited by Tim Newburn. 90–115. Cullompton, UK: Willan Publishing.

O'Connor, Anahad, and Eric Schmitt. 2009. "Terror Attempt Seen as Man Tries to Ignite Device on Jet." *New York Times*, December 25. http://www.nytimes.com/2009/12/26/us/26plane.html.

"Oregon Resident Arrested in Plot to Bomb Christmas Tree Lighting Ceremony in Portland." 2010. *United States Attorney's Office, District of Oregon*. November 26. http://www.fbi.gov/portland/press-releases/2010/pd112610.htm.

"Pakistan Reportedly Detains Five DC-Area Muslims on Suspicion of Terror." 2009. *Investigative Project on Terrorism*, December 8. http://www.investigativeproject.org/1557/authorities-search-for-five-missing-dc-area.

Pate, Antony, and Penny Shtull. 1994. "Community Policing Grows in Brooklyn: An Inside View of the New York City Police Department's Model Precinct." *Crime & Delinquency 40*(3): 384–410.

Perlez, Jane, Salman Masood, and Waqar Gillani. 2009. "5 U.S. Men Arrested in Pakistan Said to Plan Jihad." *New York Times*, December 10. http://www.nytimes.com/2009/12/11/world/asia/11inquire.html?pagewanted=all.

"Peter King's Obsession." 2011. *New York Times*, March 7. http://www.nytimes.com/2011/03/08/opinion/08tue1.html.

Pew Research Center for the People and the Press. 2011. "Muslim Americans: No Signs of Growth in Alienation or Support for Extremism". Washington DC: Pew Research Center. http://www.people-press.org/files/legacy-pdf/Muslim-American-Report.pdf.

"Profile: Umar Farouk Abdulmutallab." 2011. *BBC News*, October 12. http://www.bbc.co.uk/news/world-us-canada-11545509.

Ramirez, Deborah, and Tara Quinlan. 2008. "The Greater London Experience: Essential Lessons Learned in Law Enforcement-Community Partnerships and Terrorism Prevention." *Social Science Research Network*. http://papers.ssrn.com/sol3/papers.cfm?abstract_id=2005349.

Robbins, Liz, and Edward Wyatt. 2010. "Bomb Plot Foiled at Holiday Event in Oregon." *New York Times*, November 28. http://m.post-gazette.com/news/us/bomb-plot-foiled-at-holiday-event-in-oregon-1106671?p=0.

Shah, Allie, James Walsh, and Richard Meryhew. 2009. "Relative Confirms Death of Fourth Young Man from Minnesota in Somalia." *Minneapolis Star Tribune*, July 13. http://www.startribune.com/local/minneapolis/50588512.html?page=all&prepage=1&c=y#continue.

Skogan, Wesley. 1997. *Community Policing, Chicago Style*. Oxford: Oxford University Press.

Skogan, Wesley, Susan Harnett, Jill DuBois, Jennifer Comey, Marianne Kaiser, and Justine Lovig. 1998. "Problem Solving in Practice: Implementing Community Policing in Chicago." United States Department of Justice. https://www.ncjrs.gov/pdffiles1/nij/179556.pdf.

Smith, Thomas. 2011. "Testimony of Thomas E. Smith, Chief of Police, St. Paul Police Department, St. Paul Minnesota." *House Committee of Homeland Security*, July 27. http://homeland.house.gov/sites/homeland.house.gov/files/Testimony%20Smith_2.pdf.

"Somali-American Accused of Plotting to Bomb Oregon Tree-Lighting Event." 2010. *CNN News*, November 27. http://articles.cnn.com/2010–11–27/justice/oregon.bomb.plot_1_tree-lighting-justice-department-portland-resident?_s=PM:CRIME.

"Source: Terror Suspect's Father Tried to Warn Authorities." 2009. *CNN News*, December 26. http://articles.cnn.com/2009–12–26/justice/airline.attack_1_umar-farouk-abdulmutallab-no-fly-list-nigeria/2?_s=PM:CRIME.

Spalek, Basia, Salwa El Awa, and Laura Zahra McDonald. 2008. *Police-Muslim Engagement and Partnerships for the Purposes of Counter-Terrorism: An Examination: Summary Report*. Arts and Humanities Research Council. http://www.ahrc.ac.uk/News/Latest/Documents/Rad%20Islam%20Summary%20Report.pdf.

Stacy, Mitch, and Tamara Lush. 2012. "Muslim Man from Kosovo Charged in Fla. Bomb Plot." *Associated Press*, January 9. http://news.yahoo.com/muslim-man-kosovo-charged-fla-bomb-plot-212431556.html.

Stolberg, Sheryl Gay, and Lauri Goodstein. 2011. "Domestic Terrorism Hearing Opens with Contrasting Views on Dangers." *New York Times*, March 10. http://www.nytimes.com/2011/03/11/us/politics/11king.html.

Stone, Christopher, and Jeremy Travis. 2011. "Toward a New Professionalism in Policing." National Institute of Justice, March. https://ncjrs.gov/pdf-filesl/nij/232359.pdf.

Tilley, Nick. 2011. "Modern Approaches to Policing: Community, Problem-Oriented and Intelligence-Led." in *Handbook of Policing, Second Edition.* Edited by Tim Newburn. 373–403. Cullompton, UK: Willan Publishing.

"Umar Farouk Abdulmutallab Sentenced to Life in Prison for Attempted Bombing of Flight 253 on Christmas Day 2009." 2012. *United States Department of Justice*, February 16. http://www.justice.gov/opa/pr/2012/February/12-ag-227.html.

"Understanding Community Policing: A Framework for Action." 1994. *United States Department of Justice, Office of Justice Programs.* https://www.ncjrs.gov/pdffiles/commp.pdf.

"Underwear Bomber Abdulmutallab Sentenced To Life." 2012. *BBC News*. February 12. http://www.bbc.co.uk/news/world-us-canada-17065130.

*United States v. Abdulmutallab*, 2010. No. 2:10-cr-20005, United States District Court, Eastern District of Michigan, January 6. http://abcnews.go.com/images/Politics/abdulmutallab.pdf.

Walsh, James. 2009. "Court Records Detail Minnesota Somalis' Path to Terrorism." *Minneapolis Star Tribune*, July 15. http://www.startribune.com/local/minneapolis/50806557.html?source=error.

Yuen, Laura. 2009. "Missing Somali Men: What's Next in the Investigation." *Minnesota Public Radio*, November 24. http://minnesota.publicradio.org/display/web/2009/11/24/missing_somalI_next_day/.

Yuen, Laura, and Sasha Aslanian. 2009. "Timeline: The Missing Somali Men." *Minnesota Public Radio*, November 23. http://minnesota.publicradio.org/projects/ongoing/somali_timeline/.

Zeleny, Jeff, and Charlie Savage. 2010. "Official Says Terrorism Suspect Is Cooperating." *New York Times*, February 2. http://www.nytimes.com/2010/02/03/us/03terror.html.

# 10

# Pioneers Always Take the Arrows: LAPD Outreach to Muslim Communities in Los Angeles

*Mark G. Stainbrook*

## A Rough Start

The Los Angeles Police Department (LAPD) has led a progressive effort to work more collaboratively with Muslim communities for several years, and has experienced many notable successes. A description of these efforts, however, cannot begin without first reviewing the Los Angeles Police Department's "Muslim mapping" initiative, a derogatory label for an honest attempt to increase understanding, which presented LAPD leaders with an early challenge in their innovative drive to extend community policing to the counterterrorism arena.

On October 30, 2007, Deputy Chief Michael P. Downing, the commanding officer of the LAPD's Counter-Terrorism and Criminal Intelligence Bureau (CTCIB), gave testimony before the Senate Committee on Homeland Security and Governmental Affairs. As his new adjutant, I was tasked to assist with the writing and editing of the chief's testimony.

Chief Downing's testimony read in part:

> We need to understand the problem as it exists in Los Angeles before we roll out programs to mitigate radicalization. Historically, the temptation has been to turn to intervention programs before we have clearly identified problems within the community. In the past we have relied on interventions based on "experts," logic or previous programs that are either generic or insensitive to the constellation of issues. This has consistently produced unremarkable results. Public safety pays a high cost for this business practice....

> In order to give our officers increased awareness of our local Muslim communities, the LAPD recently launched an initiative with an academic institution to conduct an extensive "community mapping" project. We are also soliciting input of local Muslim groups, so the process can be transparent and inclusive. While this project will lay out the geographic locations of the many different Muslim population groups around Los Angeles, we also intend to take a deeper look at their history, demographics, language, culture, ethnic breakdown, socio-economic status, and social interactions. It is our hope to identify communities, within the larger Muslim community, which may be susceptible to violent ideologically-based extremism and then use a full-spectrum approach guided by an intelligence-led strategy.
>
> Community mapping is the start of a conversation, not just data sets: It is law enforcement identifying with its community and the community identifying with its families, neighborhoods, city, state, country and police. For the past 18 months, the LAPD's outreach and grassroots dialogue with Muslim communities has helped the entire command staff to observe, learn, engage and, most importantly, listen. This has helped to build more robust trust networks at the divisional level of the police service area. (Downing 2007, 7)

Directly after his testimony, Chief Downing met with prominent Muslim leaders and was praised for his insightful and forward-thinking approach. There was even an article in the *Homeland Security Congressional Quarterly* (Fowler 2007) relating their praise for the innovative ideas in the initiative, but there was some hesitancy as well—something we did not realize would become a firestorm.

Believing we had scored a victory, we were elated upon Chief Downing's return to officially move toward implementation. We were shocked when several days later there was an uproar from local Los Angeles Muslim groups and specific individuals, who had taken the initiative entirely out of context. What happened next is well documented in the media: the LAPD and the "mapping" plan were thoroughly attacked.

Welcome to the challenges of outreach to communities.

Let's be clear, this initiative was in no way racial profiling or even mapping individual Muslims in Los Angeles or anywhere else. The term was taken from the academic terms "community mapping" or "cultural mapping." Cultural mapping can be described as:

> A broadly-based mapping exercise for purposes of investigating or creating an identity profile of the community is enriching, informative and useful…the process of mapping by itself draws attention to the

> existence and importance of cultural resources. The results point out problems to be solved or strengths to build upon. (Stewart 2010, 3)

The most important part of this initiative was having the LAPD partner with an academic institution and a community organization, such as the Muslim Public Affairs Council (MPAC) or the Council for American Islamic Relations (CAIR).

The source of the outrage came from the leadership of the various Muslim community organizations with whom we had been working diligently over the previous years. Their reaction was visceral; there was a great deal of anger and confusion regarding our intentions. Whether the anger was purely an emotional response, or a calculated attempt by certain "community leaders" to increase the divide between the LAPD and the community, in either case, is unimportant when a strategic initiative went very wrong. Damage control was now the name of the game. One lesson for me was to never underestimate the level of complexity of the political dynamics within Muslim communities.

## Lessons Learned the Hard Way

We admittedly made several mistakes in how we broached this subject with the community. First, we did not lay the proper foundation with our known friendly community partners prior to the testimony. Second, we did not have a communications plan from the very beginning. Finally, we did not fully comprehend the level of anxiety Muslim communities had about interactions with law enforcement in general.

On a positive note, this crisis gave both the LAPD and Los Angeles Muslim communities a much needed impetus for dialogue and action. Even better, once the initial public outcries had run their course, neither side let emotions get in the way of working through the issues. I believe that everyone understood we needed each other.

Since the 9/11 attacks, Muslim communities throughout the United States and the world have found themselves under the glare of the media spotlight. Islam and terrorism have become all but synonymous in the eyes of some—much to the chagrin of the millions of Muslims who practice Islam peacefully and devotedly.

Even as many aspects of Muslim culture have been explored and studied, an odd thing has happened: Muslim communities have been lumped together, by many, as a monolithic presence in American society. In fact, that could not be further from the truth. Each community of Muslims has its own story—its own linguistic, cultural, ethnic, and socioeconomic history. Unfortunately, that rich, holistic picture of these communities has not yet been captured in a scientific way in Los Angeles.

As Muslim communities have struggled to be understood, American law enforcement—including the LAPD—has struggled to understand. Departments have had no road maps to use as they attempt to craft outreach strategies to communities that they know little about. Our fundamental question was this: How do you attempt to have positive interactions with Muslims in Los Angeles when you don't know who they are, where they are, or even what is important to them?

Chief Downing and I were like-minded in our views. In 2006, we had both spent time in the United Kingdom working with, and observing the police forces there, who were attempting to engage with their Muslim communities. Similar to 9/11 in the United States, the London transit bombings on July 7, 2005, served as a backdrop to the strained relationships between the UK government, particularly the police and intelligence services, and their Muslim communities. In that attack, four terrorists carried out coordinated bombings on the London mass transit system killing 52 people and wounding over 700. Unlike the 9/11 attack, in which the terrorists were not US citizens, the attackers were all British nationals, who had been born and raised in the United Kingdom. Three of the individuals were Muslims of Pakistani descent and one was a convert of Jamaican descent (Murphy 2006).

Chief Downing and I believed that the United States was approximately 5–7 years behind the United Kingdom, both in terms of the amount of violent radicalization in US Muslim communities and in the level and sophistication of police outreach to these communities. It should be noted that although individuals within a community may become violent, we did not believe that this perpetuated throughout entire communities. However a community can be vulnerable on many other levels. Vulnerability of a community to the effects of terrorism does not imply they are more likely to become terrorists; it means that they are more likely to be impacted socially, economically, mentally, and yes, possibly to the point wherein some individuals believe that violence is an acceptable alternative. *However, statistically very few actually resort to physical violence.* One source of frustration for us was, and still is, the perpetuation of the myth that Muslim communities are somehow more susceptible to becoming violent in support of Islam. This has never been academically proven, but is continually perpetuated by far-right extremists on the Internet and via pseudo-intellectual books.

Although in 2007 there was very little indication of radicalization from American citizens within the country, there were several examples of US-born citizens going overseas to wage a violent ideological "jihad." The most apparent example was from the Somali community in the Minneapolis, Minnesota area. Open sources estimated 20–40 young men have traveled to Somalia since 2007 to fight with Al-Shabab, several of whom became suicide bombers. The number of those engaging in a support activity, such as recruiting, fundraising, financing, logistics, and offering spiritual/moral support, is potentially much higher.

Additionally, since 2007, there has been a sharp increase in the number of "homegrown" terrorism plots within the United States. From a strictly preventative perspective, we believed that the only way to move from a reactive posture, which generally eroded the relationships between the police and the community due to overreaction on both sides when a terrorist attack occurred, was to move toward a preventative approach. The reactive approach generally requires those "hard policing" and intelligence methods such as surveillances, wiretaps, search warrants, interviews/interrogations, and arrests. The preventative approach involves trying to reach out to people and maintain a dialogue that builds trusting relationships, thus gaining information from a community by overt methods, such as meetings, joint projects, recruitment, and attending social/cultural events.

It's been more than 10 years since the 9/11 attacks, and in general, local, state, and federal governments in the United States are embarrassingly behind what is needed to constructively engage with our Muslim communities. Although many police agencies are indeed constantly striving toward improved community policing efforts, few have the nuanced knowledge and experience to seriously engage with those Muslim communities that are affected by international terrorism.

Other than in academia, which conducts research but little actual engagement, there is a lack of expertise on some very specific dynamics within American Muslim communities. These include: (a) the traits of Diaspora communities; (b) the perception of negative media attention; (c) perception of unfair government policies; and (d) the implications of international events. This lack of knowledge is a huge barrier to effective communication and relationship building.

In the weeks following the explosive nature of the "mapping" debate, then-LAPD chief William Bratton and deputy chief Downing engaged the Muslim communities through a series of meetings, both large and small. There were many behind-the-scenes negotiations, and outreach was done through news interviews, editorials, telephone calls, e-mails, and one-on-one meetings. The bottom line was that we agreed to scrap the community mapping plan and reengage with the communities via a quarterly "Police Chief's Forum." Chief Downing also gave me the go-ahead to form a community liaison unit that would specifically reach out to any community in the Los Angeles area which was affected by terrorism.

## Los Angeles: The Lay of the Land

It is difficult to determine the exact number of Muslims in Los Angeles. Additionally, many Muslims who do not actually live in the city are very much tied into the community there via political, social, or religious organizations, such as the Islamic Center of Southern California, the Muslim Public Affairs Council, the Iman Center (Iranian Shia), and the Omar Al-Khattab Center, as well as many other mosques and community centers. Those who grew up in Los Angeles and now live outside the city are still deeply connected to the mosques they grew up in, often attending Friday "jumah" prayers.

The earliest large Muslim communities were African American Muslims who came to Los Angeles in the 1920s and 1930s looking for work and a chance at a better life. They are very proud of the fact that they did not immigrate to America, but are American-born Muslims. They are quick to differentiate themselves from members of the Nation of Islam.

In the 1970s, students from Iran came to LA to attend the local universities, especially the University of California Los Angeles (UCLA) and the University of Southern California (USC). After the fall of the Shah in 1979, tens of thousands of Iranians fled to the region forming an instant community. The new arrivals were typically well educated and brought enough capital to buy homes and start businesses.

Arab Muslims arrived in large numbers in Los Angeles between the late 1960s and the 1980s, often fleeing political oppression. During the same period, many Arab Christians and Jews arrived from Lebanon, Syria, and Egypt fleeing Middle East wars and oppressive governments. Events in the Middle East continue to occasionally cause tensions between Muslim and Christian communities. Violence against Coptic Christians in Egypt has impacted the local Coptic communities.

The most recent immigration has come from South Asia, primarily from Pakistan. Within the Pakistani community there is something of a socioeconomic gap. A small, highly educated, economically vibrant group is contrasted by a larger group of service industry–oriented Pakistanis. A large number are Deobandi, many of whom are affiliated with the Tablighi Jama'at movement.

Unfortunately, as a political, economic, and cultural center, Los Angeles has long been a target for terrorists. Al-Qaeda–inspired plots are just the latest threat. In 2000, Ahmed Ressem was arrested while driving across the US-Canadian border with bomb-making material to be used on the Los Angeles International Airport. The downtown Library Tower was targeted by Khalid Sheikh Mohammed for the second wave of attacks after 9/11. In 2003, the Jam'yyat Al-Islam Al-Saheeh (JIS) case involved African American converts, who intended to attack local synagogues and military installations. Most recently an Angelino Muslim, also African American, was arrested in Seattle for conspiring to attack military installations there.

## Forming the Unit

It is with this background that we began to form a unit specifically designed to provide outreach and services to communities affected by terrorism. It should be noted that, unlike the Muslim Contact Unit in London, we did not intend to engage only with Muslim communities, but with any and all communities impacted by terrorism. This included nontraditional communities such as scientists from University of California Los Angeles, who were being targeted by animal rights activists.

Personnel are the key to a successful outreach unit. They will make or break the unit. Due to the complexity of the different Muslim communities, the political sensitivities, and the importance of international events to the communities, finding the right people can be difficult, but recruiting outstanding officers is imperative. The burden is made greater by the bureaucratic nature of police agencies and since 2007, the reduction of resources.

One might think that having Muslim officers, and some Jewish officers in our case, would be beneficial, maybe even a requirement. I find that this is dangerous thinking for several reasons. Especially in Los Angeles, we have very different Muslim communities, each with their own culture, shared history, perhaps language preference, but also their preferred way of practicing Islam. Rifts between individuals, groups, and organizations may exacerbate or inflame the separation from other communities. There are some mosques in Los Angeles that are very diverse in their ethnic makeup, but most are fairly homogeneous.

A Muslim officer may try to engage in a community of a different ethnic or cultural makeup, or a different tradition than his or her own, and be treated with even more suspicion than a non-Muslim officer. It may be assumed that the officer is representing his or her own Muslim community, or there may be long-standing disputes stemming from home-country rivalries, particularly if there is a tribal dimension. While this may not always be the case, it is worth considering.

Issues surrounding female Muslim officers can also be complex and frustrating. Many Muslim women and their communities are fairly Westernized in their dress and practices; however there are communities that are much stricter in their views. I participated in community events where the women's area is separated by a rope line that no men cross. This presents an unusual circumstance for male officers, who are generally used to engaging with both sexes. There are also males, generally from older generations, who would prefer not to engage with female officers. Subtle offenses of sensitivities may have an impact on relationships that may be overlooked by less experienced officers.

My first officer to the unit, and still one of the best, was actually a white, male Christian, who started out knowing little about Islam or Muslim communities. Indeed, he was assigned to me; I was not allowed to choose. As it turned out, because he was very interested in the unusual assignment, he was excited and had the dedication to learn by reading, going to training classes, watching educational programs, and meeting people who would take the time to instruct him on the religious and cultural nuances. I cannot emphasize enough the importance of hiring personnel who have the motivation and interest to self-educate. There are not many formal programs that can teach law enforcement community outreach to Muslim communities.

## Holistic Approaches to Community Engagement

As a young officer (pre-9/11), I walked into a lot of churches and synagogues while on patrol or while working in a community outreach capacity. Although I saw mosques, I never had the opportunity to visit or engage with any Muslim communities. I probably did meet individual Muslims, most assuredly when I worked the West

Los Angeles area, but I probably did not even think of their religious background. In some respect, Muslims were invisible to US law enforcement prior to 9/11.

It is often said that the police are the most visible form of government. Because of this, we are often the first government agency that new communities come into contact with, and it is very rarely due to a terrorism investigation. More than likely, it is going through customs and airport security, or receiving a traffic ticket. This is an important point, because the former is a contact with federal officers/security and the latter is with state/local police, who have very different missions. In my experience, first-generation immigrants really do not make the level of distinction between the types of law enforcement agencies, but see them all as "the government." Generally, contact with the police is not a positive experience, but especially for those who emigrate from countries with extremely repressive governments.

It is for this very reason, that the police are usually the first to come into contact with new communities, and that they work to broaden favorable interactions with police officers and government as a whole. This is an important educational step for the community in a new and sometimes scary environment. It is especially important if we value engaging new communities and weaving them into the fabric of American society. Therefore, it is imperative that community outreach officers look for opportunities to engage in less confrontational venues and that we do not always try to be the focus of engagement, but to coordinate with other government, social, and educational services.

The strength of local law enforcement is that we can engage with a wide variety of communities on a daily basis on quality of life issues, crime problems, and special projects/events in a nonconfrontational atmosphere. One of the complaints for local Muslims was that we (law enforcement in general) only wanted to talk when some major terrorism event occurred. It was the impression of some that we did not really want to build relationships on other shared interests.

## Third Party Engagement

Engagement should not be done in a vacuum. Within the LAPD, there are many units we needed to be successful, but they had to be asked. Media Relations, Community Relations Section, Community Policing Unit, the Reserve Corps, and the Police Cadet Program, among others, are important partners, who must be coordinated and communicated with, but they may not have experience working with

Muslim communities. Each unit has unique expertise or resources that our personnel did not have; and we were able to introduce them to a part of the LA community that was often underserved.

Aside from the specialized units, there was no way to really conduct the relationship building required with such a small cadre of officers. Part of our strategy was to engage with key community members and then introduce them to the local station's key personnel. In the case of the LAPD, each station has a Community Relations Office (CRO), staffed with Senior Lead Officers (SLOs), who work specifically assigned areas and projects. Many of the SLOs had never interacted with the mosques in their areas, but we were surprised to find several who had taken their own initiative to meet the imams and mosque leaders. We would invite the commanding officers to meetings and events.

As we built our networks, the importance of also coordinating with other local agencies, the Los Angeles City government, and state and federal agencies became apparent. Los Angeles is a massive city with many programs and resources, but has particularly strong connections with its religious institutions. The Human Relations Commission (HRC) is a leader in promoting interfaith dialogue between Christian, Jewish, Muslim, and other faiths within the city. Part of the HRC's work included the Middle East Advisory Board, which was made up of members from numerous prominent local religious and cultural organizations. The purpose of the board was to advise the mayor and city officials about the impact of events in the Middle East and to promote dialogue between all the major faith groups.

Perhaps the most impactful, regularly scheduled meetings that we participate in is coordinated by the Department of Homeland Security's Office of Civil Rights and Civil Liberties, and these are held quarterly. These meetings are made up of various government agencies, local, state, federal law enforcement, social service agencies, and community groups. The main audience is Muslim and Sikh communities. It is an important venue to exchange information and to deliver our message to the communities. Each agency updates their programs and answers questions from community members. Because there is sometimes confusion on the part of community members as to which agency handles what issue, it is a good opportunity for rumors to be quashed and misunderstandings addressed. We have the opportunity to educate communities to laws, policies, and procedures, and they have the opportunity to express their concerns and problems to us.

## Reengagement

Out of the large-scale community meetings held immediately after the press on the Congressional testimony, Chief Bratton decided that the Muslim communities would have quarterly access to him directly at a Chief's Forum. Chief Bratton routinely held these forums with other specific communities, including African American, Hispanic, Asian, and Lesbian-Gay Bi-Sexual, and Transgender (LGBT). The Chief's Forums were organized by the Community Relations Section, in order to maintain a separation from counterterrorism; however, the CT Liaison Section has a large behind-the-scenes role, especially as advisors and cultural experts.

## Recruitment

One area we wanted to focus on was to increase LAPD's transparency in the communities by recruiting Muslims officers into the department. We felt it was much better for fellow community members to see what was going on within the LAPD and report back, than for us to try to explain that we did not profile or participate in secret interrogations. There are very few full-time Muslim officers in the LAPD, and the budget restraints due to the poor economy have also been a roadblock to hiring more officers, in general.

A quick bit of research confirmed that the LAPD did not have a Muslim chaplain. LAPD chaplains were primarily Christian or Jewish. The difficulty for us was finding someone with the proper religious credentials and personality to pass a series of boards with the other chaplains, who sit as the gateway for admission into the Corps. The second problem was finding someone with the guts and tenacity to apply. We had broadcast a request for volunteers during meetings and through personnel contacts. The solution came in the person of Qazi Asad.

Qazi Asad, even at first blush, is a charismatic and interesting person. He can also be intimidating to non-Muslims as he wears a long beard and often dresses in full Pakistani cultural attire. Qazi is a Deobandi and a leader within the regional Tablighi Jama'at. Qazi is not an imam, and even if he were, the Chaplain Corps wanted to see papers that certified him as ordained. As this was not possible, Qazi prepared a resume of his background and experience leading prayers, burying the dead, and as an active member of his mosque, in a role that I best described to people unfamiliar with Islam as that of a church deacon.

Qazi was interviewed by a panel of chaplains for the position. The first interview went very well, by all accounts, but there was some still some concern about appointing Qazi, who would be the first LAPD Muslim police chaplain. My understanding was it centered around the number of officers in the department who were Muslim, and if a Muslim chaplain was even necessary. My perception was that there was a general nervousness about having a Muslim chaplain at all, and some resistance from well-entrenched chaplains, who were also community activists in the Jewish community. After a second interview, Qazi was voted to become a member of the Corps and was appointed on June 12, 2009.

We fully expected that there would be resistance from some officers on Qazi's appointment, especially when he began to show up at police stations. This was easily overcome by his personality and good nature when educating officers about who he was and in understanding Muslim communities. Qazi really enjoys being part of the police and recently was sworn in as a Los Angeles Sheriff's Reserve Deputy.

What was unexpected was the reaction from other Muslim communities. The Arab Muslim communities, who generally are more Westernized in their dress and mannerisms, were upset that we would choose a very conservative, first-generation Pakistani Muslim as the first chaplain. We pointed out that after repeated requests, Qazi was the only one to apply and went through the process unassisted. Neither Chief Downing, nor I, had any influence on the decision-making process and we were not completely sure he would be appointed.

What this underlined for us was the continuing divisions and competition within our different communities. Although the issue generally passed without too much heartache, it was a lesson that even when we were trying to be open and transparent, things could go wrong. For our part, we felt that if LAPD could accept a very conservative Muslim into the ranks, then we were breaking down barriers and there was no excuse for members of other Muslim communities to argue we were intolerant.

One night a new reserve officer was assigned his partner for his first night on patrol as an LAPD officer. As they patrolled, they received a call from an individual under the influence of drugs, running on the street. When they arrived, the crazed man ran from them, was hit by a car, then jumped up and ran again. When the officers chased him down, a fight ensued with the suspect and he was taken into custody.

Earlier in the evening a unique conversation took place between the new partners. It went something like this: "Hey, later in the shift we can stop by my synagogue and get some food. I want to introduce you to my rabbi." The response was, "Sure, but only if later I can take you to my mosque and introduce you to my imam!"

The newly minted LAPD Reserve Officer was Omar Ricci, a former national chairman of the Muslim Public Affairs Council, a member of the Muslim Homeland Security Congress, and a member of the greater Los Angeles Shura Council. His partner was none other than a female, Orthodox Jew, who served in the Israeli Defense Forces.

Omar Ricci was the second person I worked hard at recruiting. Omar had been a good community partner and a personal friend for several years. When he told me he was about to join another police agency as a reserve officer, I knew I had to convince him to join LAPD. He had credibility with the community, and he was passionate about wanting to become a police officer. Still he had some trepidation about working with LAPD and how he might be perceived in the community. I reminded him of his ties to Los Angeles growing up in the mid-Wilshire district and his ties as a businessman in the city. The process, including background checks, medical, and other administrative paperwork, took more than a year, but he thought it was so important to serve that he persevered through the frustration.

After about a year "on the job" he penned some of his thoughts in an editorial. As Omar describes it:

> The journey to become a police officer, no matter your background, starts with a fundamental trait. One must have an innate desire to protect and serve the public with integrity while upholding the Constitution. For an American Muslim, there is the added sense of responsibility to fight so-called Muslims who launched terrorist attacks against us on 9/11, who have done immeasurable damage to the image of Islam, and who continue to threaten us. In addition, Muslim police officers can act as a bridge between law enforcement and the Muslim community. But in becoming a police officer, I seek to carry on an important tradition of our country, and a mandate of my faith—one of public service. (Ricci 2010)

Omar is unique in many ways in that he is a bridge between cultures. His father is a Roman Catholic and his mother was a Muslim.

Omar describes goes on to describe what he calls his "transformative experiences":

> There was the Gaza flotilla crisis in May 2010, where emotions were running high, and hundreds of pro-Palestinian demonstrators gathered in front of the Israeli consulate in Los Angeles. I, along with a

> cadre of other officers, stood in a circle around a lone teenage Jewish boy waving an Israeli flag in front of an impassioned pro-Palestinian crowd. The boy was adamant in his views, and put himself in danger to express them, and while I may not have personally agreed with his views, I was equally adamant about defending his Constitutional right to express them. (Ricci 2010)

Recently, Omar took his family to Jewish services and was struck by the familiarity of the religious themes.

## STUMBLING BLOCKS

Three closely related issues were (and can still be) flash points with LA Muslim communities, and particularly the more civil rights–minded groups found them concerning. They are law enforcement fusion centers, Suspicious Activity Reporting (SARS), and the iWatch program.

There are more than 70 fusion centers in the United States. The Los Angeles regional fusion center is the Joint Regional Intelligence Center, or JRIC. Since their inception, many civil rights groups nationally have expressed concerned that fusion centers may collect intelligence on US citizens. Part of the intake of information at the JRIC is through SARS. SARS enables police officers and citizens to use a reporting mechanism for suspicious activities that do not rise to the level of a crime. Understandably, the concerns of civil rights groups center around reports being made that focus on race, ethnicity, and/or religion. For law enforcement it is an invaluable intelligence tool, but it is extremely regulated in order to ensure civil liberties are maintained.

The iWatch program was designed to increase public awareness of suspicious activity that might be related to terrorism. Through a series of public awareness videos, billboards, and classes, the iWatch program encourages the public to complete online SARS or to call the police.

These initiatives were launched separately, but became increasingly intertwined. Coming on the heels of the "mapping" issue, it made Muslim community outreach that much more difficult. Chief Downing developed a simple strategy to counter the negative aspects of these three initiatives. First, we set up several meetings with Muslim community groups to review iWatch and SARS policies and procedures. A part of those meetings was to explain how and why these policies were developed and implemented. Second, Chief

Downing arranged tours of the JRIC and briefings of the SARS process. Finally, we offered to review requested changes to our policies and procedures within reason. The result was an improved system for SARS that was aligned with the national SARS guidelines.

One of the more proactive things that Chief Downing initiated due to the concerns over these issues was to offer the informational briefings to community leaders/members at our facilities, including tours of the JRIC and the unit that processed LAPD SARS reports. This type of transparency was unheard of at the time and in some ways even surprised some members of the department who, citing security concerns, were not enthusiastic about welcoming members of the Muslim community into our workspaces. These issues aside, the tours and briefings were very successful. It gave Muslim groups the ability to tell their constituents that they were actively representing the community and had direct access to police decision makers.

Part of marketing SARS to the public meant releasing the iWatch video on the web encouraging people to report when they observed specific activity that might be related to terrorism. SARS reports are based on actions, not race, gender, religion, or ethnicity. Even language, if the reporting person can identify it, is not in and of itself used as a terrorism indicator. Our initial list of terrorism-related activities was based on research done on past terrorist attacks and the actions of the attacker before the attacks. These are collectively known as "pre-operational indicators." Unfortunately, we had over 60 listed, which was much too cumbersome to be digested by the public. Nationally, the federal government had adopted SARS by this time and used 15 pre-operational indicators. We met with community groups, who requested that we change LAPD's standards to the national standards. Chief Downing thought this made sense and took action to adjust our policies.

Another requested change was to the promotional video for iWatch. The video is on the LAPD website and promoted across the Internet on websites such as Youtube. We were careful to design the video to be a multicultural representation of Los Angeles. The theme is that "I watch my neighborhood," for suspicious activity and can report it online or via the telephone. Interestingly, the Muslim community was upset that there was not a "Muslim" on the video. We agreed that there was not a specifically "Muslim" appearing individual on the video, such as a woman in a hijab, but many of the people in the video could have been Muslim. As we are often told by community members, "what does a Muslim" look like? We used this argument back to them. The video remained unchanged.

The real test came as we unveiled iWatch, and thus SARS, at the Los Angeles International Airport (LAX) on June 3, 2010. This would come in the form of posters, flyers, and video/audio throughout the airport. The implications of this program at LAX was monstrous, as can be imagined, due to worries of American Muslims about being profiled when they fly. Our goal was to invite the attendance from all our major Muslim community partners. Before the press conference we held a number of meetings with groups and individuals inviting key members to attend and speak. It was a huge moment in the three years since "Muslim mapping" to see how far our relationships and partnerships had come, when all of the major players from the Los Angeles Muslim communities came to support and endorse the launch of iWatch at LAX.

## What We Learned

Working with Muslim communities is all about individual relationships. When you think about Islam as a religion, it is very focused on brotherhood and sisterhood. Muslims often refer to each other in such terms. The importance of close personal relationship in Islam, and in the many cultures that encompass the *Ummah*, requires that police officers who are going to engage in this work are prepared for the amount of dialogue, tea drinking, meals, and more dialogue. Mentally, they also have to be prepared for numerous emotional swings that come with success and failures during highly charged, often media-intensive projects. Even if it is not the professional media, oftentimes we were interviewed on personal cameras and phones as to our positions on any number of issues.

I believe the old rule about seeking to understand before being understood applies with Muslim communities. The ability for an officer to listen and hear grievances, even general criticism about law enforcement or government policies, while not taking it personally is critical. It has to be understood that it is not the police officer the person finds offense with. Additionally, religious and cultural norms need to be taken into consideration. For example, during Ramadan, when many Muslims are fasting, they may be irritable or grumpy by the end of the workday. I know I am when I haven't eaten or had anything to drink for 12 hours.

I counsel police officers when working with any community never to promise anything. Especially, due to the very personal nature of their relationships, sometimes there is pressure to make something happen that the officer does not have the power to implement without seeking guidance or resources from his or her chain of command. On the flip side, the more autonomy and authority the officer has from the department to make supportable decisions the better. Otherwise community members will always want to speak to the more senior decision makers.

Forming a new unit to do this type of community engagement is challenging. Again, the most important factor is choosing the right people. There are not many specific classes or programs that teach this type of outreach. Finding individuals who are motivated to read and self-educate is extremely important. Officers with military experience, higher educational levels, and experience living in foreign countries seem to have a better attitude and understanding of the nature of the work. Choosing officers who are Muslims is not necessarily an instant antidote to building better community relations. A Muslim officer who comes from a different background than the specific community being engaged may be met with apprehension or distrust. This may not always be the case, but it is worth considering what issues may arise. Imagine hiring an Iranian Shia police officer to work in an Iraqi Sunni community!

Education of both police officers and community members is the key to success. Most police officers will know little about working with Muslim community members, and there also may be skepticism or outright distrust. Conversely, many first-generation American Muslims tend to view the government and law enforcement in general with the same level of distrust. With both groups, more interaction leads to greater comfort and eventually the building of relationships. And police officers need to extend the first hand. As Chief Downing put it:

> We need to show that our democratic principles built on the values, practices, and lives of American citizens are sacred and worthy of embracing. We need to show our belief in human dignity, the family and the value of the individual. We need to show how we honor the meaning of our lives by what we contribute to others' lives. We need to show that behind the badges of American law enforcement are caring Americans "doing" law enforcement. To do this we need to go into the community and get to know peoples' names. We need to walk into homes, neighborhoods, mosques, and businesses. We need to know how Islam expresses itself in Los Angeles if we expect to forge bonds of community support. The LAPD has been involved in this process and we are now ready to evolve our outreach to a more sophisticated and strategic level. (Downing 2007, 8)

From a strategic perspective, program and policies must be carefully reviewed and forged *with* community leaders and groups prior to implementation. Use of the media and social networks must be tapped into to lay the groundwork for successful ventures. My recommendation is to outreach directly to community members through e-mails, flyers, town hall meetings, and arm officers with talking points for any individual conversations. Remember, if you allow your message to be filtered through the various community organizations or self-claimed leaders, then you may be doomed to failure before any policy or project gets off the ground.

## CONCLUSION

Someone has to take the lead in the outreach to American Muslim communities in this time of asymmetric warfare and terrorism, and state/local law enforcement agencies in the homeland are perfectly placed to do so. They have the community knowledge, experience in community policing, and the infrastructure to accomplish this task. What they often lack is the mandate, funding, and a clear plan to make that a reality.

A variety of academic researchers have offered worthwhile descriptions of community-centric responses to terrorism, especially in the United Kingdom (e.g., Lambert 2008; Spalek, El Awa, McDonald, and Lambert 2008). What we know is that terrorism cannot be defeated through military engagement overseas, law enforcement in the homeland, or global intelligence alone. The fourth leg of the table must be a holistic civic engagement of all American communities, but especially those American Muslim communities that maintain links to their homelands overseas. There are those who believe the American Muslim experience can be a catalyst for international change as dictatorial governments are falling throughout the Middle East. The best ambassadors of democracy and freedom that America possesses are those transnationally linked peoples who have sought, received, and lived religious freedom under a constitutional form of government. Only in this way can the American Muslim identity and experience be promulgated globally. Whether in the United States or across the globe, Chief Downing summed up his Congressional testimony before the Senate Committee in these terms:

> Ultimately, preventing extremism will be up to neighborhoods and communities, but thread by thread, relationship by relationship, the police can help build a network of services and relationships that will make it very hard for terrorism to take root. American Muslim neighborhoods and communities have a genuine responsibility in preventing

any form of extremism and terrorism. If the broader communities are intolerant of such things, these ideologies cannot take root in its midst. I believe no amount of enforcement or intelligence can ultimately prevent extremism if the communities are not committed to working with law enforcement to prevent it. (Downing 2007, 8)

## REFERENCES

Downing, M. P. 2007. "Statement of Michael P. Downing before the Committee on Homeland Security's and Government and Government Affairs United States Senate." October 30. http://www.hsgac.senate.gov/download/103007downing.

Fowler, Daniel. 2007. "Los Angeles Police, Muslim Group on Same Page With Mapping Plan." *CQ Homeland Security*. November 1. http://homeland.cq.com/hs/display.do?dockey=/cqonline/prod/data/docs/html/hsnews/110/hsnews110-000002620033.html@allnewsarchive&metapub=HSNEWS&seqNum=37&searchIndex=4.

Lambert, Robert. 2008. "Empowering Salafis and Islamists against Al-Qaeda: A London Counterterrorism Case Study." *Political Science and Politics 41*(1): 31–35. http://journals.cambridge.org/action/displayAbstract;jsessionid=55FF87711AA10B7B0F84E413513E750F.journals?fromPage=online&aid=1631163.

Murphy, Paul. 2006. *Report into the London Terrorist Attacks on 7 July 2005*. Norwich, UK: The Stationary Office.

Ricci, Omar. 2010. "Faith, Freedom, and a Badge." Altmuslim: Global perspectives on Muslim Life, Politics, & Culture. October 21. http://www.patheos.com/blogs/altmuslim/2010/10/faith_freedom_and_a_badge/.

Spalek, Basia, Salwa El-Awa, Laura Zahra McDonald, and Robert Lambert. 2008. *Police-Muslim Engagement and Partnerships for the Purposes of Counterterrorism: An Examination (Summary Report)*. Birmingham, UK: University of Birmingham. http://www/ahrc.ac.uk/News/Laest/Documents/Rad%20Islam%20Summary%20Report.pdf.

Stewart, Sue. 2010. *Cultural Mapping Toolkit: A Partnership between 2010 Legacies Now and Creative City Network of Canada*. Vancouver, British Columbia: 2010 Legacies Now. http://www.2010legaciesnow.com/fileadmin/user_upload/ExploreArts/Toolkits/CultureMapping.pdf.

# 11

# Hearing Community Voices to Identify Best Practices: Building Antiterrorism Partnerships with American Muslims

*Alejandro J. Beutel*

## Introduction

On 9/11, policy makers and the American public at large were suddenly and violently confronted by the threat of al-Qaeda's violent extremism. As a result, the nation's resources and thought-leaders were mobilized to devise new ways of preventing terrorism and contesting extremism.

In the decade prior to 9/11, countering terrorism was not the highest priority of federal law enforcement agencies such as the FBI (9/11 Commission 2004; German 2005a). Nor were Muslim extremists like al-Qaeda perceived to be a threat to security as they are today. At the time, right-wing extremists (neo-Nazis, Apocalyptic cults, patriot militias, etc.) intending to kill large numbers of people (Kristof 2002) also drew significant law enforcement attention (Berger 2012). Furthermore federal and local antiterrorism investigations were typically reactive, after-the-fact efforts, instead of proactively driven, meant to prevent the next attack before it occurred. Terrorism-related information typically was not shared between and among local, state, and federal law enforcement agencies (9/11 Commission 2004; German 2005b).

These approaches to antiterrorism changed after 9/11. After the 9/11 attacks, law enforcement was under intense political pressure to make terrorism its top priority and to make prevention the default orientation of any investigation. Furthermore, the main profile of antiterrorist concern began to definitively focus on al-Qaeda, and along with it, American Muslims. As a result, immigrant Muslim communities of African, Arab, and South Asian origin, as well as African American communities, have been a topic of concern and interest not just for law enforcement officials, but also for community and civil liberties advocates and academic researchers. These changes have prompted an intense and ongoing debate among many parties over what is the appropriate balance between civil liberties and national security and what types of policies are needed to achieve that balance. At the policy level, much research has been dedicated to utilizing community-oriented policing strategies that emphasize partnering up with communities to come up with appropriate solutions.

It is argued by proponents of community-oriented policing that working with communities can be an effective antiterrorism alternative to other methods, such as intelligence-led policing (which has a heavy emphasis on covert surveillance techniques like informants and sting operations), while also minimizing negative impacts on civil liberties. (Murray 2005; Innes 2006; Jensen 2006; Friedmann and Cannon 2007). However in order to be effective, community-oriented policing requires building and maintaining trust between law enforcement and communities. However, trust-building between American Muslim communities and US law enforcement agencies is easier said than done. This chapter aims to focus on community perspectives on barriers to trust with law enforcement, and provide some potential answers to this dilemma in several ways.

First, it provides an overview of the complex factors that inhibit the development of trust between law enforcement and American Muslim communities. A combination of broad-brushed surveillance, poor training, negative police experiences, internal disagreements over the utility of engagement, and anti-Muslim politics at the national level have served to heighten tensions and inhibit trust.

Second, this chapter conducts a review of studies that highlight the activities and perspectives of American Muslims to strengthen anticrime, and specifically antiterrorism, partnerships. I find that a small body of research is emerging to identify such efforts and viewpoints. Furthermore, as far as this author is aware, there has been no academic inquiry into identifying best practices from the perspectives of American Muslim leaders who regularly engage law enforcement.

Upon identifying this gap in the research, I conducted a preliminary qualitative study involving six telephone interviews with six participants in six US metropolitan areas. I then used the responses gathered from the interviews to outline five key themes for trust building. Before concluding, I provide a short analysis of the findings, arguing that they are largely a reflection of the sociopolitical factors that inhibit trust and stoke tensions between law enforcement and American Muslims.

## Barriers to Building Trust with Law Enforcement

While it is clear to many officials and community leaders that establishing relationships between communities and law enforcement—particularly through community-oriented policing—is important, the lack of trust is perhaps the biggest barrier to forming these relationships. Missteps and misunderstanding by both sides have inhibited better partnerships. There are five main barriers to effective partnerships between law enforcement and American Muslim communities.

The first barrier deals with concerns over civil liberties. Although American Muslims overwhelmingly express strong attachment to America (Reske 2011), live in a socio-political-economic context that is less conducive to violent extremism relative to their co-religionists in Europe (even with the recent rise in anti-Muslim bias over the past two years, Beutel 2007), and overwhelmingly reject terrorism at both mass (Pew 2007; Khan 2011; Naurath 2011) and elite levels (Musaji 2011), they have still been the subject of wide-ranging and invasive surveillance policies of both local (Associated Press 2012; Hassan 2012;) and federal law enforcement (Heymann 2002; BBC 2005; Muslim Advocates 2009) since 9/11. Community members and activists have voiced concerns over policies such as wholesale surveillance of activist groups, community centers, and houses of worship without any evidence indicating criminal activity and highlighted instances of racial and/or religious profiling[1] at airports, border crossings, and other means of travel (ACLU 2008; Tu 2008; Harris 2009; Syed 2010; Barakat 2011; Jones 2011). Discontent over such policies creates distrust among American Muslims and thereby makes some individuals less likely to cooperate or even engage with law enforcement.

The second barrier has to do with imperfect information. Unfortunately much of the confrontational nature that characterizes the relationship between many Muslim communities and law enforcement officials has to do with the training the latter receive on Islam and Muslims. Unfortunately, there is a subset of self-styled private industry counterterrorism "experts" who have sought to distort the image of Islam and Muslims under the guise of law enforcement training. Such training creates bias and hostility toward communities before there is even a chance for interpersonal engagement. This situation mainly exists due to the flawed training that has been continuing unchecked due to lack of regulatory frameworks and structural incentives to promote non-biased, evidence-based training (Cincotta 2011; Griffin and Johnston 2011; Muslim American Civil Liberties Coalition 2011; Stalcup and Craze 2011; Temple-Raston 2011).

Third, is cultural and historical. All the community leaders and activists stressed that some Muslim community members—immigrant or indigenous African American—may have skewed perceptions of law enforcement due to some prior negative experience. For some, such as African American community members, these experiences are based on the legacies of racism and discrimination in America. Others, such as Muslim immigrants, may harbor such misconceptions due to the oppressive nature of law enforcement agencies in their homelands[2] (Wasserman 2010, 14–15). Another way to describe these experiences is that many Muslim immigrants are accustomed to law enforcement "serving and protecting" *the regime*, not "serving and protecting" *the community*. In the current political climate of intense anti-Muslim bigotry, the policies and unscrupulous actions of a minority of law enforcement actors have not been helpful, adding to these varied anxieties.

Fourth, are political reasons. Certain organizations have been placed on an "un-indicted co-conspirator list" (United Stated District Court for Northern Texas 2007), which has no legal significance (Robbins 2006, 442), but politically is the equivalent of a blacklist. At least one federal law enforcement agency has used this list to justify complete disengagement—rightly or wrongly—with such organizations (Federal Bureau of Investigation 2009). Reflected in official public correspondences, this immediately strained relations with other Muslim community organizations engaging federal law enforcement at the time (Islamic Shura Council of Southern California 2009).

Fifth, it has to do with internal disagreements over the utility of engaging with law enforcement. Concerns over civil liberties and other factors have created a great deal of intracommunity discussions about working with police. Although such discussions generally take place in private, they have occasionally spilled over into the public spotlight. One example was community uproar over the Craig Monteilh scandal. Montelih, an ex-convict in Southern California, publicly claimed in 2009 that he was a paid FBI informant asked to do surveillance over mosques and other Muslim community centers.

In response, a number of Muslim civil liberties and advocacy groups stated they were considering cutting ties with the FBI (American

Muslim Task Force 2009). Even those advocacy organizations that had previously affirmed their commitment to maintaining engagement with law enforcement (Kuruvila 2009; Marks 2009) noted that the controversy surrounding the allegations had the FBI, "Losing Partnership with [the] American Muslim Community" (Muslim Public Affairs Council 2009).

In the next section, I conduct a brief overview of the current state of research that seeks to identify best practices and frameworks for strong partnerships from the perspectives of American Muslim community members and identify potential gaps in the literature.

## Literature Review and Critique

It is in this post-9/11 context that academics, law enforcement officials, and even community advocates have engaged in research on identifying which theoretical policing paradigms, policy frameworks, and concrete practices are the most effective at eliciting community antiterrorism assistance. With this broader research movement, there is a small but growing body of literature that examines the impact and effectiveness of certain policing practices from the perspective of American Muslim community members. Three studies are worth briefly examining.

The first study is a 2010 study by a trio of law and psychology professors, Tom Tyler, Stephen Schulhofer, and Aziz Huq, at New York University and the University of Chicago (Tyler, Schulhofer, and Huq 2010). Their inquiry involved an empirical examination of whether people respond to counterterrorism policing out of a belief that police are a legitimate authority, or because they perceive cooperation brings them greater benefits than costs. Their research found that American Muslims are much more likely to say they would cooperate with the police based on factors that support a normative model of policing: when police are viewed as a legitimate authority. The research design involved conducting a telephone survey with 300 Muslim respondents living in New York City.

The second and third studies are a pair of reports published in 2010—one from Duke University, *Anti-Terror Lessons of Muslim Americans* (Schanzer, Kurzman, and Moosa 2010), and the other produced by this author on behalf of the Muslim Public Affairs Council, *Building Bridges to Strengthen America* (Beutel 2010). Both reports conducted extensive literature reviews and compiled data to provide antiextremism and antiterrorism policy recommendations to both Muslim communities and law enforcement. The Duke study had the additional benefit of conducting over 120 interviews with American Muslims in four cities across the country.

Though each of the studies makes important research contributions, all of them also have their limitations. *Building Bridges* conducted only one formal interview with a community member actively engaged with law enforcement. The Duke University and NYU/University of Chicago studies interviewed hundreds of community members. The Duke study, however, deliberately excluded interviews in large cities such as Chicago, New York, and Los Angeles and did not examine any small-size cities. Meanwhile the NYU/University of Chicago study limited itself to New York City.

However, it is unclear whether or not these included any individuals who are actively involved in law enforcement engagement. Regardless, none of the studies looked into the specific elements in creating a successful partnership between communities and law enforcement. It appears, as far as the author is aware, there is no prior research that seeks to identify best practices for strong antiterrorism partnerships with American Muslims, based on the perspectives of leaders who regularly engage with law enforcement.

## Why This Specific Topic Matters

There are three main reasons why we look at Muslim community leaders and activists who regularly engage law enforcement. First, they are primary means for law enforcement to engage with the broader grassroots groups in a community. Often these individuals will host community events and other forums in which they can invite police to participate and speak.

Second, such individuals are usually considered to be trusted figures in their communities and can leverage that position of authority to play to ordinary community members who might otherwise be hesitant to communicate with police. Even if ordinary community members are unwilling to directly contact law enforcement, engagement leaders and activists can act as an intermediary for communication between the parties.

Finally, these community members often play other roles that are helpful to antiterrorism policing. The case of Mohamed Elibiary in Texas is worth mentioning because it provides an instance of a community member who was involved in a grassroots effort to prevent acts of violence. With the case of Elibiary, prevention of violence was possible through a program that made use of religion-based counseling to effectively dissuade at-risk individuals from engaging in acts of ideologically motivated violence (Robberson 2009; Iftikhar 2010; also see: Harwood 2012).

## RESEARCH DESIGN

This study conducted six interviews with six community leaders and activists in six US metropolitan areas. Interviews were semistructured and conducted over the phone from July 23, 2011, to August 7, 2011. A preliminary pool of interview candidates was identified by the author based on his professional expertise as a staffer for an American Muslim advocacy organization (Muslim Public Affairs Council), at that time, which works on law enforcement issues.

Identified individuals were those people known by the author to have at least five years experience and *ongoing* engagement (at the time of the interviews) with local and/or federal law enforcement officials. All individuals at the time of the interviews had held formal titles of authority—either as an active member of a specific committee whose responsibilities included law enforcement outreach or as an individual with broader executive institutional responsibilities—within his/her local mosque and/or *majlis ash-shura* (regional Muslim coordinating body) in order to demonstrate some measurement of sensitivity to the opinions of local Muslim grassroots opinion.

The interviewee pool was then narrowed to six individuals based on where they lived. As a result, individuals living in the following metropolitan areas were chosen:

- Los Angeles, CA,
- New York, NY,
- Washington, DC,
- Chicago, IL,
- Buffalo, NY, and
- Iowa City, IA

The areas were chosen based on four criteria. First was *varying city and metropolitan area sizes.* New York, Los Angeles, and Chicago are all municipalities that have more than 1 million people. However, all the cities in our study, except Iowa City, have *metropolitan areas* with over 1 million people. The second criterion was *geographic location.* Three of the metropolitan areas are located on the East Coast, two in the Midwest, and one on the West Coast. The third criterion was *location of terrorism-related events.* With the exception of Iowa City, all the cities where phone interviews were conducted had at least one al-Qaeda–related[3] violent conspiracies prevented and/or occur, while New York, Washington, DC, and Chicago have had at least two or more such cases (Bergen, Lebovich, Banks, et al. 2012; Beutel 2012).

The fourth criterion was *likely clusters of sizable Muslim populations.* Although timely and reliable data on American Muslim population sizes and geographic locations are difficult to come by, the author contacted leaders and activists from these specific metropolitan areas because of their likelihood to contain large Muslim populations. This chapter based its estimates of American Muslim geographic population distribution off the Association of Religion Data Archives (ARDA) data of the year 2000, and from the 2009 data by InfoGroup, a private marketing and data collection and analysis consulting company (ARDA 2000; Social Explorer 2011).

Before going further, some caveats are in order. First, this is a preliminary qualitative study with a small sample size ($N = 6$). As a result, this study is not necessarily representative of the opinions of all local American Muslim communities and community leaders engaging with law enforcement officials. However given this-chapter's earlier-mentioned criteria for selecting interviewees, its findings may potentially have some transferability to similar sociopolitical Muslim-law enforcement contexts in other parts of the United States.

Since this study aims to fill the existing gap in the research literature, similar studies need to be replicated in order to test whether or not these findings are valid. Finally, it is important to note that all of the individuals who were interviewed are anonymous to maintain confidentiality and reduce the likelihood of any desirability bias in their responses, to the maximum extent possible.

## Community Feedback on Solutions to Building Trust

Based on the interviews, five recurring themes stood out. First, was a *commitment* on both sides "to stay the course" and remain engaged. This required dealing with internal and external pressures to divide both sides and effectively respond to arguments against partnership. As noted earlier, relations between various communities and law enforcement have fluctuated at different times and different places.

Underlying this commitment to remain engaged is the need for *consistency and sustainability.* Discussions were not a one-time event; meetings were regularly scheduled and conducted. In several metropolitan areas, such as Washington, Chicago, and Buffalo, the initial conversations, particularly in town hall and community round-table forums, were rocky. However through patience, persistence, and professionalism, relations were gradually transformed, in the words of one interviewee, "from mutual suspicion to partnership" (Chicago interviewee).

Maintaining this consistency, however, can be particularly difficult in light of law enforcement personnel rotations from one field office to another. As the Washington interviewee half-jokingly remarked, "Over the last 8 years because of agents constantly coming and going, I have accumulated enough business cards from the FBI that filled an entire shoebox" (Washington DC interviewee).

*Programs* that nurture communication and understanding are also necessary for maintaining the consistency and sustainability of engagements. Chicago and Buffalo interviewees cited the FBI Citizen's Academy as an important mechanism for fostering understanding and awareness of law enforcement operations. The Buffalo interviewee noted the academy helped him to develop a curriculum that was later used to educate community members about standard border security procedures, which might otherwise be potentially misconstrued as profiling. The Los Angeles interviewee also described local programs, such as the LA County Sheriff's Muslim American Homeland Security Congress, as a similarly important program to sustain communication and understanding.

*Which people are present at the discussions and what is discussed.* These are equally important. Interviewees noted that engagement with government officials cannot be limited to federal law enforcement officials about antiterrorism; many community members may interpret this as a sign that they are being stigmatized as suspects. Instead, interviewees emphasized the importance of a whole-of-government style of outreach involving representatives from multiple local, state, and federal departments.

Different communities have different needs. In the unique case of Iowa City, the interviewee noted little friction exists between federal law enforcement and local Muslim communities; however this may be attributed to the fact that there is also little interaction between the two. Most engagement efforts and friction is with local law enforcement and the fault lines of tension are not religious per se; they are mostly race based probably involving sizeable segments of the local community (African Americans and Sudanese immigrants).

Even at events focused on crime prevention, several of the community activists and leaders interviewed specifically noted the visible presence of local and state law enforcement, as well as the regional US attorney (Los Angeles, Washington, DC, Buffalo, NY, and Chicago interviewees). Issues discussed ranged from protection against Internet pedophiles to finding better ways of reporting hate crimes.

Finally, providing specific *mechanisms for input and redress on issues of particular concern must also be taken into consideration.* Ultimately, in addition to contributing to the nation's safety, communities must also seek to ensure that their civil liberties and civil rights are being protected. For instance, the Chicago interviewee noted that the roundtable discussions with DHS helped remove backlogs on immigration-related delays on visas, green cards, and citizenship applications. Los Angeles, Chicago, and Buffalo interviewees specifically pointed out that engagement with law enforcement allowed better cultural competency education to local and federal agencies to ensure effective job performance without infringing or hurting religious sentiments.

## Discussion

Taken at face value, an immediate observation about these responses is that they run contrary to assertions by those who doubt the commitment of American Muslims to partnering with law enforcement, such as US representative Peter King. Representative King had previously asserted that American Muslims are not doing enough to work with law enforcement, criticizing people who, he claims, "are in mainstream Islam, leaders of mosques, leaders of Muslim organizations who do not come forward and denounce, officially denounce, officially cooperate with the police against those extremists and terrorists" (Imus 2010). The level of detail suggesting how to maintain and improve partnerships is a clear indication of their commitment to antiterrorism efforts.

Beyond that, however, it also appears to indicate how fragile some Muslim leaders perceive the partnership to be. Each of the steps outlined also appears to be a reflection of the various barriers, outlined earlier, that community leaders face when building trust.

The need for commitment, consistency, and sustainability appears to be linked to the need for overcoming the internal disagreements and skepticism within communities toward law enforcement and mitigating the effects of anti-Islam material on law enforcement members who may be equally suspicious of partnership with Muslims. Mechanisms of input and redress are clearly an enduring reflection of the ongoing civil liberties concerns of American Muslims in a post-9/11 world. Programs serve as a tangible way for community members, especially those who have had prior negative experiences with law enforcement (outside of post-9/11 civil liberties concerns), to start overcoming those perceptions. Finally, advice on who is at the discussion table and what is being talked about is most likely a way of effectively coping and mitigating the negative institutional effects of anti-Muslim politics by trying to bring as many people to the table as possible and move discussions beyond a particular topic that is felt to have stigmatized their communities.

Unfortunately, none of those issues have been resolved; in fact they have become more intense. While it is difficult to accurately measure factors that influence law enforcement relations with American Muslims, such as fluctuations in the level of surveillance of American Muslim communities, the news of these challenges continues to spread. For instance, since the completion of these initial interviews in July 2011, media has confirmed or revealed the existence of new events that likely contribute to negative community perceptions of law enforcement, and hence damage relations, including:

- Warrantless surveillance of New York City area Muslim communities by the New York City Police Department (NYPD) (Associated Press 2012)
- Evidence of CIA involvement in NYPD surveillance ( Associated Press 2012)
- The pervasive use of anti-Muslim training material by the FBI (Ackerman 2012a and US Department of Defense; Ackerman 2012b)
- FBI abuse of community outreach programs to illegally collect intelligence on Muslims (Huus 2012)

It will be interesting to see what observations and suggestions, if any, these community members would currently offer in light of these recent challenges. While this analysis may seem to imply a certain level of pessimism, that is not necessarily the case. For instance, community engagement prompted swift reviews and thorough removals of anti-Islam material in law enforcement training seminars (Ackerman 2012a). At the local level it has also helped win civil liberties reforms to an antiterrorism program run by the Los Angeles Police Department (Schulz 2012). As a result of this and similar successes, some are now seeing partnership between LAPD and its local Muslim communities as a potential alternative model to the NYPD's approach (Finnigan 2012).

## Conclusion

American Muslims are a part of our nation's growing cultural and religious pluralism and play important roles in keeping our nation safe. With this growing diversity, new opportunities and new challenges are presented on ways to best protect and serve these communities.

The focus of this chapter was to provide a community perspective on barriers to trust with law enforcement and to examine what has been done to overcome those hurdles. Given the historical and current experiences of American Muslims, a conscious and careful effort to build trust is needed. These experiences are strongly reflected in the responses of our interviewees. Although the challenge of trust building is a tough one, particularly in light of recent developments, it is not impossible.

## Notes

1. This chapter defines racial and religious profiling as, "The practice of targeting individuals for police or security interdiction, detention or other disparate treatment based primarily on their race, religion or ethnicity in the belief that certain racial, religious and/or ethnic groups are more likely to engage in unlawful behavior." Alejandro J. Beutel, *Building Bridges to Strengthen America: Forging an Effective Counterterrorism Enterprise between Law Enforcement and Muslim Communities.* (Washington, DC: Muslim Public Affairs Council, 2010). Available at: http://www.mpac.org/assets/docs/publications/building-bridges/MPAC-Building-Bridges–Complete_Unabridged_Paper.pdf.
2. For a comparative case study between community policing in Minneapolis among African American and Somali communities, which illustrates this point, see: Dennis L. Jensen, Enhancing Homeland Security Efforts by Building Strong Relationships Between the Muslim Community and Local Law Enforcement." *Naval Postgraduate School* (March 2006). Available at: http://edocs.nps.edu/npspubs/scholarly/theses/2006/Mar/06Mar_Jensen.pdf.
3. Our conception of al-Qaeda related would include those groups who share a *jihadi* ideological affinity but may not be formally allied with al-Qaeda or its affiliates. This would also include individual lone-wolf actors that are formally not affiliated with any particular group.

## References

9/11 Commission. 2004. "Law Enforcement, Counterterrorism, and Intelligence Collection in the United States Prior to 9/11." Washington, DC: National Commission on Terrorist Attacks Upon the United States. http://bit.ly/QYhJpo.

Ackerman, Spencer. 2012a. "Exclusive: Senior U.S. General Orders Top-To-Bottom Review of Military's Islam Training." Wired.com. April 24. http://bit.ly/Ib6swo.

———. 2012b. "FBI Purges Hundreds of Terrorism Documents in Islamophobia Probe." Wired.com. February 15. http://bit.ly/xGmMbt.

American Civil Liberties Union. 2008. "Fact Sheet—New Attorney General Guidelines." American Civil Liberties Union. October 8. http://www.aclu.org/national-security/fact-sheet-new-attorney-general-guidelines.

American Muslim Taskforce on Civil Rights and Elections. 2009. "U.S. Muslim Coalition Considers Suspending Relations with FBI." American Muslim Taskforce on Civil Rights and Elections. March 17. http://www.americanmuslimtaskforce.net/pView222b.html?action=viewPDetails&pageId=11102&pCatName=%20&pGrpName=%20&pT=Community%20Relations.

*Associated Press*. 2012. "AP's Probe into NYPD Intelligence Operations." http://www.ap.org/Index/AP-In-The-News/NYPD.

Association of Religion Data Archives. 2000. "Muslim Estimate—Number of Congregations (2000)." Association of Religion Data Archives. http://bit.ly/phGWf3.

Barakat, Matthew. 2011. "Frequent Flier Fracas: Muslims Face Travel Woes." *Associated Press*, August 16. http://www.taiwannews.com.tw/etn/news_content.php?id=1680441.

BBC News. 2005. "US Mosques Checked for Radiation." December 24. http://news.bbc.co.uk/2/hi/4557224.stm.

Bergen, Peter. Andrew Lebovich, William Banks, et al., 2012. *Post-9/11 Jihadist Terrorism Cases Involving U.S. Citizens and Residents: An Overview*. Washington DC: New America Foundation.

Berger, J. M. 2012. "PATCON: The FBI's Secret War against the 'Patriot' Movement, and How Infiltration Tactics Relate to Radicalizing Influences." New America Foundation. May, 2012. http://newamerica.net/sites/newamerica.net/files/policydocs/Berger_NSSP_PATCON.pdf.

Beutel, Alejandro J. 2007. "Radicalization and Homegrown Terrorism in Western Muslim Communities: Lessons Learned for America." Minaret of Freedom Institute. http://www.minaret.org/MPAC Backgrounder.pdf.

———. 2012. *Data on Post-9/11 Terrorist in the United States."* Washington DC: Muslim Public Affairs Council. http://www.mpac.org/assets/docs/publications/MPAC-Post-911-Terrorism-Data.pdf.

Buffalo NY Muslim Leader. 2011. Interview by author. Phone interview. Buffalo. August 6.

Chicago Muslim Leader. 2011. Interview by author. Phone interview. Chicago. July 24.

Cincotta, Thom. 2011. *Manufacturing the Muslim Menace: Private Firms, Public Servants & the Threat to Rights and Security*. Somerville, MA: Political Research Associates. http://www.publiceye.org/liberty/training/Muslim_Menace_Complete.pdf.

Federal Bureau of Investigation. 2009. "Letter to Senator John Kyl." Federal Bureau of Investigation, April 28. http://www.investigativeproject.org/documents/misc/265.pdf.

Finnigan, David. 2012. "LAPD Modifies Surveillance Program of Muslims." Religion News Service. May 21. http://wapo.st/JscTxU.

Friedman, Robert, and William J. Cannon. 2007. Homeland Security and Community Policing: Competing or Complementing Public Safety Policies?" *Journal of Homeland Security and Emergency Management* *4*(4): 1–20.

German, Michael. 2005a. "Squaring the Error." In *Law vs. War: Competing Approaches to Fighting Terrorism*. Carlisle, PA: Strategic Studies Institute. http://www.au.af.mil/au/awc/awcgate/ssi/boyne_law_terr.pdf.

———. 2005b. "An FBI Insider's Guide to the 9/11 Commission Report." GlobalSecurity.org. 2005. http://www.globalsecurity.org/security/library/report/2005/guide-iii.htm.

Griffin, Drew, and Kathleen Johnston. 2011. "'Ex-Terrorist' Rakes in Homeland Security Bucks." CNN. July 14. http://www.cnn.com/261011/US/07/11/terrorism.expert/index.html.

Harris, David A. 2009. "Law Enforcement and Intelligence Gathering in Muslim and Immigrant Communities After 9/11." *New York University Review of Law and Social Change 34*(1).

Harwood, Matthew. 2012. "Building a Tenuous Trust." *Security Management*, April 10. http://www.securitymanagement.com/news/building-a-tenuous-trust-009770.

Hassan, Anwer. 2012. "SFPD Secret Agreement with FBI Puts Muslims in Spotlight." *Illume Magazine*, January 27. http://www.illumemagazine.com/zine/articleDetail.php?san-francisco-police-fbi-joint-terrorism-task-force-muslim-community-civil-rights-13942;

Heymann, Philip. 2002. "Muslims in America After 9/11: The Legal Situation." Harvard University. http://www.ces.fas.harvard.edu/conferences/muslims/Heymann.pdf.

Huus, Kari. 2012. "ACLU: FBI 'Mosque Outreach' Program Used to Spy on Muslims." MSNBC. March 29. http://nbcnews.to/Qpoo7K.

Iftikhar, Arsalan. 2010. "Life of a Muslim de-Radicalizer." Altmuslimah.com. April 21. http://www.altmuslimah.com/a/b/print/3659/.

Imus, Don. 2010. Interview with Peter King. Don Imus Show. October 28. http://www.youtube.com/watch?feature=player_embedded&v=Chn4TfQ89m4#!.

Innes, Martin. "Policing Uncertainty: Countering Terror through Community Intelligence and Democratic Policing." *The ANNALS of the American Academy of Political and Social Science 605*(1): 222–241.

Iowa City Muslim Activist. 2011. Interview by author. Phone interview. Iowa City. July 31.

Islamic Shura of Southern California. 2009. "Letter to FBI LA Office Assistant Director Salvador." Islamic Shura Council of Southern California.

February 11. http://www.shuracouncil.org/images/special/onlineDocs/Shura-DOJ_Re_CAIR_Feb2009.pdf.

Jensen, Dennis L. 2006. "Enhancing Homeland Security Efforts by Building Strong Relationships between the Muslim Community and Local Law Enforcement." Naval Post-Graduate School. http://www.dtic.mil/cgi-bin/GetTRDoc?AD=ADA445337.

Jones, Liz. 2011. "Muslims to Protest Mistreatment at US-Canada Border." KUOW.org. July 15. http://www.kuow.org/program.php?id=23960.

Khan, Azmat. 2011. "America and Muslims: By the Numbers." *PBS Frontline,* September 26. http://www.pbs.org/wgbh/pages/frontline/religion/man-behind-mosque/america-and-muslims-by-the-numbers/.

Kristof, Nicholas D. 2002. "All-American Osamas." *New York Times,* June 6. http://www.nytimes.com/2002/06/07/opinion/all-american-osamas.html.

Kuruvila, Matthai. 2009. "U.S. Muslims Debate How Much to Help F.B.I." *San Francisco Chronicle*, April 6. http://articles.sfgate.com/2009–04–06/news/17193854_1_american-muslim-taskforce-muslim-community-american-islamic-relations.

Los Angeles Muslim Activist. 2011. Interview by author. Phone interview. Los Angeles. July 23.

Marks, Alexandra. 2009. "FBI and American Muslims at Odds." *Christian Science Monitor*, March 25. http://www.csmonitor.com/USA/Society/2009/0325/p02s01-ussc.html.

Murray, John. 2005. "Policing Terrorism: A Threat to Community Policing or Just a Shift in Priorities?" *Police Practice and Research* 6(4): 347–361.

Musaji, Sheila. 2011. "Muslim Voices—Part I Fatwas & Formal Statements by Muslim Scholars & Organizations—Updated." *The American Muslim*, January 28. http://theamericanmuslim.org/tam.php/features/articles/muslim_voices_against_extremism_and_terrorism_part_i_fatwas/0012209.

Muslim Advocates. 2009. "Unreasonable Intrusions: Investigating the Politics, Faith & Finances of Americans Returning Home." *Muslim Advocates.* http://www.muslimadvocates.org/documents/Unreasonable_Intrusions_2009.pdf

Muslim American Civil Liberties Coalition. 2011. "MACLC Concern Over NYPD Use of the 'Third Jihad' Film." Muslim American Civil Liberties Coalition. January 28. http://maclc1.files.wordpress.com/2011/02/maclc_letter_-_nypd_-_28_january_2011–1.pdf.

Muslim Public Affairs Council. 2009. "FBI Losing Partnership with American Muslim Community." Muslim Public Affairs Council. February 25. http://www.mpac.org/programs/government-relations/fbi-losing-partnership-with-american-muslim-community.php.

Naurath, Nicole. 2011. "Most Muslim Americans See No Justification for Violence." Abu Dhabi Gallup Center. August 2. http://www.gallup.com/poll/148763/muslim-americans-no-justification-violence.aspx.

New York City, NY, Muslim Leader. 2011. Interview by author. Phone interview. New York City. August 7.

Pew Research Center. 2011. *Muslim Americans: No Signs of Growth in Alienation or Support for Extremism*. Pew Research Center. http://www.people-press.org/2011/08/30/muslim-americans-no-signs-of-growth-in-alienation-or-support-for-extremism/.

———. 2007. *Muslim Americans: Middle Class and Mostly Mainstream*. Washington, DC: Pew Research Center. http://pewresearch.org/assets/pdf/muslim-americans.pdf.

Reske, Henry J. 2011. "Gallup Poll: Most Muslim-Americans Loyal to US." Newsmax.com. August 2. http://www.newsmax.com/US/gallup-muslim-americans-poll/2011/08/02/id/405835.

Robberson, Tod. 2009. "A Better Way to Fight Radicalism." *Dallas Morning News*, October 30. http://www.waayaha.net/view.php?articleid=9243.

Robbins, Ira P. 2007. "Guilty without Charge: Assessing the Due Process Rights of Unindicted Co-Conspirators." *The Federal Courts Law Review 1*: 442.

Schanzer, David. Charles Kurzman, and Ebrahim Moosa. 2010. *The Anti-Terror Lessons of Muslim-Americans*. Duke University. January 6. http://fds.duke.edu/db/attachment/1255.

Schulz, G. W. 2012. "LA Police Agree to Modify Suspicious Activity Intelligence Gathering." Center for Investigative Reporting. May 25. http://cironline.org/reports/la-police-agree-modify-suspicious-activity-intelligence-gathering.

Social Explorer. 2011. "Religion 2009 (InfoGroup)." Social Explorer. http://bit.ly/nPz6VO. (Downloaded "Excel 2003 [xls]" file).

Stalcup, Meg, and Joshua Craze. 2011. "How We Train Our Cops to Fear Islam." *Washington Monthly*, March 3. http://www.washingtonmonthly.com/features/2011/1103.stalcup-craze.html.

Syed, Nafees. 2010. "Screening for 'Flying While Muslim.'" CNN. January 29. http://articles.cnn.com/2010–01–29/opinion/syed.muslim.while.flying_1_profiling-muslim-women-head-scarf.

Temple-Raston, Dina. 2011. "Terrorism Training Casts Pall over Muslim Employee." National Public Radio. July 18. http://www.npr.org/2011/07/18/137712352/terrorism-training-casts-pall-over-muslim-employee.

Tu, Janet I. 2008. "Privacy Vs. Border Security: Critics Say Laptop Searches Cross the Line." *Seattle Times*, July 23. http://seattletimes.nwsource.com/html/localnews/2008067440_searches23m0.html.

Tyler, Tom, Stephen Schulhofer, and Aziz Huq. 2010. "Legitimacy and Deterrence Effects in Counter-Terrorism Policing: A Study of Muslim Americans." New York: NY, New York University/University of Chicago. http://papers.ssrn.com/sol3/papers.cfm?abstract_id=1559923.

United States District Court for the Northern District of Texas. 2007. "United States v. Holy Land Foundation for Relief and Development—Attachment A: List of Unindicted Co-conspirators and/or Joint Venturers." United

States District Court for the Northern District of Texas. http://www.investigativeproject.org/documents/case_docs/423.pdf.

Washington, DC. Muslim Activist. Interview by author. Phone Interview. Washington DC. July 24.

Wasserman, Robert. 2010. *Guidance for Building Communities of Trust.* Washington, DC: COPS Office US Department of Justice.

12

# Building Bridges: The Experience of Leaders in Detroit, Michigan

*Ihsan Alkhatib*

The 9/11 attacks constitute a transformational event in American history. A community that suffered and still suffers from the aftermath of these attacks is the Arab and Muslim American community.[1] Due to the challenges faced in the aftermath of 9/11, the Arab American community leadership in Detroit and law enforcement started having frequent meetings to deal with issues of concern. Recognizing the importance of regular dialogue, Imad Hamad of ADC (Arab American Anti-Discrimination Committee) Michigan, then US attorney Jeffrey Collins, and then FBI Detroit agent-in-charge John Bell agreed to institutionalize these meetings by having them held in a forum under the name of BRIDGES (Building Respect in Diverse Groups to Enhance Sensitivity). BRIDGES was co-chaired by Mr. Hamad and Mr. Collins. This chapter seeks to answer questions about BRIDGES based on interviews of a number of its members who agreed to answer questions about their participation in that forum. The answers make it clear that the participants value BRIDGES, and see it as primarily a communication channel between the government and the community that is still relevant and needed even ten years after the attacks of 9/11 and that can serve as a model of community–law enforcement interaction elsewhere as well.

I write this chapter as a participant in BRIDGES from its inception. I have been involved with BRIDGES in my capacity, at various times, as an ADC volunteer, ADC Detroit chapter chair, ADC Michigan advisory board chair, and currently as advisory board member. I have attended most of the meetings over the years and I know personally many of the participants. I am indebted to my friend Imad Hamad for involving me in ADC, and am thankful for all of those interviewees who agreed to be interviewed for this chapter.

## COMMUNITY RELATIONS AND TERRORISM

In *Domestic Terrorism: A National Assessment of State and Local Preparedness*, Kevin Jack Riley and Bruce Hoffman (1995) identify seven future research areas: preventive intelligence, border security, training, monitoring and evaluation, technology developments, community relations, and conferences. Regarding community relations they write:

> How can law enforcement relations with often closed, scared and in many instances, isolated communities such as religious and messianic sects be affected and improved so that law enforcement can better respond to, and have fewer misunderstandings with, these groups? This project takes on particular relevance after the incident in Waco, and in light of the terrorism threats many smaller communities reported. (Riley and Hoffman 1995, 44)

The BRIDGES experience is useful to shed light on the subject of community relations. Is BRIDGES a useful tool in improving relations with the Arab American and Muslim community? Does it contribute to fewer misunderstandings between law enforcement and the Arab American community?

## BRIDGES: BETWEEN TEMPLATE AND DOUBTFUL SUCCESS

The experience of BRIDGES has caught the attention of academics interested in Arab American issues and those interested in law enforcement and civil rights and civil liberties.[2] Ramirez, O'Connell, and Zafar (2004) write about BRIDGES approvingly, seeing it as a mutually beneficial arrangement for both the government and the Arab American community, an experience that can serve as a model for law enforcement-community engagement.[3] The benefits include providing a forum to "debunk growing negative stereotypes" and include "effective hate crime protocols" (Ramirez, O'Connell, and Zafar 2004, 4). Scholars who study Arab Americans who examined the BRIDGES experience had a mixed evaluation of BRIDGES, highlighting the positive of the experience as well as criticism. On the positive aspect of the experience, in *Being and Belonging*, Howell and Jamal write:

> In 2005, several of the people we interviewed for this project were cautiously, if also strategically, optimistic about the benefits that flowed from the BRIDGES alliance, pointing to sustained dialogue between the state and the community that enabled all parties to clarify legal, linguistic, and cultural matters in ways that improved the application of federal laws on the ground. Arab leaders argued that the process made the law enforcement community more accountable to Arab concerns, and law enforcement agreed, adding that it also brought greater trust and public support. Both sides recognized that the familiarity encouraged by an ongoing airing of principles, concerns, and grievances was able to produce better law enforcement and greater cooperation among those involved. Both groups were also able to monitor and safeguard another in ways not yet operative in other parts of the country. (Howell and Jamal 2008, 68)

In the interviews this author conducted for this chapter, the respondents echo these themes of BRIDGES serving as a communication tool, one that is mutually beneficial and as well as trust building. Howell and Jamal continue their discussion of BRIDGES with the criticism that "BRIDGES has not yet been able to challenge the status quo in which the presumption of innocence seems to have been reversed and due process is lacking for Arab and Muslim defendants" (2008, 69). They conclude with doubts about its survival and continuity: "As time passes, the volatility of the BRIDGES alliance has made it less effective and less easy to sustain" (68).

On September 9, 2011, BRIDGES celebrated its tenth anniversary, and a meeting was held by BRIDGES as recently as April 17, 2012. A community leader who knew about BRIDGES but attended it the first time this April related how she was pleasantly surprised by the turnout and the presence of the "government bigwigs" and shared her satisfaction with the arrangement (Anonymous, personal communication, April 2012).[4] What sustained BRIDGES? What made it survive ten turbulent years? The interviews conducted for this chapter are meant to shed light on this reality.

## THE CREATION OF BRIDGES

It has been more than ten years since the creation of BRIDGES. Before 9/11 the interaction between the Arab American community and law enforcement was limited. Due to the challenges faced in the aftermath of 9/11, the community leadership and law enforcement started having frequent meetings to deal with issues of concern. Within three months of these meetings, recognizing the importance of regular dialogue, Imad Hamad of ADC Michigan, then US attorney Jeffrey Collins, and then FBI Detroit agent-in-charge John Bell agreed to have these meetings regularly. On May 16, 2003, almost one year after the regular meetings were first held, the name BRIDGES was given to this arrangement. BRIDGES was co-chaired by Mr. Imad Hamad and the US attorney in Eastern Michigan, Mr. Jeffrey Collins. The fact that Mr. Collins co-chaired BRIDGES signaled the importance of BRIDGES and the commitment of the government to this forum. BRIDGES members are federal law enforcement agencies in Michigan, the US attorney, and community leaders—a total of 22 members.

## ALPACT: History of Community-Law Enforcement Dialogue

Regular meetings between the diverse Michigan community groups and law enforcement are not a new development in Michigan according to Noel Saleh, a veteran attorney and community activist (personal communication, January 24, 2008). Many years before 9/11, regular meetings were held between diverse community groups and law enforcement agencies. ALPACT (Advocates and Leaders for Police and Community Trust), of which ADC Michigan is a member, has for many years held regular meetings with law enforcement and still does. However, ALPACT was not focused on Arab American and Muslim issues, issues that have become front and center after 9/11. It is important to note the ALPACT experience to understand the BRIDGES experience. Noel Saleh emphasized that the legitimacy and acceptance of BRIDGES derives directly from the fact that ALPACT existed and had legitimacy and credibility. This precedent of statewide regular community-law enforcement interaction meant that the stakeholders invited to participate were willing to be part of BRIDGES because they were used to that type of community-law enforcement interaction. Therefore, it was not difficult to recruit community groups and law enforcement to participate in BRIDGES and accept the idea of sitting together to engage in regular dialogue. Imad Hamad agrees that without the existence of ALPACT, more work would have been required to explain the concept and convince both law enforcement and community groups to participate (Imad Hamad, personal communication, January, 2008).

## THE KEY ROLE OF ADC

BRIDGES was set up as a forum that includes both community leaders and law enforcement officials. ADC Michigan regional director Imad Hamad understood the importance of engaging the top leadership of law enforcement. He recognized that people at the top set the tone and that it is at this level that policy is set, attitudes are formed, and accountability is measured. Mr. Hamad saw that ADC as an institution, whose mission was to protect the civil rights and liberties of Arab Americans, needed the federal government as an indispensable partner to achieve this mission. The rationale behind BRIDGES is the recognition by ADC Michigan that having dialogue builds confidence and faith in law enforcement and that the absence of that dialogue builds mistrust. Mr. Hamad had no doubt that in a time of crisis there would not be any difficulty to call for a meeting and have the community leaders and government officials meet. However, he also understood that crisis-driven interaction is far from an ideal mechanism to discuss issues in an environment of mutual trust. He believed that regular meetings help develop rapport and enable the participants to bring up issues and concerns before they grow into full-blown problems. The sense of the need was validated by Senator Carl Levin's advice to Mr. Hamad to get to know government officials working in the Arab and Muslim American community in the Greater Detroit area (Imad Hamad, personal communication, January 2008). ADC Michigan takes individual complaints of discrimination against the private sector as well as against government agencies. Hamad understood that having an established channel of communication between law enforcement and the Arab and Muslim communities could be used by ADC as a mechanism to deal with these complaints received against government agencies.

## THE FUNCTIONS OF BRIDGES

According to Hamad the functions of BRIDGES are the following:

1. Providing a forum for discussion of issues of importance to Arab and Muslims communities.
2. Meeting and knowing the implementers of national policy, implementers who have discretion in carrying out their mandate.
3. Putting a face to the name of the individuals who are major stakeholders. The attendees are the heads of the agencies, not their representatives.

4. Enabling face-to-face communication versus impersonal telephone, letter, and e-mail communication.
5. Communicating concerns of the community freely and directly to those in charge.
6. Understanding the law enforcement issues from the government's point of view.
7. Establishing useful contacts that can help in dealing with issues that come up with specific government agencies (access).
8. Getting accurate information that helps debunk myths and rumors on the street.
9. Holding town hall meetings to address pertinent issues directly with the greater community.
10. Solving problems.

## THE BRIDGES EXPERIENCE: TEN YEARS LATER

BRIDGES came into existence ten years ago, and the faces of the participants, especially on the government side, have changed. However, the meetings are still held regularly. BRIDGES today is as relevant as it was at the time of its inception. The global war on terror, the fear of future attacks on the United States, and US foreign policy in the Middle East, all put stresses on the Arab and Muslim American community. Mr. Imad Hamad, as a participant in the community side of the equation, believes that the community's confidence in its organizations, including ADC, and the belief in the importance of reaching out and enabling dialogue, provide the necessary setting for the continued engagement with the government.

To get a better understanding of BRIDGES, Mr. Hamad, the co-chair of BRIDGES, was approached with the idea of interviewing BRIDGES members about their experience with BRIDGES. He e-mailed the participants and encouraged them to agree to be interviewed. The following discussion is based on phone and e-mail interviews with seven members of BRIDGES who responded to the invitation. The following questions were asked:

1. How long have you been involved with BRIDGES?
2. What percentage of its meetings have you attended?
3. What are the goals of BRIDGES?
4. Has BRIDGES been able to achieve these goals? Please give examples.
5. What issues has BRIDGES been successful at dealing with? Unsuccessful at?

6. How has BRIDGES impacted the Arab American and Chaldean community as well as law enforcement?
7. What is your overall evaluation of BRIDGES?
8. How do you see the future of BRIDGES? Is it still needed?
9. What improvements/changes, if any, could be made to improve BRIDGES and help it better achieve its goals?
10. Do you think that BRIDGES is a model of community-law enforcement forum that can be replicated nationwide?

Interviewees were told to feel free to share any ideas or raise any issues that were not part of these questions, but they think are important.

## The Goals of BRIDGES

The interviewees all agreed that communication was key for the success of BRIDGES. The sole interviewee from the government side stated that the goal of BRIDGES was "to foster dialogue, to share information, to improve understanding, and to build trust between members of the Arab, Muslim, Chaldean and other Middle Eastern communities and law enforcement in the Eastern District of Michigan." The government participant was the only interviewee who mentioned the issue of trust as a goal. One participant who recently started attending the meetings stated that the goal was to "bring leaders and government employees together to discuss outstanding issues." A longtime participant and community leader stated that the goals are

> primarily to bring about a better and more accurate understanding of the culture, religion, norms, traditions and the way of thinking of people from the Middle East region and to create and maintain open channels of communication between the law enforcement community and the community at large. Its basic premise was that: diversity and differences can and shall be used as a source of strength and not weakness. Create awareness that being different should not be viewed as being non-patriotic, inferior or hostile.

The communication aspect was singled out by three other participants with one stating "it's a communication tool between the government and the community," "it's a forum for discussion of issues with the government," and "it provides a communication tool that helps dispel misconceptions. The government made it clear that we are not here to change the policy but to talk about implementing things. It's a back and forth communication process." Only one participant mentioned the other goals that are stressed by ADC such as solving problems and knowing the implementers of policy on the ground.

The goals are multifold. They include but are not limited to (a) bridging the understanding between government officials and community leaders from different persuasions (i.e., Arab, Chaldean, Muslim, Christian, clergy, imam, civil advocates, cultural advocates); (b) dispelling myths that exist between/among the attending parties; (c) addressing common community concerns; (d) devising solutions in a collaborative fashion; (e) knowing persons on a first-name basis; and (f) and educating the community about its mission.

## Success at Achieving Goals

There is a consensus that BRIDGES has been able to achieve its goals. In evaluating the success of BRIDGES, the general tendency of the interviewees was to think of BRIDGES as a communication channel and consider it a success as such. The government interviewee was unequivocal about the success: "BRIDGES has been successful in achieving its goals, though we constantly strive to do more." The community interviewees considered BRIDGES as a communication and educational tool mainly for the government, and therefore saw that BRIDGES was successful in achieving its goals. One longtime participant and community leader stated:

> BRIDGES has come a long way since the date of its formation and succeeded in creating awareness and better understanding which prompted sensitivity training by numerous federal agencies in the Detroit Area. The net result of this was that law enforcement became better educated and more comfortable dealing with the community and had a more profound understanding of why certain things happen in a certain way in the community which also helped the community. Federal Agencies have also benefited from learning that matters and events are not necessarily the way they are portrayed via the news media. If I may give an example, federal prosecutions that were taken place in Detroit went through a period of time during which any Arab American charged with illegal activities which were not different in nature or type than activities other ethnic Americans were engaged in always carried an added charge of terrorism or supporting terrorist organizations regardless of whether merited or not. Charges against Arab Americans and Muslim Americans in the Detroit Area were tried on the pages of newspapers and evening news casts rather than in courts where they belonged. BRIDGES takes pride in the fact that its efforts succeeded in eliminating this practice which helped both law enforcement and the community in avoiding a great deal of hardship,

> polarization and alienation and forged a closer relationship between the community and law enforcement."

Others stated that "the government hears from the community and sees its reaction"; another stated that it was a two-way education process: "Community leaders became more educated about how the government operates; law enforcement became more educated about religious and cultural sensitivities."

## Examples of Successes and Failures

In evaluating the particular instances of successes and failures of BRIDGES the government interviewee emphasized the forum-for-discussion aspect of BRIDGES:

> BRIDGES has been successful in a number of ways. BRIDGES organized a program on charitable giving for members of the community, featuring speakers from the U.S. Department of Treasury. BRIDGES has also facilitated Arab and Muslim cultural training for Customs and Border Protection officers. In addition, BRIDGES has served as a forum for discussions of issues such as the no-fly list, TSA practices, CBP border inspections, the FBI's use of informants in mosques, the defacing of a prayer calendar by a federal agent, and the fatal shooting of a local imam by the FBI during an arrest, among others. Even when we disagree, these discussions help enhance understanding between law enforcement and community leaders. BRIDGES also has challenges. For example, we are always seeking ways to reach all of the varied Arab, Muslim, Chaldean and Middle Eastern communities in our district.

Two participants when asked about successes and failures remarked about specific cases that were brought up in meetings and their resolution:

> BRIDGES was able to address many of the issues facing the community in terms of law enforcement, ethnic profiling and border crossing. Being in Michigan presented a unique problem where members of the Arab American and Middle eastern communities living in the United States and Canada were faced with many border crossing issues which resulted in the unnecessary waste of resources on the part of the government and resulted in prolonged delays at border crossings. BRIDGES was instrumental in rectifying many of the problems and improved the then unsettled state of affairs. However, many issues remain unresolved and cases of long unjustified detentions continue to linger.

The second participant mentioned the specific cases resolved as successes but the inability to change policy as a failure:

> BRIDGES has been successful with dealing with particular cases. People put on the no-fly list for no reason at all. There are border stop and search cases that were resolved. There is the case of a three year old child named Saddam Hussein. The family used to be stopped for 8–9 hours when traveling outside the country. After bringing the matter up a number of times, the matter was resolved. They said they will fix the problem and finally they did something. We are unsuccessful at changing policy and having the question is how to change the policies to better ones. We barely scratch the surface of the problem.

Another participant alluding to the inability to change policy stated that BRIDGES succeeded in reducing suspicion of the government but was unsuccessful at having the government "follow through with community concerns."

One veteran activist who attended BRIDGES from the beginning of the meetings praised its success as a communication tool and educational tool, but was suspicious of the government and its sincerity in reaching out to the community. To him, the forum did not build trust in the government's intentions, a goal that the government participant and ADC had in mind as a goal for BRIDGES:

> At some of the meetings the government clarified the difference between material support of terror and freedom of speech. That was useful to learn. We get to learn how the government is thinking on issues of concern to us. But the trust issue. Sometimes we feel that the government does not see us as partners. That they see us more as a liability. We get the sense that they are not interested in real solutions. This does not apply to all government participants in BRIDGES. We conveyed to the government the need to hire people from our community not as informers but in positions in law enforcement. Although we are serious, we sometimes get the sense that the government is more interested in the project as PR. We keep bringing up the same issues, over and again. We don't see ourselves in the DHS or the FBI? Where is our voice from within government? We need the government to hire our people. The successes have been with individual issues/cases. How about the community systemic issues?

## IMPACT ON COMMUNITY AND LAW ENFORCEMENT

While all the interviewees saw BRIDGES as having a positive impact on the community and on law enforcement, they disagreed on what that impact is. None of the community participants raised building trust as a goal for BRIDGES, one young participant saw the impact of BRIDGES as building trust between the two parties. The government participant emphasized the trust factor with law enforcement trust in the community implicit in her answer:

> I am hopeful that the Arab American and Chaldean communities have gained trust and understanding of law enforcement efforts and practices. For our region to thrive, we need immigrant communities to feel welcome to live and do business here. By meeting with law enforcement leaders and learning more about their work, I am hopeful that community members have greater trust in the men and women performing these important jobs. I am also hopeful that because of improved trust, law enforcement benefits from community members who feel confident to report when they are victims of or witnesses to crime.

Four participants identified awareness of issues/learning on both sides as the impact of BRIDGES.

Only one participant saw the impact of BRIDGES as reducing community fear of government, though he was cynical about the government using the forum as a tool to collect intelligence about the community:

> The biggest impact is on reducing the fear of government. In this area there is no fear about interacting with the government. In other areas I have visited I see a fear of the government. They wonder how I sit and interact with the government. There is no fear of government in Dearborn, whether it is the DHS or FBI—if it exists—it is not at the same magnitude as other areas I have visited. Other communities are afraid to speak that they have a problem. I meet people in other areas who are afraid to complain or even hire an attorney if they have an issue with the government. In the Detroit area I don't sense this problem and I believe at least part of the reason is BRIDGES. The impact on law enforcement is that they know our concern, it's like collecting intelligence. BRIDGES benefits the government more than benefits us—they get information and insight into our community.

## Overall Evaluation of BRIDGES

Interviewees were asked for an overall evaluation of BRIDGES. Even those who had strong concerns about BRIDGES saw it as mostly valuable and wished that it continued. The government interviewee had the most positive evaluation: "I think that BRIDGES is an outstanding example of government of, by and for the people. BRIDGES enhances both the community and law enforcement in all of the ways discussed above." One community participant interviewee was almost as positive as the government interview, but added a government-community open-conflict prevention dimension to BRIDGES: "While we continue to have a long road ahead of us, BRIDGES has been very instrumental and extremely successful in resolving many of the issues facing Arab Americans and Chaldean Americans and in no uncertain terms created a mechanism and venue to address issues of mutual concerns before escalating out of proportion." Another focused on BRIDGES being a connection between the community and the government: "I think it's an excellent tool to serve its name as bridge."

Two interviewees emphasized the information-exchange element of the arrangement. One interviewee stated that the "meetings are educational and increases awareness of both sides. It minimizes the fears of the community," while the other said that BRIDGES is "still needed as a communication channel." Another interviewee mentioned the importance of BRIDGES as a communication tool but saw the arrangement as mainly benefiting the government:

> Meeting with the government helps them more than helps us. It's more to the government's advantage. They come to us and say this is how things are and how they will affect their community. The question [the government officials ask] is not how we can change things. It is a good forum of communication though. Sometimes I find that the government takes it more seriously than some of those attending from the community.

Two interviewees saw BRIDGES as a much needed communication tool between the government and the community, and they focused on BRIDGES undergoing different phases with the government and community participants' attitudes toward the forum changing with time. One interviewee stated:

> BRIDGES goes through phases. From the government side you see that some are more interested in the project than others. At one point there was a sense that the government was not serious about engaging the community. As to the community, in the past 2–3 years I have seen low turnout. My overall evaluation is that there are no real tangible results.

## The Future of BRIDGES

The interviewees' consensus is that, ten years after 9/11, BRIDGES is still needed. All the interviewees were certain that there still existed a need for BRIDGES, though their reasons for its continuance varied. The government interviewee linked BRIDGES to 9/11 backlash: "I think that BRIDGES is still needed as members of our community continue to face the backlash of 9/11." Two interviewees answered along the same lines as the government interviewee, with one stating that "given the political environment we are in, I see that it is still needed. It is a direct line to government. It is very valuable." The other said that "it is needed. The more the community is afflicted, the more bridges are needed."

One longtime member linked the need for BRIDGES to continue into the future to the persistent discrimination that exists in American society at large:

> No matter how advanced our system will become, biases, prejudices and pockets of discrimination will continue to exist and as such, I see BRIDGES as an ongoing need for both government and the community to continue to have a venue to address issues of common concern. It is our hope that the need to rely on it will diminish as we grow into nation at peace with itself, but as long as we continue to have vestiges of discrimination and segregation, it is my opinion that BRIDGES will continue to be needed to serve a useful and needed role.

Again the theme of communication reappears with one interviewee stating that "BRIDGES is needed because there are always issues coming up," referring to the need for a forum to discuss these issues.

An interviewee linked the need for the continuation of BRIDGES to the political weakness of the community and what he sees as lack of effective community organization:

> Most people who attend say that they are frustrated. We are sincere and the government is not responsive enough. We get nice talk, they are pleasant, but nothing happens. Some people want to cancel it. It is still needed. Despite the criticisms, it is needed as a communication tool. We are a weak community, not organized. BRIDGES is not ideal but we have no other options. The response we get is basically I am doing my job. What can you tell someone who says that? Please convey our concerns to top officials at Justice and DHS. We get no results.

## Changes Needed

All the interviewees spoke about changes that were need to be made in BRIDGES. One interviewee expressed surprise that not many in the community know about the existence of BRIDGES and that changes needed to be made to promote it in the community: "More people need to know about it. I have met many people who are active in the community and yet never heard of BRIDGES."

The government interviewee indicated that changes have been made due to the increased interest in BRIDGES, that there are two tiers of membership—general membership and a steering committee. The government interviewee indicated interest in expanding dialogue to other communities:

> In light of the tremendous growth of BRIDGES, which attracts large crowds to its meetings, we have recently created a small steering committee to help set agenda items and foster more meaningful dialogue. We are hopeful that this model will help define issues. In addition, we are always looking for ways to reach more groups in our varied Arab, Muslim, Chaldean and Middle Eastern communities.

One interviewee who was involved with BRIDGES from its inception concurred with the government interviewee's position of the need to include others but hinted about the problematic division within the Arab and Chaldean communities by stating: "It is my opinion that there will always be a need and room for improvement to BRIDGES which also applies to any community organization. Inclusivity without compromising the quality and the nature of discussion will always be a challenge. Competing interests, agendas and goals of the various ethnic communities undermine the overall success of the organization, at times, and it is in this area that BRIDGES can and should improve."

Two participants expressed frustration that the same issues keep coming up in every meeting: "It seems we always revisit the [same] issues." The second interviewee to raise this point expanded on the complaint:

> The same questions come up. Who is at the table, who determines membership, the leadership issue? The same questions come up. Housekeeping issues are still a hindrance. I would like to see a concrete format. Everybody can't be involved? We are always sidetracked by questions of why we are here. There is the Arab and Chaldean issue that comes up a lot.

Two interviewees who saw the role of BRIDGES as vital and worthy as a communication channel focused on the need for substantive changes to make BRIDGES more than a communication channel. One said: "Perhaps have official appointments as part of the team, increased role in policy making, congressional sessions." The second interviewee to make the same point was more critical of BRIDGES and its other participants questioning whether all those who attend are really community leaders or people looking out for their self-interest:

> [Changes are] Very difficult. Perhaps meeting with top-level people at the policy-making level. Every three months there is a meeting but even that is PR. There is a secular dominance in composition of BRIDGES. It needs to include more clergy and leaders of institutions and organizations. There is an issue of who is attending from the community side. 10 % are real leaders. Some who attend simply bring personal issues or emotional issues. One person who was mistreated at the border came nervous to the meeting. Only 50% of the attendees understand what BRIDGES is about. Some misunderstand it as a magic solution to all our problems.

## BRIDGES as a Model

The participants that were interviewed were all in agreement that BRIDGES is needed and useful primarily as a communication tool between the government and the community. Given the success of BRIDGES, having survived ten tumultuous years, it is a model that can be replicated elsewhere. One person who recently began attending the meetings was not sure if the model could be replicated elsewhere. The government interviewee's answer was "yes," with conditions related to the demographic presence of the community: "I think that the BRIDGES model can be replicated in other communities similar to ours—with sizeable and diverse Arab, Muslim and Chaldean communities." The other interviewees were in agreement that it could be implemented elsewhere.

An interviewee who attended more than 90 percent of the meetings of BRIDGES from the beginning stated:

> Based on the input from the different law enforcement agencies and in light of the fact that the Detroit Metro Area and the State of Michigan is home of the largest Arab American concentration outside of the Middle East, BRIDGES has been given high marks and it seems to have set the bench mark and the role model that others have attempted to emulate which gives me the confidence to say that BRIDGES is the role model to follow and it will perhaps benefit others from its experiences.

One person agreed that it is a model but added: "We suggested that [the BRIDGES model to community leaders] to other areas. They [The community leaders] did not seem convinced of the concept."

The most involved member in BRIDGES, a founding father, Imad Hamad of ADC, who has served as the co-chair of BRIDGES from its inception, offered the following explanation to Howell and Jamal (2008) when asked about why the model has not been successfully replicated elsewhere in the nation:

> Imad Hamad laments the fact that BRIDGES, though replicated in other locations, has met with only local success in eastern Michigan and has been able to intervene positively only on a case-by-case basis. "Of course, the dialog needs to be with policy makers and not just those who implements policies," he argues. "For BRIDGES to make a difference outside Michigan, we need to communicate with those in D.C. and not only those who are in Detroit." (Interview, 2005) (2008, 70)

To assess the reasons for the failure to recreate BRIDGES in other parts of the country one needs to interview the stakeholders involved, the law enforcement, and the community leaders who have tried to build on this model but failed, as well as those who did not consider using such a model. Future researchers will need to examine this issue.

## CONCLUSION

A forum developed in the aftermath of the attacks of 9/11 to deal with the challenges facing the community and law enforcement is still in existence ten years later. Participants who included those with a two-year or less involvement and those whose involvement dates back to the group's inception were asked for their opinion concerning this important community-law enforcement forum. There were areas of agreement and areas of disagreement among the interviewees. The interviewees disagreed on the goals, successes and failures, and the changes needed, but were in agreement about BRIDGES being successful in achieving its goals, being overall a worthy arrangement that is needed in the future and that can serve as model of community-law enforcement relations. The answers given reveal that while different participants see the goals, successes and failures, and the changes needed differently, these differences do not go to the core of BRIDGES and its mission. Despite the shortcomings that a number of participants highlighted, and a dose of cynicism that some participants revealed, all the members agree that it is needed as a communication tool and that it is a model of community-law enforcement forum that can be duplicated nationwide.

## NOTES

1. The ADC Michigan regional office witnessed a substantial increase in claims of discrimination by Arab Americans in the Greater Detroit area in the aftermath of the 9/11 attacks. These incidents and others were documented in the ADC report of 2002: "The Arab American Experience After September 11: Healing the Nation."
2. See, for example, Sally Howell and Amaney Jamal discuss the BRIDGES experience in the context of the post-9/11 Arab American experience. The same discussion appears in three books, *Being and Belonging: Muslims in the United States Since 9/11* (2008); *Citizenship and Crisis: Arab Detroit after 9/11* (2009); and *Race and Arab Americans: Before and After 9/11: From Invisible Citizens to Visible Subjects.* Ramirez, O'Connell and Zafar (2004) discuss BRIDGES in the context of relations between targeted ethnic communities and law enforcement in the post-9/11 environment.
3. Deborah Ramirez wrote and spoke extensively and approvingly at a number of meetings that this author attended in the United States and abroad. Professor Ramirez wanted to establish a law-enforcement training center that trains law enforcement on the lessons of successful community engagement such as the BRIDGES examples. Her efforts were defeated by political intervention that contributed to the FBI backing out from the project.
4. Anonymous refers to a state government employee who is not authorized by her agency to speak on record.

## REFERENCES

Arab American Anti-Discrimination Committee (ADC). 2002. "The Arab American Experience After September 11: Healing the Nation." Washington, DC: Arab American Anti-Discrimination Committee.

Howell, Sally, and Amaney Jamal. 2008. "Detroit Exceptionalism and the Limits of Political Incorporation." In *Being and Belonging: Muslims in the United States since 9/11.* Edited by Katherine Pratt Ewing. New York: Russell Sage Foundation.

Ramirez, Deborah, Sasha Cohen O'Connell, and Rabia Zafar. 2004. *A Promising Practice Guide: Developing Partnerships between Law Enforcement and American Muslim, Arab, and Sikh Communities.* New York: Open Society Institute.

Riley, Kevin Jack, and Bruce Hoffman. 1995. *Domestic Terrorism: A National Assessment of State and Local Preparedness.* Santa Monica, CA: RAND.

13

# Lessons Learned and Best Practices: The Outreach Efforts of the Los Angeles County Sheriff's Department Community Policing Method with Emphasis on the Muslim Community

*Mike Abdeen*

## History

After the 2005 London bombing, Sheriff Leroy D. Baca, the sheriff of Los Angeles County in Southern California, invited the leaders of the Muslim community to meet with him and discuss methods of cooperation to prevent any further such acts in Los Angeles. The sheriff understood that building relationships and trust with the Muslim community in his county, rather than alienating them, would encourage the community to be an important partner in finding a solution to extremism, and it would also reduce the tension and the fear of law enforcement among the community. Several meetings and discussions were held, and the result was the establishment of the Muslim American Homeland Security Congress also known as MAHSC. It consists of leaders of Muslim organizations (the Muslim Public Affairs Council, the Council on American Islamic Relations, the Shura Council) and members of some of the larger-sized Islamic centers in the Los Angeles area (Islamic Center of Southern California, Islamic Center of San Gabriel Valley, Omar Ibn Al Khattab Center, and the Iranian American Muslim Association of North America and Cultural Center).

The sheriff envisioned MAHSC playing a leading role in developing programs to benefit the community and offer training and education to staff members on community concerns and cultural awareness. The relationship and trust between law enforcement and the Muslim community was at its lowest then due to increased government surveillance and investigations conducted on members of the community after the events of September 11, 2001. As regards this, the experience of Muslims in Los Angeles County was no different from that of Muslims in other cities in the United States. In addition, the role of MAHSC changed to having a more political and social relationship with the sheriff, largely due to the fact that most MAHSC board members were either volunteers or active members of various Muslim organizations with their own goals and agendas that did not necessarily represent the community on a grassroots level. In order to accommodate this shift, the sheriff established the outreach program with full-time Sheriff's Department staff.

## Community Liaison

The position of a Muslim community liaison officer was established in 2007 to complement the efforts of the MAHSC and to develop an outreach program with the intent of restoring community trust, building bridges, and developing educational programs that would benefit the Muslim community as well as the sheriff's personnel. A Muslim Arab American sergeant from the Sheriff's Department was tasked with this duty on a full-time basis. At first, the sergeant worked on his own, without any other dedicated staff for support.

Generally speaking, the interaction between the liaison officer and imams and community leaders was cordial. However, MAHSC members felt threatened that a liaison officer could replace their organization and jeopardize their relationship with the sheriff. In addition, the selection of leaders was done so quickly, without proper vetting of true leadership and community representation, and therefore cooperation at first from MAHSC board members was limited. Trust and relationship building takes time, and it was not until a year later and changes in MAHSC leadership that the efforts started to pay off. The phone was ringing, requests for attendance to community events increased, and relationships began to be fostered on a personal basis, one mosque at a time.

## Growth, Development, and Staffing

Success and hope of a better relationship requires that you maintain it while continuously working on developing new ones, and that requires more resources and staffing. The sheriff believed in the outreach efforts and the philosophy of community trust policing, and therefore did not hesitate to assign another full-time Muslim American deputy sheriff to assist in the development of the program. The selection of one full-time Muslim deputy and four part-time deputies to work with the Muslim community proved to be of great value in gaining the trust and building stronger relationships. The addition of another deputy and access to some other staff for assistance when needed allowed the expansion of the program and took it to the next level.

## The Muslim Community Affairs Unit

Eventually, the Muslim Community Liaison Officers assignment became the Muslim Community Affairs Unit. The unit was developed with the mission of building trust and a stronger relationship with the Muslim community for better understanding and cooperation with law enforcement. For the community to understand the importance of their participation, the approach of the outreach had to bring in some benefits to Islamic centers and their congregations; several programs were developed to assist with the daily quality of life issues. A phone number, an e-mail address, and a website were eventually developed to assist community members in connecting with the Sheriff's Department and learning how to express their concerns. Although building trust and relationship with the community was a major component of the outreach program, the Muslim community comprised various ethnic groups with different backgrounds and issues and learning the community and identifying leaders was a constant challenge. There were a lot of people who claimed leadership in the community to gain status, but had little influence on the members. Identifying an effective leader who possesses the quality and charisma to influence people in the center required close observation during events and functions at the particular location.

## Interaction with Youth and Young Leaders

Besides reaching out to the community and community leaders, it was equally important to reach out to the younger generation; this was a challenge by itself. We wanted to develop a youth group and engage them in programs that would be good for them, from a basic community policing approach, to protect them from getting into trouble and offering them an alternative. Muslim youth are no different from any other youth in America, they want to play sports, explore, and have fun. However, we found that some Muslim youth often had an identity problem: as much as they wanted to be all-out American boys and girls, parents and immigrant community members wanted them to be Muslims first and attached the ethnic background of their parents' home country to them. You could meet a young high school kid whose parents are from Jordan, Pakistan, Syria, or India identifying themselves as if they were from that country although they might have never been there physically. All they know is what their parents have told them. The first meeting we initiated for youth was at a Sheriff's Department building, and I remember about 15 kids showing up with their parents. When I introduced myself and my ideas of a youth group, parents were very skeptical of our motives and true intentions. Our youth meetings continued to include parents for many months before we earned the parents' trust for talking to their kids without their presence. I asked one of the parents why would he not drop off his kid and his friends and allow them to speak freely without the intimidation of adults. He responded that he was protecting them from being recruited to work with the police. Eventually our youth programs were developed to be for young adults over the age of 18. We did not do this out of intimidation by the parents but rather for logistical reasons, and decided to have our meeting at various locations where youth (14–17 years of age) almost always had to be dropped off and picked up by an adult. Currently, our young adults' program participants are between the ages of 18 and 30 with access to their own transportation as well as access to companies, organizations, and other resources that helped in the expansion of the activities offered to the group.

## YOUNG MALAC

Interaction with young Muslims and adults led to the development of the Young Muslim American Leaders Advisory Council, or Young MALAC. The word "malac" in Arabic means angel, and the group seemed to like the fact that it symbolized something important in their faith, which is the presence of angels. The advisory council now advises the Sheriff's Department on issues of concern to Muslim youth and young adults such as education on domestic violence, work, and participating in civic duty and doing volunteer work in cooperation with law enforcement. In turn we were able to present to youth groups the dangers of radicalization, via the Internet, by using education on Internet safety in general as the topic. Some youth participants shared some of the websites they visited and useful information they came across without knowing how dangerous it might be. Having an advisory council allowed us the opportunity to identify and develop new leadership that we can work with in the next 10, 15, or 20 years.

## Education

Early on during the development of our program we realized the importance of educating not only the community on the functions of the various law enforcement agencies, but also our officers and staff on the communities they serve. It is basic community-oriented policing: you think, *get to know your beat.* However, the Muslim community is somehow often seen as different. The vast majority of Muslims in the United States are well integrated into society and are good law-abiding citizens; they are business owners, doctors, lawyers, cops, professionals, and so on. However, when it comes to practicing the faith, very few officers truly understand what Muslims believe in and how they practice Islam, and officers often lack understanding about the cultural differences and the background of Muslims in the United States. This presented a problem.

A cultural awareness program was developed to educate new officers at the academy on the basics of Islam and the customs of Muslims and their ethnic background, whether they were of Arab, African, Asian, or South Asian descent.

A video titled "Law Enforcement Interaction with the Muslim Community" was developed in partnership with a national Muslim organization in an attempt to help officers on all levels have a better understanding of the cultural differences, which can in turn help them interact with the Muslim community better while performing their duties.

## Coordination

Several police and law enforcement agencies tuned in to the idea of outreach to the Muslim community as a possible method of potentially partnering to solve problems of radicalization or preventing future terrorist activities. On a local level, in Los Angeles and Southern

California, an outreach coordinators' group was developed by the Los Angeles County Sheriff's Department in partnership with Los Angeles Police Department (LAPD) and Los Angeles city office of Human Relations and Community Development. The idea and mission of the group was to coordinate outreach efforts to avoid duplication, share experiences, challenges, and best practices. The group now has developed to include representation from various local, state, and federal agencies such as the Department of Homeland Security, office of the Attorney General, office of the US Attorney, the Federal Bureau of Investigations, and several other branches of government. The coordination among law enforcement agencies reinforces the message of inclusiveness in the community rather than alienation while sharing experiences and expressing consistency and unity in the government stance toward the Muslim community and the genuine efforts to equally protect all citizens.

## CUSTODY ENVIRONMENT

Los Angeles County has one of the largest inmate populations in the United States, with an average of about twenty thousand inmates in five county jails. Prisoners are susceptible to recruitment and radicalization in custody facilities by extremists who teach them a violent form of Islam, or as some call it "prislam." A jail outreach program was developed to address some of these issues as well as to connect inmates with support organizations and centers upon their release from custody, while also ensuring that jails propagate nonviolence in their teachings. Imams and chaplains are not paid for their work and their services to inmates. Rather, they work as volunteers. This creates a challenge of sometimes taking what you get just to fill a need. However, by having an organized custody outreach program, more volunteers could be recruited and encouraged to participate in such a program by partnering with the outside outreach coordinators and utilizing the relationships built with local imams and mosque leaders to promote the idea of volunteering in jails and prisons. This promotes a safe teaching environment and accountability while building bridges between incarcerated Muslims and a mosque they can connect with outside once released from custody.

The Los Angeles County Sheriff's Department's custody outreach program in our jails is not only a bridge between inmates and the outside world. It is also is a counterradicalization effort by ensuring that nonviolent teachings are promoted by having the right educators, material, and well-qualified chaplains and imams with proper credentials. Similar efforts are in place with other faiths as well. The process would not have been possible without the cooperation of the local Muslim community who provided volunteers and vetted religious texts that do not incite violence, but rather teach the proper peaceful message of the religion. An example of this was an incident wherein the so-called vetted material was an inaccurately translated copy of the Quran that was printed by an unauthorized vendor and somehow distributed in the jails before it was discovered and recalled out of circulation.

## Success

The Los Angeles County Sheriff's Department's experience with the Muslim community in the Los Angeles area, although challenging at times, has been very rewarding. The level of trust and cooperation the members of the Sheriff's Department continue to experience has been very good and continues to improve on a daily basis. Members of the MCA unit and the department in general have been invited and have attended many social, religious, and educational events to include holiday festivities, Ramadan Iftars, and family celebrations. The mosques and Islamic centers in the Los Angleles area have been kept open and made available to any member of law enforcement to visit and to attend any cultural or religious event.

The MCA unit and the sheriff have hosted several town hall meetings with the Muslim community to answer questions and to address concerns. Some of the topics of the educational programs that were provided to the community include:

- Domestic violence
- Gang activities and awareness
- Youth and teens driving education
- Terrorism
- Narcotics education and awareness
- Identity theft avoidance and awareness
- Immigration laws and the process to obtaining citizenship

We measure our success by the trust that we enjoy with community leaders, members of the community in general, and the organizations that represent the community. Sheriff's Department cars and uniform personnel are no longer seen as a threat to the community in Los Angeles County, but rather as a pleasant and welcome part of the community and the Islamic centers.

Many tips, leads, and reports of suspicious activities have been provided by either Muslim community members or organizations. These reports of possible suspicious activities might not have been communicated to law enforcement personnel if we had not gained their trust by building these bridges. The trust that was earned provided the mechanism for the community to communicate its concern and therefore report the criminal activity.

## Lessons Learned

Our experience continues to teach us that implementing "community trust policing" methods is the best way to succeed and gain the cooperation of any community you serve and work with. The Muslim community is not different from any other community we serve daily. Build trust, solicit cooperation, and establish methods of communication with the community and the result will be crime reporting, reporting of suspicious activities, and countering violent extremism at all levels.

*Know your community.* Outreach to the Muslim community is a broad term; the Muslim community is more like many communities within a community. To truly understand your community, the liaison officer or the community relations unit must have an interest in learning about different cultures and attempt to understand the difference between a Muslim of Arab, South Asian, African, or European descent. This relates back to the importance of education for law enforcement members: an officer needs to know his or her beat and know who he or she is working with. Muslims speak different languages and come from every country in the world; it is of great importance that we understand their ethnic background and try to understand the different categories that they fall under. The approach of outreach is going to differ and might be totally changed to investigative in some categories.

Engagement with the African American Muslim community has been limited and continues to be challenging. It is quite likely that the lack of understanding of the culture and the history of African American Muslims in America contributes to the lack of partnership and trust between law enforcement and the African American community, whether native Muslim Americans or converts to Islam, the challenge is the same. I have found that although many African American Muslims are highly educated and patriotic, engagement with the police is still not very common, and it requires more analysis of our own community and the dedication of several resources to help with the daily quality-of-life issues, before we even consider engagement on a higher level to discuss cooperation and participation in government programs. The criminal element attached to converts who received their education about Islam in prisons presents a challenge, and they are understandably afraid of contact with the police, and the contacts they gain in custody refers them back to mosques that have little or no relationship with the police departments.

Muslims differ on how they practice Islam; the majority choose to be "mainstream" Muslims. They identify with Islam but may or may not adhere and practice everything. Some are more conservative, and some are extreme with their views or even radical. We must value everyone's choice as long as it is practiced within the law and does not threaten the safety of other members of the community.

*Terminology and government programs.* Whether we call it outreach to the Muslim community, countering violent extremism, or countering radicalization within the community, we all agree that the government and law enforcement agencies are reaching out to partner with the community. However, it is very important that we are clear in describing our mission when working with the Muslim community. Building a relationship and trust of the community takes years of effort that you do not want to jeopardize by choosing the wrong terminology. With the creation of Intelligence Fusion Centers throughout the country and the continued change in government programs in countering terrorism, everyone is looking to learn from best practices around the country. This could cause some redundancy of programs and create some confusion in the use of terminology that the community may perceive as a threat or a way to target them rather than solicit their partnership; therefore the use of terms such as countering violent extremism or "home grown terrorism" or any local police "suspicious activity reporting" might be confusing or create fear in the local Muslim community. One way to eliminate or avoid problems that may jeopardize relationships is to include respected community organizations or representatives in the development of such programs before they are initiated out and promoted to the community in general. A good example of that is the "see something say something" initiative by the LAPD. The LAPD involved community leaders and organizations in the development of the initiatives thus ensuring its success and getting the support of the community, which will promote it and be part of the success story.

## Areas of Challenges

Now that we know community policing and outreach efforts to our communities, and in this case to the Muslim community in Los Angeles County, work, what do we do next? We need to continue to build on our relationships with the communities that we serve, and work on preventing ideological violence through continued education and partnership.

In spite of an overall successful model, there are several areas of challenges and gaps, both external and internal. Some of the external challenges pertain to the dynamics of the communities, while others are specific to intergovernmental barriers.

## External Challenges (Community Dynamics)

- For the most part, most of the challenges are due to lack of community infrastructure and minimal organizational avenues.
- There have been some difficulties in terms of power struggles among the various community leaders and challenges in reaching the grassroots community at large. Often, these challenges come in the form of difficulties in organizing events and attempts to disseminate needed information to the community.
- Perceptions of biased practices in government and a lack of understanding of the basic government structures.

## Internal Challenges (Intergovernmental Barriers)

- Highlighting the significance of outreach and community engagement as it relates to areas of counterterrorism.
- Shifts in political priorities and the will to emphasize inclusion in the government processes. Consistently promote government-community relations and its importance across the board for all communities.
- Budgetary priorities and recognizing the significance of outreach and long-term benefits.
- Identifying appropriate resources to support programming areas (i.e., academic, demographic data, trends, grants, other government).
- Lack of financial support and federal funding specific to outreach efforts.

## CONCLUSION AND RECOMMENDATIONS

Community policing and the development of an outreach program to the Muslim community has great potential to improve the relationship between American Muslims and law enforcement agencies. However, it is important to understand that it is a process that will take time.

Several considerations have to be in place including the careful selection of staffing, the coordination among local, state, and federal agencies, and above all *the genuine interest in working with the community to help solve quality-of-life issues that matter to American Muslims as much as it matters to all other communities.*

In LASD's experience, the Muslim community has been eager to participate in programs that law enforcement agencies are proposing to engage them in a meaningful dialogue that will lead to a better relationship; however, civil rights and civil liberties issues have to be addressed as well to ensure the success of any program.

# Conclusion

## *P. Daniel Silk, Mary O'Rawe, and Basia Spalek*

### Introduction

This chapter will commence with a re-articulation of the difficulties of defining "success" in the context of employing community policing strategies to prevent ideologically inspired violence. In so doing, it will acknowledge the challenges that are experienced by communities, police, and activists as they seek to address terrorism in the post-9/11 era. We will also look more deeply at how this struggle is predicated and articulated, and what this might tell us about how violence itself is viewed, experienced, understood, and responded to within the police-community paradigm.

The chapter will then highlight, by way of example, four key themes emerging from the case study chapters that may be indicators of, or at times even barriers to, "success." Thereafter the chapter will move to address whether some of the more obvious obstacles to success in this area might be moderated or turned to broader societal advantage by subjecting to critical questioning the underlying assumptions of counterterrorism strategies themselves, as well as the fitness of the mechanisms employed to achieve them.

The chapter will conclude by pointing both to the potential benefits of certain kinds of police-community engagement in a given context, while challenging simple assumptions that engagement per se is always a straightforward, well-defined tactic.

The chapter, in this context, wonders whether the types of initiatives outlined by contributors such as Loughran (Chapter Six), and Rooney and Maskey (Chapter Five) in this book are indicative of an evolution toward different and more holistic ways of doing business. In these examples, reflective of the empowerment end of Myhill's typology of community policing (Myhill 2006, 7), communities have taken their own initiatives to enhance community safety, and engaged the police as one statutory partner among several (rather than the main or only relevant government organization), to address issues, not just violence as it is manifested subjectively, but also the structural violence of poverty and social exclusion. Resources, credibility, education, empathy, capacity building, agenda-setting, and action by appropriate community and other participants seem to be important parts of the "success" equation in these approaches.

No one will deny that are better ways to do "business." The contributors to this book suggest ways to accomplish this narrating their own experiences, even when they candidly admit mistakes and failures. Forms of broader engagement clearly raise their own particular dilemmas in terms of ownership, funding, management, selection of priorities and partners, and buy-in to such initiatives, but many of these are part and parcel of "normal" bilateral projects in any event. A more holistic and informed understanding of what violence is and where it comes from might point to the benefits of an approach that addresses violence in all its different facets as a public health epidemic (Gilligan 2000b; 2000c; 2001) rather than exclusively as a law enforcement issue. Capacity building in this regard, within police, communities, and other statutory and nonstatutory agencies may co-create the valuable synergy required for new and creative processes to flourish and, in the process, diminish the hold of terrorism and counterterrorism as watchwords for our future. At the same time, increased attention to the construction of perceptions of "procedural justice" as suggested by Tyler and his colleagues (e.g., Tyler and Huo 2002; Sunshine and Tyler 2003; Tyler 2004; Tyler, Schulhofer, and Huq 2010) may indeed offer a useful counter to older understandings of policing, crime, and the role of police-community interaction.

## What We Know and What We Don't

Northern Ireland, Britain, and the United States are linked in many ways, not least by their status as active participants in broad efforts to fight terrorism on a global scale. These three jurisdictions, at the same time, offer vastly different backdrops for the type of police-community interaction that is our emphasis here. While some common themes have emerged in the course of this study, the contributions to this book are best understood against the specific landscape that envelops both the individual jurisdictions and the actors involved in each particular chapter. How criminal justice is provided for and administered, the different legal and political systems, and significant contextual influences—for example, the legacy of the "Troubles" in Northern Ireland and the "war" on drug and gun crimes in the United States—are key to seeking a deeper understanding of how policing and police-community engagement operate in each of the territories under consideration. Within a contextualized framework for understanding, we believe that this collection of essays represents an innovative contribution to the debate on outreach and engagement as a tool for countering violent extremism in the jurisdictions studied. One of the commonalities in these different jurisdictions is that policing in its various forms currently combines and seeks to accommodate the twin imperatives of national security and community safety. An adherence to community policing, within this context is generally, though not always, portrayed as a facet of an effective form of law enforcement, at least on a theroetical level, with initiatives based around notions of community engagement and partnering (see examples in HM Government 2011; The White House 2011), deemed law enforcement's most acceptable and accessible face.

With this acknowledged, although a focus on community safety may coexist with a broader national security agenda, the two foci can also be in direct tension with one another (see, e.g., Lambert, 2008a; 2008b). There is always the potential for conflict to arise between local policing priorities and national security efforts. This has very particular implications in terms of outreach, expectations, partnering, and trust building to combat violent ideological extremism, and the potential for one priority to sideline another is real and must be recognized.

Crucially, criticisms of the application of counterterrorism strategies, whether overt or covert, at the local level, particularly as described by McGovern in Chapter Three, and Lambert in Chapter Four, must be accorded attention alongside any reading of "success stories," as a source of reflection on past practices and their effects. While there is ample evidence that many of the contributors here have looked at their own activities with a critical eye (see Stainbrook, for example), there are no guarantees that this will always be the case.

As McGovern insightfully argues in Chapter Three, "getting policing wrong, most obviously through echoing the failures of the past, still has a capacity to have profound political consequences." In the "real world," experienced police personnel and community leaders know this fact well. The points that follow should, therefore, be weighed with the recognition that policing has consequences—positive and negative—that deserve close consideration by any state and the people whom that state is designed to serve. As Mackenzie and Henry (2009) point out, because community policing is so optimistically and powerfully portrayed, labeling all manner of interventions as community oriented can serve to gloss over the complexities and challenges inherent in policing in a democratic society while seeking to increase the participation of the civilian populace in that endeavor. Skogan (2006) is clear, in his 13-year evaluation of Chicago's Alternative Policing Strategy (CAPS), described by MacKenzie and Henry as "probably the best-known and the most rigorously researched [community policing] strategy in the world" (2009, 16), that the success of such ventures cannot be determined by a specific set of strategies or be evaluated in terms of concrete outcomes or particular projects rolled out. Any understanding of success must, in this view, instead be intimately process based, connected with the extent to which approaches change organizational cultures and decision-making processes within the police, leading, through administrative decentralization and community engagement, to the actual solving of real problems (Skogan 2006, 5–12).

## THINKING SUCCESS

Judging and evaluating "success" within such contours is clearly fraught with difficulty—a reality that practitioners and academics alike will recognize. Despite our best efforts, we are far from consensus regarding what may or may not constitute appropriate, effective, and ethical community policing in a given context. Does setting up a community relations unit or forum with no real decision-making powers qualify? Should special teams be tasked with this work, or does the community policing ethos need to be internalized and mainstreamed through all police units within a department, from the public information office to special branch? Does engagement need to lead to empowerment of communities to make decisions on their own terms, sometimes *with* and sometimes *without* police involvement? Given all of the above, attempts to evaluate the utility and effectiveness of community policing in concrete terms so far suggest very mixed results (see, e.g., Myhill, 2006), with academic analysis of community-police engagement as an effective tool to combat violent extremism particularly thin on the ground.

An unraveling of all these conundrums is beyond the scope of this book. We merely aim here to provide a snapshot of police-community outreach and engagement happening "on the ground" in the jurisdictions under study, and to highlight some of the generic and particular challenges posed when community policing is employed in the service of broader counterterrorism strategies. Any evaluation of the success of such efforts is likely, at this point, to be both unscientific and highly subjective, with no broad agreement emerging as to what kind of metrics would be valuable to determine whether community policing–inspired counterterrorism efforts bear fruit, or indeed which fruit is good fruit, in the context of international, national, and local efforts to prevent ideological violence.

Research suggests that there is indeed a relationship between police-community engagement, attention from police on the way in which they treat the public, public compliance with the law, and public willingness to cooperate with police initiatives (see, e.g., Sunshine and Tyler 2003; Tyler 2004; 2011), including involvement in police efforts to combat terrorism (Huq, Tyler, and Schulhofer 2011; Tyler, Schulhofer, and Huq 2011). However, a great deal is involved, not the least of which is continued emphasis on police legitimacy in the eyes of the public, itself a characteristic strongly framed by police dedication to "procedural justice."

Anecdotal evidence of the success of community-police engagement clearly exists of the type outlined by Ramirez, Quinlan, Shutt, and Malloy in Chapter Nine, and any number of examples can be proffered to demonstrate that a trusting and aware public is more likely to offer information to the police than one which fears or holds police in contempt. However, how best to create and sustain a trusting public may be linked into what information is sought, and how it is obtained and used, and more foundationally, how police and communities interact and view one another. While we can find evidence of success in the examples summarized in Chapter Nine, at the same time we need only look at the complexities in other chapters to be reminded that a variety of views exists in any of these endeavors. As we state repeatedly, success is hard to define.

For every successful arrest, there will be any number of stories to be told about those either detained or released without charge or wrongly prosecuted (e.g., Azmy 2012). Such may be the nature of any imperfect human endeavor, especially one as challenging as policing in a democratic society. However, the human toll and the alienating impact such events have on individuals, families, and wider communities rarely make the headlines, but must nonetheless still be factored into any trust-building equation. Our contributors here would certainly agree. Meetings and other voluntary engagement with police may reassure participants they are part of the solution, but when participants are stopped and searched on the way home, detained for hours at an airport, or are the subject of sweeping intelligence-gathering measures, this will only serve to reemphasize they can still be treated as part of the problem. Police treatment of the public and perceptions of fairness have ramifications (e.g., Sunshine and Tyler 2003), including in the counterterrorism context (Tyler, Schulhofer, and Huq 2010; Huq, Tyler and Schulhofer 2011). The question then becomes, can and will localized policing efforts impact more broadly on regional and national policy in these regards? If not, can they truly be said to be successful or contributing to solving the problems leading to violent extremism?

Success in this arena does not lend itself to measurement in statistical terms. In part, this is again linked to different understandings of what might be considered success, and also the need for success in this area to manifest in substantive and qualitative manners, rather than in strictly numerical terms. Further, behind every successful statistic might be a number of other realities attesting to success as a highly contested and problematic descriptor as regards the core aim of diminishing extremist violence.

For instance, the extent to which success can be read from numbers of people attending a particular awareness-raising training progam is minimal, as so much depends on both the quality of the learning interaction (O'Rawe and McManus 2004; O'Rawe 2005), and whether it actually impacts positively on attitudes and behaviors (Rowe and Davis 2003; O'Rawe 2007). Similarly, measuring success in terms of an increased number of arrests or prosecutions is not straightforward. First, it may be difficult to ascertain, with certainty, a causal link between information supplied and involvement in a specific community engagement scheme, as opposed to the cumulative effect of a series of factors of which the particular scheme may or may not be a feature. The manner in which arrests and prosecutions happen is also substantively significant in terms of the potential for such occurrences, even where the right person is targeted, to alienate whole sections of a suspect community (Hillyard 1993; McGovern, Chapter Three in this collection). A forceful arrest at 4 a.m. and the media hype around it can confirm suspicions and stereotypes in dominant communities, and normalize the need for aggressive modus operandi, regardless of whether the system operates to determine that person as innocent at some later date. Clearly, educational efforts and information networks can prove fruitful, but the way in which they are harnessed can itself prove difficult, and efforts to plot the success they engender are elusive.

So, if success can't be measured by anecdotes and statistics, where do we go? If there is a tangible feeling that police and communities are being brought closer by a given interaction, or if police officers are now being welcomed into schools and community events, can this not be deemed success? Perhaps, and such sentiments such as involvement in decision making and improved treatment may indeed have broader, positive implications (e.g., Sunshine and Tyler 2003). Again, this is a difficult measurement to make, depending of course on what one is attempting to gauge. For one, it fails to take any account of the potential strength of feeling of those outside the engagement process. Seeing police adopting a high-visibility presence in a given area might carry connotations of overpolicing or signal an area as somehow unsafe. Also, given the contention of Gilligan (2000) and others (see e.g., Stern 2004) that violence is first and foremost linked to shame, an eye has to be cast toward whether the sight of police officers at a local house of worship or school might actually *heighten* feelings of shame and humiliation among the very people police seek to engage in the first place. This is not to overstate the point, or to suggest in any way that police and community need to stay at more than arm's length. The question is raised merely to counsel that even the most apparently innocuous win-win situation should be carefully thought through for potential downsides. If someone who has become, or is in the process of becoming, "radicalized" feels they need to distance themselves from a local religious institution deemed too friendly with the police, a potential opportunity for that community to work constructively with that individual to diminish potential recourse to violent action might be lost.

Rather than defining success, this concluding chapter seeks to consider a small number of themes coming through the case study chapters themselves to help reflect on the extent to which the "success" of any particular engagement program can currently be defined, particularly against the backdrop of a "new" antiterrorism agenda. While leaving the case study chapters to present themselves to the reader, in their own terms, as indicative of what successful ventures look like in practice, and seeking to take nothing away from the time and effort expended and the goodwill and positive results generated, the chapter will also reflect on some of the contributors' own frustrations. What is evidenced from the case study chapters is an evolving practice. Whether the evolution is proceeding in the best direction is ultimately for the reader to discern. We can applaud the effort involved while still respectfully seeking to question whether or not a particular police or community initiative has "worked."

## TRENDS AND THEMES FROM CASE STUDY CHAPTERS

Four key themes emerge persistently through the case study chapters, and in our opinion are deserving of further attention in the context of preventing ideological violence:

1. Outreach between communities and police is educational in nature, with the potential to be humanizing at different levels.
2. Relationships, trust, and dialogue are valued.
3. Outreach between communities and police occurs against politically contentious backdrops, and wider government agendas can serve as barriers to engagement.
4. The role of partnerships must be broader than singular government concerns such as individual strands of violent extremism.

We do not try here to simplify these discussions, or to suggest that the viewpoints expressed in the case study chapters can be packaged into easily digestible commonalities. The list is certainly not presented as exhaustive. Neither do we suggest that each author (or indeed editor) necessarily agrees on each of these themes. We identify these particular issues simply because each writer has given these ideas at least *some* attention (directly or not), and they appear to us to be particularly pertinent in a context of deploying community-police engagement strategies for the explicit ends of countering violent ideological extremism. To experienced practitioners, policy writers, and researchers, none of the above points will offer surprising revelations—except perhaps in the consistency of their inclusion in such a wide variety of experiences. That should not minimize their relevance, however, but rather serve to underscore areas where additional attention requires to be focused.

## OUTREACH AND ENGAGEMENT BETWEEN COMMUNITIES AND POLICE IS EDUCATIONAL IN NATURE

The educational aspect of police-community outreach is often identified as a key function of engagement activity by practitioners. It is clear from the foregoing chapters and the literature in general that community members and police often feel anger and frustration at the misinformation spread regarding their communities, organizations, actions, and intentions. Islamophobia has undoubtedly increased exponentially in the United States and the United Kingdom since the attacks of 9/11 and 7/7. Irish nationalists have long known what it is to be a "suspect" community. Distrust of the police by those on the hard edges of policing in any society is an age-old problem, as is the concern voiced by the police themselves that they are often demonized and misunderstood.

Tyler points in this respect to the educational nature of *every* police-community contact:

> From a legitimacy perspective, every encounter that the public have with the police, the courts and the law should be treated as a socializing experience that builds or undermines legitimacy. Each contact is a "teachable moment" in which people learn about the law and legal authorities. (2011, 257)

Tyler argues that trust and legitimacy are "learned" in each of these contacts, and, therefore, the quality of these interactions is of paramount importance. In a similar vein, McGovern contends in Chapter Three that "long term experiences of state policy and practice will invariably shape community perceptions of policing." This equally works both ways, in terms of the molding and cementing of police views of community and its constituent parts, as well as community views of police. Indeed, the most successful practitioners in this arena are likely well aware that they are constantly involved in an effort to "teach" and influence opinions.

It is not surprising therefore, that many of the initiatives described in the preceding chapters were framed in a manner that included a distinct educational aspect. A sense is conveyed through the case study chapters that there is much merit in the types of learning opportunities that can be harnessed to reverse, for example, the increasing Islamophobia exacerbated by 9/11 and 7/7, a view of police as not intervening when they should (or should not), or a notion that Loyalists in Northern Ireland have nothing of value to contribute to the peace process there. Communities want to be understood by governments, decision makers, and police. Police personnel, for their part, similarly wish for educational opportunities to thwart perceptions of law enforcement activities as close-minded, secretive, and brutal.

The power of concrete, tailored exposure and awareness-raising initiatives to educate and alter viewpoints and understandings as to different realities also comes across strongly in some case study chapters. On the engagement continuum, this can involve anything from police working with community organizations to secure the welcome attendance of law enforcement personnel at community festivals, to police learning about particular religious, social, and cultural realities with a view to informing more sensitive police practice in these regards to, at the far end of the community policing spectrum, communities being empowered to make their own decisions as to what their policing and security needs are, and to engage with those best suited to help fulfill them.

Some of the case study initiatives (such as CAPT and Connect, as well as those in London, Los Angeles, and Detroit) have taken steps both to challenge stereotypes and encourage empathy, through a deliberate educational focus, geared loosely or more explicitly around the age-old philosophy of "walking a mile in another's shoes." Honesty and openness during such engagements, and exposure to the competing demands experienced by others, if properly facilitated, can clearly be powerful catalysts for change in the way people with different identities, concerns, and agendas come to view and treat each other. Trust built, sometimes painstakingly, through such encounters can lay a basis for solid relationships and help realistic expectations to evolve of what a particular process or a particular person can and cannot deliver. Initiatives seem to work best where there is space and capacity for difficult conversations to be had in a safe environment, recognizing the contested political backdrop that renders such conversations both necessary and possible. However, just because individuals come to the "table" to inform and learn from one another, it does not ensure that issues of power, competing interests, and "voice" will be sufficiently recognized and handled, even in settings where education is a key aim (for more on this, see Cervero and Wilson 2006).

Having established that educational encounters can serve in the right circumstances to accomplish a range of outcomes—from humanizing and encouraging empathy to changing attitudes and fostering better understandings—we must consider if educational endeavors in the context of police-community engagement truly make a difference in terms of preventing or reducing misunderstanding or even violent extremism? Irvine, Stainbrook, Alkhatib, and others seem to suggest they can. This could lead to the conclusion that if community-police engagement serves no other purpose, it at least allows those involved to gather information about situational contexts and about each other. Whether in terms of a discrete training initiative such as Connect or CAPT in Northern Ireland, or more diverse forms of learning through interaction, simply coming together provides a format to gain some insight into police institutional and community pressures, expectations, and limitations, and possibly other ways of working.

However, all of this said, gathering information and convincing people of the justness of your cause and your realities is not value neutral and, if abused, can serve covert or unstated agendas capable of running at cross purposes to what certain participants (and also those who either choose not to or have not been "selected" to engage) would want or expect from such engagement. This issue is worth the attention of all involved in police-community outreach for the purposes discussed here. There is also a question of who "needs" to be educated, by whom, about what, and to what ends. Without a doubt, misinformation and unhelpful stereotyping does not exist solely at the level of the communities described here and the police. Other groups in society may feel similarly or even more so that there is a need to educate police, policy and decision makers, and their neighbors about themselves and/or to learn about and from the experience of others. Meaningful forums are in short supply, making it difficult to add in these other experiences and realities, and share fuller information about the experiences and frustrations of different societal constituencies in terms of defining problems and posing solutions. Someone is always left out, and this may have implications.

Safer societies clearly do not come about simply through police learning more about communities and vice versa. What avenues exist for sharing the full gamut of societal experiences necessary to address violence in meaningful ways? How can police and communities work to optimize these learning opportunities? It is not as simple as suggesting, "more educational opportunities are needed," as the quality and content of any training itself must equally be an area for constant scrutiny (e.g., O'Rawe 2005; 2007).

Given all of this, how can partnerships between communities and police better harness the potential for learning, ensure that all "sides" of important issues are addressed, and at the same time guard against the learning encounters being hijacked or exploited for other purposes? These are only some of the questions requiring more fundamental research in this area.

## Relationships, Trust, and Dialogue Are Valued

Much has been written in academia and government policies regarding the value of quality police-community relations, and this is therefore certainly not a new revelation. The point may have been emphasized nearly 200 years ago in Peel's era in Britain (Lentz and Chaires 2007). Current police strategies in Northern Ireland, Britain, and the United States all seek to capitalize on philosophies situating police in a favorable position vis-à-vis communities (e.g., LASD's "community trust policing," or the PSNI's latest brand of policing with the community-"personal policing"). However, the new infusion of attention, effort, and funding to support police-community relations to counter violent extremism (see, for example, the 2011 versions of the UK "Prevent" strategy and the 2011 US "Empowering Local Partners to Prevent Violent Extremism in the United States" document) also increases the need to better understand the role of concepts such as "relationships," and "trust" as they are used in outreach and partnerships in this terrain (see Spalek 2010).

It is attractively straightforward to suggest that improved police-community relations are needed to address ideological violence, and Irvine's observation of the "humanizing" effect achieved through shared police-community experiences is commendable, and perhaps a goal sought by many community and police leaders. It is obvious that a strong human and personal relationship with someone in this setting may result in a more realistic understanding of the pressures they are under and their capacity to "deliver." However, this is insufficient in and of itself to necessarily engender mutually satisfactory concrete action. Visible short-term victories can enhance trust, but in their absence, or to the extent that these diminish the possibility of bigger picture goals, these circumstantial relationships can remain fragile and may not be easily rebuilt once trust breaks down. There is a potential downside in that strengthening certain relationships might diminish the potential for others. Where there is a perception that relationships within these initiative are too cozy, this can lead to those outside the circle of participation feeling sold out by their representatives who they come to view as police or community "apologists," too ready to accept excuses, and unwilling to be too critical of their partners in a given endeavor. Maintaining a critical, helpful edge while gaining necessary insight into organizational processes and human fallibilities is a difficult balancing act. It is not just relationships and trust "inside the circle" that matter, but credibility beyond meeting-room walls. Education and capacity building in this regard is highly important, yet often overlooked.

As Irvine suggests in Chapter Seven, the context behind the need for relationships is itself a reflection of the problem:

> Perversely, the main opportunities for sustaining and developing the relationships are predicated mainly around issues of conflict or citizens

> having negative experiences. The challenge, therefore, must be to continue to create positive and mutually beneficial experiences that facilitate and foster relationships and strengthen partnership working while at the same time reducing levels of conflict.

Not all of these relationship-building experiences, of course, will be comfortable—and might actually be viewed as healthiest where they avoid becoming *too* comfortable. As Rooney and Maskey recognize in Chapter Five: "Engagement ha[s] to be meaningful, facilitate and encourage unpalatable conversations and recognise everyone [is] not starting from the same page or with the same destination in mind." Experienced practitioners in this field are all likely to agree on this point: *relationships are needed to address problems, yet the problems that require effective police-community relationships also make developing and sustaining those relationships more challenging in the first place.* These same challenges also make the process of discerning with whom one should seek a relationship difficult.

A further difficulty is that the strength and character of relationships in this context will necessarily be a factor of what needs they fulfill and, to put it bluntly, what can be "got" out of them. If all participants are agreed on both aims and process, this issue might be less problematic—but in turn it raises further concerns as to the nature of selection of participants. If participants on the community side are all "law abiding," "right thinking," people who share the dominant community view of the nature of the problem and what is to be done about it, one question might be about why outreach is needed in the first place. These kinds of people, first, might be likely to assist police in any event (regardless of outreach efforts); second, are less likely to know the kind of information that police might really need; and third, in a spirit of wanting to help, might actually contribute to blame and suspicion being located where it should not be. Where civilian participants on the other hand contain elements deemed less trustworthy by the police, it is difficult to get over the fact that police seeking to build trust with members of a particular community has echoes of the same kind of grooming and trust building involved in covert policing for more clandestine purposes.

When considering the role of relationship-building efforts between communities and police to tackle violent extremism, a variety of further questions come to mind. How are inherently ambiguous—but often used—terms such as "relationships" and "trust" best defined? How are these concepts best built or utilized, and when do ends justify means when it comes to information and intelligence gathering?

Relationships built on false premises have a substantial capacity to wound individuals and damage broader agendas in the long term. There is indeed a great deal more research and understanding needed on this topic alone, particularly given tactics adopted by undercover agents insinuating themselves within groups deemed to be subversive, to the point of forming intimate relationships in the intelligence-gathering endeavor. Complex inquiry is required into how relationships and trust are fostered and sustained, the role of the affective (feelings and emotion) facets of countering violent extremism, and the practical personnel issues (hiring, selection, and training) that this type of policing involves. Moreover, how can police forces and community groups work to develop common understandings of their "relationship" roles so that some sort of joint ethical understanding is achieved regarding boundaries and expectations? What are the limits to what police can ask (or demand) of community contacts, and how do academics and practitioners demarcate the distinction between community contacts, useful resources, legitimate informants, and "spies"? What is to be done when relationships are abused by either "side," and what are the repercussions? This realm raises a range of concerns regarding the place for "hard" and "soft" aspects of counterterrorism (see Spalek and Imtoual 2007). This conceptual terrain will assuredly remain precarious, and is unlikely to ever be settled with any finality. Nevertheless, this facet of attempts to police violent extremism in policy and practice is key, and should continue to be studied and scrutinized. So, too, should the potential value of relationship building and partnership with a range of statutory agencies over and above the police. Certain case study chapters (e.g., Loughran) suggest this more rounded problem-solving approach can have the dual effect of taking some of the sting out of distrustful communities engaging (and/or being seen to engage) with the police, as well providing its own added value in terms of defining both problems and solutions more holistically.

## Outreach between Communities and Police Occurs against Political and Contentious Backdrops, and Wider Government Agendas Can Serve as Barriers to Engagement

The contributing authors—whether in the academic realm or the practical (or a combination of both)—clearly recognize that the world of police-community partnerships is deeply influenced by politics and competing interests. This is not to ascribe nefarious motives to those involved (or to deny that possibility), only to acknowledge aloud that police, activists, and community members each have their own reasons and goals for engagement, and that issues of power and the influence of stated and unstated agendas all play a role. To fail to recognize the very real influence these topics have is, to borrow a phrase, "like walking across a busy intersection with one's eyes closed" (Forester 1989, 7).

In the current law enforcement environments in Britain, Northern Ireland, and the United States, police-community engagement clearly takes place in a challenging political space. This underlines the value of Irvine's following observation from Chapter Seven:

> Overall there is a paradox in the concept of community policing especially in conflict-related regions such as Northern Ireland. The necessity to transform relations between the police and community into strong effective partnerships which build mutual confidence and trust, appears to be at odds with the context in which the police operate. Any police framework that allows systems and/or agendas to operate, albeit under the auspices of *national security*, without any real or robust civic accountability mechanism, will invariably prove to be problematic in restoring confidence and trust with communities, especially those that are historically and traditionally suspicious of policing agendas.

It is also clear that, to varying extents, the contributors to this book recognize that outreach between police and communities for the purpose of preventing ideological violence takes place on a contested and public stage, with influence coming from a variety of powerful sources—at the national government level, within local police organizations, from within communities, and from commentators, the media, and researchers. Perhaps this contested space is healthy and required, contributing to what Beutel calls in Chapter Eleven the "intense and ongoing debate among many parties over what is the appropriate balance between civil liberties and national security."

However, the precise degree of influence and the sources of power that hold sway over counterterrorism, in terms of both agenda setting and promoted practices, is itself an area worthy of fuller attention. While the relationships that community members and police personnel form may indeed be personal, they develop and are maintained within a context that is, at the same time, formed by input from disparate actors—whether their influence is desired or not.

Engagement does not take place in a vacuum. Context must be factored into engagements, and difficult conversations need to be facilitated in a way that takes due account of competing positions in manner that does not render critics of police and government policy prone to be labeled as subversives or nay-sayers, or leave people feeling there is no room for being "off message." The type of space required needs to facilitate people moving beyond political posturing or giving "the official line" to each other points of view. This brings in the controversial notion that space may need to be made for police officers to describe things how they see them, even where this is contrary to organizational mandate, and even when a more senior officer is in the room. This whole area is replete with difficulties in a disciplined organization that functions by command and control principles. Police officers are involved in these efforts as representatives of their organization—so their own voice and feelings may not be relevant, particularly to the extent that it conflicts with the message the organization wants to put out there at any given time. However, where does this sit with the trust, honesty, and credibility principles already outlined? Clearly it would not be appropriate for an officer to act as a "loose cannon" in terms of positions stated or promises made on behalf of his or her organization. Yet to what extent can and should organizational politics be allowed to influence both who is at the table and what they can say? If an officer does not appear to adopt the party line, this could be taken by communities in any number of ways: a genuine expression of solidarity with their own situation, an indicator that the police agency is undisciplined, or even as evidence of a plant, strategically placed to lure them into greater intimacy and outspokenness to serve a covert agenda. All of this requires much careful thinking in individual contexts to ensure encounters move beyond window dressing.

Politics does not just operate at an organizational level. Bigger questions are just a tiptoe away. For instance, who decided, and why, that "terrorism" or ideological violence was the biggest topic to be addressed at a societal, and more specifically a community policing level—and can this be objectively determined to be the "right" choice? What if communities disagree? How, in particular do police and communities address the "sense of injustice generated by government policy...in terms of reactions to the very measures introduced by the state to supposedly 'counter-terrorism'" (McGovern in Chapter Three)?

If, as McGovern contends in Chapter Three, "the overarching framework of government policy and practice will invariably shape, frame, and in large part, ultimately determine any localized agenda," then the role and potential effect of national policing and counterterrorism directives at the local level is paramount, and must at the very least be openly acknowledged by all involved. How is this different, in the model of the United Kingdom with its Home Office, as opposed to the United States, which has much more decentralized policing and no direct equivalent to the Home Office and its authority?

Lambert, here and elsewhere (see Lambert 2008a; 2008b), contends that national security-centric policies and practices may actually subvert meaningful partnerships at the local level, and other authors similarly recognize how past experiences, politics, media coverage, and national agendas have a similarly negative effect. The other side of the coin is that sometimes problems are not prone to localized solutions and require more meaningful access to a higher-level polity of decision makers. To what extent does localized police-community engagement facilitate or guard against this recognition, and to what extent might initiatives be framed to deliberately exclude those who would ask and demand answers to more searching questions?

The research by Lambert (2008a; 2008b), Spalek et al. (2008), and others challenges policies and practices whereby those perceived to be too radical or different are denied a place at the table. Their research stresses that engagement and partnerships with Islamist and Salafi groups, for example, is not only desirable but essential in reducing al-Qaeda linked terrorism in Europe, the United States and other areas. Here is a situation where religion, politics, cultural identities, and practices should be embraced rather than viewed as dangerous or antithetical to social cohesion. In this approach, community members are encouraged to cooperate with the police on what is viewed as a common aim, the protection of society at large from crime committed in the name of Islam (Spalek et al. 2008). Where are lower-level police personnel and communities to turn when they jointly recognize that they have identified a potential path to local safety that runs counter to national policies?

What is apparent here is that law enforcement agencies are operating within a conflicting counterterrorism environment. On the one hand "hard" policing tactics are encouraged in order to flush out potential criminal "subversives." On the other hand, where liberal freedoms within democracies are emphasized, "softer" counterterrorism tactics involving wider engagement and partnerships tend to be pursued. Future research could usefully examine the tensions and overlaps between these different styles of law enforcement approaches as part of a wider exploration of the complex refashioning of identity and affiliation within the "new age of terror" in relation to sovereignty, "extreme" identities, countersubversion, and counterterrorism (Spalek and McDonald 2011; see also, Spalek forthcoming).

It is not just organizational and government, but also media influence that has to be taken into account in terms of agenda setting and shining light into dark corners. How the media responds to a counterterrorism agenda and police-community engagement under this rubric may be highly influential on both local and national security policies. Stainbrook's chapter offers a candid snapshot of the real influence media attention can have on local policing efforts, even when the police program itself was designed with the best of intentions and with an element of community input. Consider, also, criticisms of the New York Police Department and its surveillance of Muslim communities in and around the city (Goldstein 2012), and enduring questions regarding whether or not "Prevent" counterterrorism efforts in the United Kingdom amount to spying (see, e.g., Dodd 2009; Kundnani 2009). It is clear that news media reporting efforts can have tangible effects on policing practices, sometimes at the highest levels. Often this fourth estate is truly needed. For example, would large-scale effort to eradicate bias in counterterrorism training in the United States have taken place without scathing media attention (Ackerman 2012)? Communities and police partners must therefore be extremely aware of potential media coverage and its effects. It may be tempting to cast such attention in a negative light, and indeed certain media can be guilty of whipping up Islamophobia and have other unhelpful effects, but what role do related discussions have in promoting transparency and ethical police and community practices? While having an eye to these issues may make action more difficult for practitioners, it also appears that focus on these issues can support democratic values and accountability. Police and the communities, therefore, also need to conduct their business in a way that factors in both media and social networking sites as relevant to the work being done.

## The Role of Partnerships Must Be Broader Than Singular Government Concerns Such as Individual Strands of Violent Extremism

Whatever the "official" reason behind seeking police-community partnerships, it is clear that communities often expect the end result of these efforts to transcend artificial boundaries limited by government agendas. Communities expect not only engagement but action on a range of topics, even if the driving concern for the executive at a given moment is ideologically influenced violent extremism. Abdeen recalls the value of this understanding when he emphasizes that law enforcement must show "*genuine interest in working with the community to help solve quality of life issues that matter to American Muslims as much as...to all other communities*" (emphasis in original). This is not to imply that communities fail to feel the effects of both terrorism and related policies, because as Alkhatib notes in Chapter Twelve, "The global war on terror, the fear of future attacks on the US, and US foreign policy in Middle East, all put stresses on the Arab and Muslim American community"—which seem to often go unrecognized. But however compelling the counterterrorism mission may be, it is crucial that police remember that the communities they serve also have concerns about other forms of violence, property crimes, and general neighborhood disorder, as well as their own political views on their governments' broader foreign and domestic policy.

Of course, this has been recognized by many of the authors, and some of the partnership programs evidence a variety of ways in which police and communities may engage around, between, and underneath these realities. The Rooney and Maskey example of the CAPT program in Northern Ireland explicitly seeks to attend to broad community policing issues, *as well as* paramilitarism and sectarianism, while aware of how the context and legacy of both continue to impact on broader quality-of-life issues. Stainbrook's Los Angeles story situates a police-community partnership under a counterterrorism command, but designs it to openly address much wider policing and community safety issues. Both of these solutions appear well informed for a variety of reasons.

First, from a law enforcement point of view, there is little doubt that if initiatives are too exclusively focused on al-Qaeda–inspired terrorism, Republican or Loyalist violence in Northern Ireland, or sectarianism, there would be pushback from community partners who would instead demand engagement linked to the full range of police services they require. Just as no police department would want to be seen by communities exclusively through a narrowly defined focus on police excessive force, communities resist frameworks that view them only in terms of their potential to assist police in their efforts to confront ideologically inspired violence. Furthermore, increasing the reach of counterterrorism police officers into the ordinary lives and experiences of communities carries its own attendant dilemmas. Will officers become conditioned to see their professional world in terms that minimize other police responsibilities?

In the contexts discussed here, it is important to recognize how singular government attention on terrorism in specific communities can serve to "securitize" police-community relationships and effectively label broad segments of society as suspect (see, e.g., Hillyard 1993; Poynting and Mason 2008; Spalek, El-Awa and McDonald 2008; Pantazis and Pemberton 2009; Choudhury and Fenwick 2011; Silk 2012).

Many police in the United States and United Kingdom are likely not fully aware of the way in which communities perceive outreach tailored to specific policy goals. How have such efforts fared in Northern Ireland in the context of the current peace process (Byrne and Monaghan 2008; Topping 2008)? How might Catholics, Nationalists, Republicans, and Loyalists in Northern Ireland interpret and respond to the reach of special branch officers into community policing modalities? What would the explicit linkage of the two do to trust in the processes? How do Muslims in Britain and the United States contend with their inclusion in outreach programs designed to prevent violent extremism? To what extent can police reasonably recognize and mitigate against unhelpful and sometimes dangerous stereotypes while still fulfilling their outreach mission within potentially affected communities? These and related topics deserve much more attention.

## Alternative Views of Violence and Collaborative Responses

Given all of the challenges, frustrations, and points of contention outlined here, might the time be right to deconstruct some of the assumptions and premises on which community-police engagement efforts tend to be built? Perhaps this deconstruction is both warranted and necessary by virtue of the very difficulty we have in quantifying what we mean by success in terms of police-community engagement to address violent extremism.

Loughran in Chapter Six suggests that "a new social and political space has evolved that is no longer preoccupied with the safety of the nation so much as the safety of communities." If this is or is ever to be the case, local agency is clearly necessary—but to what ends should it be deployed? Is this reality different in a country with truly decentralized police service, such as the United States, as opposed to the United Kingdom? The police seem, in many ways, the most obvious partners to tackle extremist violence, but should this be the case in a new or evolving social and political space?

James Gilligan, (1996; 1997; 2000a; 2000b; 2000c; 2001) a North American psychotherapist with decades of experience working within the US prison system, suggests a public health approach is required to the problem. Precisely what this means can be gleaned from reading his various works on the topic, which are worthy of much more study than any attempt to summarize here would allow. We content ourselves with the following insight to demonstrate that further reading of Gilligan is indeed worth pursuing:

> Condemning violence or forgiving it are irrelevant once you see violence as a problem in public health and preventative medicine. No one supposes that because doctors do not waste their time and energy on "condemnations" or "punishments" of cancer of heart disease, they are somehow "soft on cancer" or "permissive" towards heart disease. They need all their time and energy to prevent and cure those diseases, which one does first and foremost by learning whatever one can about what causes them and how one might prevent them. It can be productive of knowledge to conceptualize violence as a health problem, but as long as we think of it as a moral problem, we will never be able to learn what causes it or what prevents it.
>
> For three millennia our main social hypothesis—that the moral and legal way of thinking about and responding to violence (by calling it evil, forbidding it—"just say no" and punishing it) will prevent violence (or at least bring it under control)—has been singularly unsuccessful in reducing the level of violence. Three thousand years should be an adequate length of time to test any hypothesis. That is why I am suggesting that it is time now to retire the moral way of thinking about violence for one capable of utilizing all the methods and concepts of the human sciences; time, in fact, to build a truly humane science, for the first time for the study of violence. (2000c, 93–94)

Gilligan is not alone in the conclusions he draws, and work toward countering violent extremism could be propelled forward exponentially if these views were mainstreamed into police and community conversations.

At least theoretically, the community and problem-oriented policing police philosophy already recognizes that the role of non–law enforcement stakeholders is key in addressing persistent public safety challenges (e.g., Goldstein 1990). But how might this realization be better harnessed systemically, in the hopes of facilitating truly holistic responses to ideological violence? Can we move beyond expecting law enforcement to always play the leading role in addressing the causes of violent crime, including violent ideological extremism? Can this be done in a way that addresses concerns that broad partnerships for countering violent extremism are just attempts to coopt more agencies into the counterterrorism "spying" agenda?

Further, if such a shift were possible, could it not free police to work in a manner that substantively assists in reenvisioning the lens through which police-community relations (at least in the counterterrorism realm) are viewed? If Tyler and his colleagues (e.g., Tyler and Huo 2002; Sunshine and Tyler 2003; Tyler 2004; Tyler, Schulhofer, and Huq 2010) are correct, and qualities of procedural justice can have an influence on crime in some instances—perhaps even more so than "instrumental" explanations—then how would community opinions of police be affected if the onus for violence prevention shifted away from the shoulders of law enforcement? Might police personnel have more ability then to address the question of their own legitimacy in the eyes of those they serve, were they instead assisting in the fight against a broadly recognized public health challenge as opposed to an exclusively criminal issue?

## Concluding Remarks

There is certainly a great deal of potential in police-community engagement for the purpose of preventing ideologically influenced violent extremism, but a dizzying variety of factors is involved, and the impact of such initiatives also carries inherent dangers. Local agency, responsibility, and input are vital, but how problems are conceived and the allowable parameters for seeking solutions might usefully benefit from further study along the lines Gilligan sets out, and from broadening both the parameters and the conversations. A multiagency approach that does not target violent extremists so much as violence per se, and its hold on our communities and our psyches (the seeds of which are perhaps apparent, for example, in the work set out by Loughran in Chapter Six as happening in Northern Ireland), is likely where police-community initiatives need to be heading.

In the end we should conclude by recognizing that outreach between police and communities for the purpose of preventing ideologically inspired violence is, and will remain, an ambiguous and imperfect practice. Like other human endeavors, it will never be agreeable to everyone involved or observing. This is not, however, necessarily to suggest that it is not worthwhile. Inasmuch as communities and police strive with their best efforts to improve safety in their cities and neighborhoods, and, mindful of the concerns featured throughout this book, concurrently work to uphold the highest values of policing in a democratic society, impressive results are possible. Community-police engagement in this context might best be viewed as a pathway rather than a destination. It is useful to the extent it opens eyes, hearts, and minds to different possibilities and better realities. It is less so to the extent that it closes down possibilities for learning and holistic forms of action that engage more honestly and meaningfully to understand and reduce violence in all its shapes and forms.

## REFERENCES

Ackerman, Spencer. 2011. "Obama Orders Government to Clean Up Terror Training." *Wired*, November 29. http://www.wired.com/dangerroom/2011/11/obama-islamophobia-review/?utm_source=Contextly&utm_medium=RelatedLinks&utm_campaign=Previous.

Azmy, Baher. 2012. "The Face of Indefinite Detention." *New York Times*, September 14. http://www.nytimes.com/2012/09/14/opinion/life-and-death-at-guantanamo-bay.html?_r=0.

Byrne, Jonny, and Lisa Monaghan. 1993. *Understanding Key Issues for Local Communities and PSNI.* Coleraine, Northern Ireland: Institute for Conflict Research,

Cervero, Ronald M., and Arthur L. Wilson. 2006. *Working the Planning Table: Negotiating Democratically for Adult, Continuing, and Workplace Education*. San Francisco, CA: Jossey-Bass.

Choudhury, Tufyal, and Helen Fenwick. 2011. *The Impact of Counter-Terrorism Measures on Muslim Communities* London. Equality & Human Rights Commission.

Dodd, Vikram. 2009. "Government Anti-Terrorism Strategy 'Spies' on Innocent: Data on Politics, Sexual Activity and Religion Gathered by Government." *The Guardian*, October 16. http://www. guardian.co.uk/uk/2009/oct/16/antiterrorism-strategy-spies- innocents.

Forester, John. 1989. *Planning in the Face of Power*, Berkeley: University of California Press.

Gilligan, James. 1996. *Violence: Our Deadly Epidemic and Its Causes.* New York: Grosset/Putnam.

———(Ed.). 1997. *Violence: Reflections on a National Epidemic.* New York: Vintage Books.

———. 2000a. "Punishment and Violence: Is the Criminal Justice System Based on One Huge Mistake?" *Social Research 67*(3): 745–772.

———. 2000b. "Violence in Public Health and Preventive Medicine." *Lancet 355*: 1802–1804.

———. 2000c. *Violence: Reflections on Our Deadliest Epidemic.* New York: Jessica Kingsley.

———. 2001. *Preventing Violence.* London:Thames and Hudson.

Goldstein, Herman. 1990. *Problem Oriented Policing.* New York: McGraw Hill Publishing.

Goldstein,Joseph.2012."KellyDefendsSurveillanceofMuslims." *The New York Times*, February 27. http://www.nytimes.com/2012/02/28/nyregion/new-york-police-commissioner-defends-monitoring-of-muslims.html?_r=1&ref=opinion.

Greenberg, Karen, and Joshua Dratel. 2005. *The Torture Papers: The Road to Abu Ghraib.* Cambridge, MA: Cambridge University Press.

Hillyard, Paddy. 1993. *Suspect Community: People's Experience of the Prevention of Terrorism Acts in Britain.* London: Pluto Press.

HM Government. 2011. *Prevent Strategy.* Norwich, UK: TSO. http://www.homeoffice.gov.uk/publications/counter-terrorism/prevent/prevent-strategy/prevent-strategy-review?view=Binary.

Huq, Aziz Z., Tom. R Tyler, and Stephen. J. Schulhofer. 2011. "How Do the Purposes and Targets of Policing Influence the Basis of Public Cooperation with Law Enforcement?" *Psychology, Public Policy and the Law 17*(3): 419–450.

Kundnani, A. 2009. *Spooked ! How Not to Prevent Violent Extremism.* London: Institute of Race Relations.

Lambert, Robert. 2008a. "Empowering Salafis and Islamists against al-Qaeda: A London Counter-terrorism Case Study." *PS: Political Science & Politics 41*(1): 31–35.

———. 2008b. Salafi and Islamist Londoners: Stigmatised Minority Faith CommunitiesCountering al-Qaida. *Crime, Law and Social Change 50*(1–2): 73–89.

Lentz, Susan. A., and Robert H. Chaires. 2007. "The Invention of Peel's Principles: A Study of Policing 'Textbook' History." *Journal of Criminal Justice 35,(1)*: 69–79.

MacKenzie, Simon, and Alistair Henry. 2009. *Community Policing: A Review of the Literature* (Web only publication). Edinburgh, Scotland: Scottish Government Social Research. http://www.scotland.gov.uk/Publications/2009/11/19091609/0.

Myhill, Andy. 2006. *Community Engagement in Policing: Lessons from the Literature.* London, UK: Home Office. http://www.wales.nhs.uk/sites3/Documents/420/Communityengagement.pdf.

OPONI. 2007. "Investigative Report: Statement by the Police Ombudsman for Northern Ireland on Her Investigation into the Circumstances Surrounding the Death of Raymond McCord Junior and Related Matters." Belfast: OPONI.

O'Rawe, Mary, and Jim McManus. 2004. *Human Rights in Police Training Report 4: Course for All.* Belfast: Northern Ireland Human Rights Commission.

———. 2005. "Human Rights and Police Training in Transitional Societies: Exporting the Lessons of Northern Ireland." *Human Rights Quarterly* 27(3): 943–968.

———. 2007. "Human Rights, Transitional Societies and Police Training: Legitimating Strategies and Delegitimating Legacies." *St John's Journal of Legal Commentary* 22(1): 199–259.

Pantazis, Christina, and Simon Pemberton. 2009. "From the 'Old' to the 'New Suspect' Community: Examining the Impacts of Recent UK Counter-Terrorist Legislation." *British Journal of Criminology 49*(5): 646–666.

Poynting, Scott, and Mason, Victoria. 2008. "The New Integrationism, the State and Islamophobia: Retreat from Multiculturalism in Australia." *International Journal of Law, Crime and Justice 36*(4): 230–246.

Rowe, Michael, and Jon Davis. 2003. "'Have You Been Diversified Yet?': Developments in Police Community and Race Relations Training in England and Wales." *Policing and Society 13*(4): 399–411.

Silk, P. Daniel. 2012. "The Complexity of Police-Muslim Community Relations in the Shadow of 9/11." *Arches Quarterly 5*(9): 73–82.

Skogan, Wesley G. 2006. *Police and Community in Chicago: A Tale of Three Cities.* New York: Oxford University Press.

Spalek, Basia. 2010. "Community Policing, Trust, and Muslim Communities in Relation to 'New Terrorism.'" *Politics & Policy 38*(4): 789–815.

———. (forthcoming). *Governing Terror: Trust, Community and Counter-Terrorism.* Basingstoke, UK: Palgrave.

Spalek, Basia, Salwa El Awa, and Laura Zahra McDonald. 2008. *Police Muslim Engagement and Partnerships for the Purposes of Counter-Terrorism: An Examination.* Birmingham, UK: University of Birmingham.

Spalek, Basia, and Alia Imtoual. 2007. "Communities and Counter-Terror Responses: 'Hard' Approaches to Community Engagement in the UK and Australia." *Journal of Muslim Minority Affairs 27*(2): 185–202.

Spalek, Basia, and Laura Zahra McDonald. 2010. "Anti-Social Behaviour Powers and the Policing of Security." *Social Policy and Society 9*(1): 123–133.

Stern, Jessica. 2003. *Terror in the Name of God: Why Religious Militants Kill.* New York: Ecco/HarperCollins.

Sunshine, Jason, and Tom. R. Tyler. 2003. "The Role of Procedural Justice and Legitimacy in Shaping Public Support for Policing." *Law & Society Review 37*(3): 513–548.

Topping, John R. 2008. "Diversifying from Within: Community Policing and the Governance of Security in Northern Ireland." *British Journal of Criminology 48*: 778–797.

Tyler, Tom R. 2004. "Enhancing Police Legitimacy." *Annals of the American Academy of Political and Social Science 593*: 84–99.

———. 2011. "Trust and Legitimacy: Policing in the USA and Europe." *European Journal of Criminology 8*(4): 254–266.

Tyler, Tom R., and Yuen J. Huo. 2003. *Trust in the Law: Encouraging Public Cooperation with the Police and Courts.* New York: Russell Sage Foundation.

Tyler, Tom. R., Stephen J. Schulhofer, and Aziz. Z. Huq. 2010. "Legitimacy and Deterrence Effects in Counter-Terrorism Policing: A Study of Muslim Americans." *Law & Society Review 44*(2): 365–402.

The White House. 2011. *Empowering Local Partners to Prevent Violent Extremism in the United States.* http://www.whitehouse.gov/sites/default/files/empowering_local_partners.pdf.

Williamson, Tom. 2005. Editorial—"Community Policing." *Journal of Community and Applied Social Psychology 15*: 153–155.

# Contributors

**Sergeant Mike Abdeen** is a 21-year veteran of the Los Angeles County Sheriff's Department. His assignments have included working in the Custody Division, Patrol Division, Detective Division, and Homeland Security Division. He also worked as an investigator and a task force officer on the Joint Terrorism Task Force for three years. Sergeant Abdeen is an Arab American, and he is also the Arabic language examiner for the Los Angeles County Sheriff's Department.

Sergeant Abdeen is currently assigned to the Homeland Security Division's Emergency Operations Bureau. Together with Sheriff Lee Baca, he established the Muslim Community Affairs Unit, the first of its kind in the State of California and the nation, with the objective of building a meaningful relationship with the Muslim community in Los Angeles County. Sergeant Abdeen also serves an instructor for cultural awareness and sensitivity training for Los Angeles County Sheriff's Department staff and academy recruits, and coordinates outreach efforts with other local, state, and federal agencies. He maintains contacts with Muslim leaders and organizations in Los Angeles County and accompanies the sheriff to community town hall meetings. In May 2010, Mike received the Award of Distinction from the California Peace Officers Association for establishing the Muslim Community Affairs Unit.

**Dr. Ihsan Alkhatib** is an assistant professor at Murray State University's Department of Government, Law and International Affairs. He teaches International Law, Business Law, Middle East Politics, and Business Ethics. He is also a volunteer attorney and advisory board member for American Arab Anti-Discrimination Committee (ADC) and a columnist for the Arab American newspapers *The Independent Monitor* and the *Forum and Link*.

Dr. Alkhatib taught Political Science as an adjunct professor at a number of colleges while practicing law for 10 years in the Greater Detroit area, representing mainly Arab American clientele. He is heavily involved in issues of civil rights and liberties, serving as president of the Detroit Chapter Board of Directors of ADC-MI for a number of years. He currently serves on the ADC-MI Advisory Board. In that capacity he represented ADC in a number of national and international forums and spoke to local, national, and international media on issues of concern to Arab and Muslim Americans.

Dr. Alkhatib has been interviewed by local, national, and international media. He appeared on Al-Jazeera and UPN 50 Detroit, and radio station Sawt al Mahjar, and was interviewed by *The Detroit News and Free Press* as well as the *Washington Post* and *The New York Times* to comment on issues relating to the civil rights and liberties of Arab and Muslim Americans in the post 9/11 era, the war on terror, and the war in Iraq.

**Alejandro J. Beutel** is an independent analyst specializing in counterterrorism and American Muslim policy issues. From 2009 to 2012 he was the government and policy analyst at the Muslim Public Affairs Council (MPAC), a faith-based advocacy group. At MPAC he authored and directed over 20 publications, including "Building Bridges to Strengthen America," a framework establishing a partnership-based strategy between American Muslims and law enforcement to fight terrorism.

**Winston Irvine** has been involved in community activism for over 16 years. Throughout that period, Winston has worked on issues affecting working-class Unionist communities in Northern Ireland, including housing, community education, community safety, community relations, and peace building. Winston is a steering group member and a "key area contact" with Belfast Conflict Resolution Consortium.

Recently, Winston has been actively involved in high-profile negotiations surrounding the issue of parades and protests across the city of Belfast and has played an important role in supporting and developing dialogue processes in other areas where there have been problems associated with Republican and Loyalist parades and protests.

His other work includes developing working relationships between police, local, community, and statutory agencies within North and West Belfast, and he is a founding member of the Greater Shankill Community Safety Network. In the context of peace building and transforming relationships, Winston has contributed both strategically and at a grassroots level, assisting positive change on various levels.

**Dr. Robert Lambert** lectures on responses to threats of terrorism and political violence at the Centre for the Study of Terrorism and

Political Violence (CSTPV) at the University of St. Andrews. He has written and teaches a module on far-right terrorism and political violence. Lambert first monitored far-right political violence when he joined Metropolitan Police Special Branch (MPSB) in 1980. In *Countering al-Qaeda in London: Police and Muslims in Partnership* (2011), Lambert reflects on his final MPSB role as head of the Muslim Contact Unit (MCU) from January 2002 to December 2007. In 2010 he coauthored two reports on Islamophobia and Anti-Muslim Hate Crimes in London and the United Kingdom.

**Zubeda Limbada** works for the Birmingham (UK) City Council and has over 10 years of local government experience around policy and project management and preventing violent extremism (PVE). She developed an operational accredited mentoring program on behalf of statutory agencies and partners for individuals vulnerable to violent extremism during a two-year assignment with West Midlands Police Counter Terrorism Unit.

Alongside an international team, Zubeda is a codirector of "ConnectJustice," an organization that researches, evaluates, trains, and facilitates communities and states experiencing social and political conflicts. Zubeda is an alumnus of the US Department of State's "International Visitors Leadership Program," the Wilton Park British-German Forum, the Oxford University Young Muslim Leadership Program, and the British Council (Africa) Interaction program. She speaks and writes extensively on communities, community policing, trust and confidence, and extremism. She graduated from the University of Manchester with a BA in Politics and Modern History and an MA in Middle Eastern Studies.

Her chapter has been submitted in a personal capacity and remains her personal views and not representative of any organization.

**John Loughran** has been employed at Intercomm in the design and delivery of track two peace-building programs since 1996. Having undertaken a number of duties, John is currently program lead on the 2028 Peace Building Program, which is designed to build the competency and confidence of the underrepresented to actively contribute to postconflict peace building. John attended Queen's University Belfast (QUB) and obtained a degree in Politics and Scholastic Philosophy (1995). In 2001, QUB awarded John a Master of Arts degree in Irish Politics. He also successfully completed the prestigious US Government, International Visitors' Program, at Boston College.

John has also engaged in a wide variety of fieldwork, investigating and experiencing the dynamics and diversity of peace processes:

in Nicaragua (1999), the Basque Country (2000), Israel/Palestine (2005), and South Africa (1996, 1999, 2010, 2012). He worked with the United Nations Development Program in Cyprus, and acted as program mentor on the Journeys Out program to South Africa (2010). At the invitation of the UK government he has also shared lessons on the Northern Irish peace process with the Thailand government (Bangkok 2011) and was also part of an Intercomm/PSNI team, which at the request of SAFERWORLD delivered community safety programs to the Nepalese Police.

**Sean P. Malloy** graduated from Northeastern University School of Law in 2011, and is currently an attorney in Boston, MA, focusing on litigation. Mr. Malloy contributed to "Community Partnerships Thwart Terrorism" as the legal fellow and senior editor for the Partnering for Prevention and Community Safety Initiative. In law school, he served as a research assistant to Professor Deborah A. Ramirez on national security, civil rights, and counterterrorism issues. Mr. Malloy also has experience in plaintiff personal injury, product liability, and employment law. He obtained a degree in Political Science from Boston College in 2005, and worked for a global law firm and a US presidential campaign before entering law school.

**Liam Maskey** is the founder of Intercomm, an internationally recognized peace-building agency and has been working on issues of Track Two Peace Building, Widening Access to the Economy, Building Better Communities, and Community Renewal since the 1980s. In addition Liam has significant experience in the governance and administration of European Union peace programs. Liam has been recognized both locally and internationally for his work, receiving the US President's Peace Prize as well as the President of Ireland's Peace Prize.

Liam was instrumental in the design and delivery on a number of PEACE III–funded programs to enhance community confidence in the peace process. These programs are delivered in partnership with the Police Service of Northern Ireland (PSNI), INCORE, An Garda, Peace and Reconciliation Group, Groundwork NI, Irish Congress of Trade Unions, and the Glencree Centre for Reconciliation.

Liam was the Intercomm program lead in the design and facilitation of an inter-ethnic policy dialogue in Kosovo that was financially supported by the US-based National Democratic Institute. This work involved facilitating collaborative working relationships with local municipality staff in a country blighted by sustained ethnic and political conflict. Liam was also Intercomm lead at the request of the international NGO SAFERWORLD to deliver community safety programs with the PSNI to the Nepalese Police. Liam is currently a commissioner with the Equality Commission (NI).

**Dr. Mark McGovern** is a professor of Sociology and coordinator of the Power, Conflict and Justice Research Group at Edge Hill University, Lancashire, UK. His main areas of research are concerned with human rights, state violence, and transitional justice, particularly in Northern Ireland. His work has focused on community approaches to truth recovery and state collusion in political violence. He has also conducted research on comparing the impact of counterinsurgency policy and law on Irish communities and Muslims in Britain. His publications include *Ardoyne: The Untold Truth* (2002), the report *Countering Terror or Counter-Productive: Comparing Irish and British Muslim Experiences of Counter-insurgency Law and Policy* (2010), and articles in *Sociology, Terrorism and Political Violence, Law and Society, International Journal of Transitional Justice, Capital and Class*, and *Studies in Social Justice.*

**Dr. Mary O'Rawe** is a barrister and senior law lecturer at the University of Ulster. She is currently counsel to the senior coroner for Northern Ireland in a range of legacy inquest cases, linked to allegations of a shoot to kill policy being operated by the security forces in Northern Ireland during the 1980s.

Mary has over 20 years of academic and applied experience in the field of criminal justice and human rights, with her main focus being on policing in societies in transition. She has worked in a strategic advisory, policy formulation, evaluation, and training role with various governmental and nongovernmental organizations such as An Garda Síochána (the Irish Police Service), the PSNI (Police Service of Northern Ireland), and the Northern Ireland Human Rights Commission. She was legal advisor to the Northern Ireland Bill of Right Forum on criminal justice and victims' rights, and has contributed, on different levels, to a wide range of international processes and research initiatives aimed at placing human rights at the center of policing reform initiatives. For example, she has been involved in evaluating and advising on antitorture training for police in China and producing commissioned strategic think pieces on Security System Reform and Identity for the International Center for Transitional Justice in New York. Mary is a former chairperson of the internationally respected civil liberties organization, the Committee on the Administration of Justice, and was cofounder of the Northern Ireland Lawyers' Section of Amnesty International. She is coauthor of *Human Rights on Duty: Principles for Better Policing* (1997), an international comparative work exploring lessons to be learned from policing reform in a range of jurisdictions worldwide. She has also authored several book chapters and journal articles in the area of human rights and policing, most recently examining the role of gender in security system reform initiatives. Mary lives in Belfast with her husband and six children.

**Tara Lai Quinlan** is a licensed New York attorney pursuing a Doctor of Philosophy at the London School of Economics and Political Science in the Department of Sociology, where she is an LSE PhD Scholarship recipient, and affiliated with the Frederick Bonnart-Braunthal Trust and Centre for the Study of Human Rights. Ms. Quinlan's research focuses on policing, community partnerships, counterterrorism, racial profiling, and Islamophobia. Ms. Quinlan also serves as the director of the Partnering for Prevention and Community Safety Initiative (PfP) at Northeastern University School of Law, where her research focuses on law enforcement–community partnerships.

Ms. Quinlan has coauthored a number of publications, including *Defining Racial Profiling in a Post-September 11th World*, American Criminal Law Review (Summer 2003), and opinion pieces for the *Huffington Post* and American Constitution Society.

Ms. Quinlan received her Master of Laws (LLM) in Criminal Law, Criminology and Criminal Justice at King's College London, her Juris Doctor (JD) from Northeastern University School of Law, and her BA from the University of California, Berkeley.

**Deborah Ramirez** is a professor at Northeastern University School of Law, as well as the founder of the Partnering for Prevention and Community Safety Initiative (PfP). In connection with PfP, Professor Ramirez works with academia, law enforcement, and community leaders in the United States and Europe to implement community partnership–based counterterrorism programs. Her belief is that we will only truly be safe from terrorist attacks when law enforcement adopts a strategy focused on building trust and strengthening relationships with the American Muslim, Arab, and Sikh communities. Her written work includes a "Promising Practices Guide" on how to develop partnerships between law enforcement and these communities. She teaches criminal justice for first year students, along with advanced courses in criminal procedure and national security. She also seeks to actively engage the student body in topics relating to criminal law, including participation with Northeastern's Criminal Justice Society.

**Noel Rooney**, BSc, MSC, CMS, was appointed chief executive of the Probation Board for Northern Ireland from 2003 to 2007. He is a graduate of the University of Ulster at Coleraine and gained a scholarship at the Federal Executive Institute Program in Virginia, US in 1997.

Noel had worked in Health and Social Services for over 20 years holding a number of senior management positions including as the director of Health and Social Services from 1993 to 2003. Prior to taking up his appointment with the Probation Board, he was the director of operations/executive director of social work at the North and West Belfast Health and Social Services Trust, with responsibility for the provision of integrated health and social services across North and West Belfast.

From 1989 to 2005 he was a member of a European Association "Quartier en Crise," an association of 25 European cities promoting a community development approach to regeneration in cities. He was on the executive committee as a treasurer from 1999 to 2005. Noel was a member of the Criminal Justice Board for Northern Ireland between 2003 and 2006. He was also a member of the Local Strategy Partnership Belfast, which dealt with European peace funding, representing the statutory sector for a number of years.

Since 2009, Noel has served as the program manager for the European program "Through Peace III." This program, Communities and Police in Transition (CAPT), involves a number of partners including INTERCOMM and both police services, the PSNI and the Garda Siochana. It also includes a number of cross-community organizations throughout the North and the border counties.

**Taylor Shutt** is a 2012 graduate of Northeastern University School of Law. She contributed to "Community Partnerships Thwart Terrorism" while working as lead research assistant for Professor Deborah Ramirez. As a student, Ms. Shutt was instrumental in advancing the goals of the Partnering for Prevention (PfP) and Community Safety Initiative. In addition to her interest in community partnership–based counterterrorism programs, she is experienced in criminal prosecution, juvenile defense, and education law. Ms. Shutt has a BS in Communications from the Florida State University, and spent six years in broadcast news before entering law school.

**Dr. P. Daniel Silk** is a teacher, researcher, and 19-year veteran of local and federal law enforcement in the United States. In 2002 he was part of the first permanent staff at the newly reopened US Embassy in Kabul, Afghanistan; he has also served as a captain with the Athens-Clarke County (Georgia) Police Department, where at various times he commanded a community policing unit, internal affairs, training, and vice. He currently works for the University of Georgia, where he manages police communications and teaches in the Criminal Justice Studies Program.

Dan also works with the UK-based organization ConnectJustice, which emphasizes the study and application of community and government partnerships designed to prevent violence. Dan is frequently requested as a trainer or advisor on a wide variety of issues linked to community policing in democracies, and has also published a number of articles on related topics.

As a Fulbright Police Research Fellow in the UK in 2009, Dan studied outreach between Muslim communities and British police, and a similar topic was the emphasis of his PhD dissertation. His bachelor's degree is in Religion, as is his master's degree, with an emphasis on Islamic Studies. Since 1999 he has had the opportunity to study or work in a variety of Muslim communities around the world.

**Dr. Basia Spalek** is a reader in Communities and Justice within the Institute of Applied Social Studies at the University of Birmingham, UK. Basia has led a number of research projects funded by the Arts and Humanities Research Council and the Economic and Social Studies Research Council, looking specifically at community-based approaches to counterterrorism.

Basia has recently put together a new edited collection on counterterrorism: *Community-Based Approaches to Preventing Terror Crime* (2012), and she is currently writing *Governing Terror: Trust, Community and Counter-Terrorism* (forthcoming). Basia is an ambassador to the Make Justice Work campaign and has acted as an advisor/consultant to the Royal United Services Institute, the Organization for Security and Cooperation in Europe, Department for Communities and Local Government, the Equality and Human Rights Commission, and is part of a new collaboration: ConnectJustice.

**Mark G. Stainbrook** retired as a lieutenant from the Los Angeles Police Department, where he served in a variety of assignments including patrol, gangs, internal affairs, intelligence, and counterterrorism. Mark currently serves as the assistant chief of the San Diego Harbor Police Department, which is the premier police presence in San Diego Bay, the San Diego International Airport (also known as Lindbergh Field), and on all tidelands around the bay. Mark is also a lieutenant colonel in the United States Marine Corps Reserve with over 25 years of military service. He is currently assigned to the Office of the Inspector General, Intelligence Oversight Division.

Mark graduated with honors from California State University Long Beach with a masters degree in Public Policy Administration. His thesis, *Attitudes of American-Muslims towards Law Enforcement: A Comparison of before and after September 11, 2001*, was the catalyst for his selection to a Fulbright Police Research Fellowship. During his Fulbright, Mark was a visiting fellow at Leeds University in the Theology and Religious Studies Department, and was also seconded to the West Yorkshire Police Force. He studied and worked in local West Yorkshire Muslim communities for six months, including the suburbs of Beeston, where the "7/7 London bombers" resided. Mark is the author of several law enforcement articles in *Police Chief Magazine*, including, "Learning from the Lessons of the 2008 Mumbai Terrorist Attacks" and "Policing with Muslim Communities in the Age of Terrorism."